EX LIBRIS

G.A. RAWLYK

THE CANADIAN FRONTIER

THE

CANADIAN

FRONTIER

1534-1760

△

W. J. ECCLES

University of Toronto

HOLT, RINEHART AND WINSTON

New York • Chicago • San Francisco • Atlanta

Dallas • Montreal • Toronto • London • Sydney

FOREWORD

THE COURSE OF AMERICA'S WESTWARD EXPANSION during the seventeenth and eighteenth centuries was shaped not only by the natural obstacles that barred the path of advancing pioneers, not only by the Indian foes who disputed their progress, but by the titanic conflicts that were remaking the map of Europe during that day of emerging nationalism. Three powers were the principal contenders for the empire that could be carved from eastern North America: England, Spain, and France. By the accident of discovery no less than by design, each monopolized one segment as a base for operations against the others: Spain, the Southwest; England, the coastal lowlands from the Carolinas to New England; and France, the St. Lawrence River valley. Almost from the day these outposts were established each contending nation sought to extend its holdings into the territories of its rivals, using the three classic weapons in the arsenal of conquest: trade with the natives, diplomacy, and war. For nearly two centuries the conflict raged, ending only in 1763 when the last of the wars for empire ended with Britain victorious and its rivals ousted from eastern North America.

In this struggle the principal antagonists were France and England, for Spanish power was already waning in America as in Europe. Their battleground spanned the continent, from Hudson Bay on the north to the Louisiana bayous on the south, from the Appalachian highlands on the east to the Shining Mountains on the west. Their shock troops were the merchants and traders who gambled their lives to barter for furs along these distant frontiers, for these venturesome wanderers were no less empire builders than were diplomats mapping the strategy of expansion in London and Paris, or the ill-fated Redcoats who marched with General Edward Braddock against the French at the Forks of the Ohio to touch off the French and Indian War. Clashes in these remote borderlands merged into four major conflicts and any number of minor skirmishes. In the retrospect of history the outcome was seldom in doubt, for New France extended its borders too

v

far to be guarded by the small population that Old France could release to its colony. The wars ended with Britain in control of the eastern half of the continent, the French elbowed aside by the sheer force of numbers. Yet a century and a half was needed to prove that superiority—a century and a half of conflict that rocked the western world.

The story of this epic struggle has been often told. More than a century ago the brilliant Boston historian, Francis Parkman, began the preparation of the series of volumes that endowed the struggle with classic proportions: *La Salle and the Discovery of the Great West, Count Frontenac and New France Under Louis XIV, A Half Century of Conflict,* and *Montcalm and Wolfe.* Others have followed, some with greater historical dexterity, none with comparable literary skill. Yet all of Parkman's successors have but slightly altered the story told by the master, and none has challenged the basic interpretation that he advanced to explain the outcome of the years of conflict.

This long-accepted version is in this volume seriously disputed by Professor W. J. Eccles of the University of Toronto. Already widely known for his revisionist volumes on *Frontenac: The Courtier Governor* (1959) and *Canada Under Louis XIV* (1964), Professor Eccles has established himself as not only a leading modern student of French Canada, but as a trampler of legends and toppler of traditional beliefs. With the true historian's determination to test even the most widely accepted truths, with an instinct for ferreting out fresh evidence, with a bold lack of respect for time-tested "facts," he has successfully challenged established doctrine at a number of points in Canadian history. In this book he applies his questioning mind and fresh viewpoints to the entire French era in Canadian history.

The result is a remarkable volume, and one certain to influence the course of scholarship for years to come. No oft-told tale is too sacred to be challenged, no individual too venerated to be pushed from his pedestal. Louis, Count de Frontenac, Francis Parkman's hero and the hero of Canadians for a generation, emerges as a self-seeking second-rater whose inept policies did more to injure than extend the French empire. The Marquis de Montcalm, long viewed as a military genius beyond compare, is revealed as a faulty tactician whose precipitous action doomed the cause of New France on the Plains of Abraham. Nor are other legendary figures treated with traditional respect. Pierre Esprit Radisson and the Sieur des Groseilliers are scarcely mentioned, while such previously acclaimed explorers as Father Jacques Marquette and Louis Jolliet are relegated to a minor role in the history of expansion. Even the famed Sieur de La Salle is painted as a minor figure whose exploits warrant only scant attention.

Instead of glorifying the mighty, Professor Eccles shifts the spotlight to the merchants, whose search for status and profits (and status was more important than profits as an incentive) paved the way for the expansion of New France. His appraisal of the economic impact of the fur trade on colony and mother country is based on extensive use of hitherto unexploited sources on both sides of the Atlantic, while his vivid picture of the techniques of the trade is so grimly realistic that little is left for the reader's imagination. Professor Eccles similarly casts the Indians in a new and more important role. They were, he demonstrates, not mere pawns in the power struggle between France and England, to be manipulated at will by British or French agents, but a third party with a status and influence equaling that of the other two. Time and again he shows that Indian diplomacy was better conceived, and better executed, than that originating in Quebec, London, or Paris.

The interpretative skills that Professor Eccles applies to his analysis of trade and diplomacy are demonstrated again when he describes the emergence of the frontier social order in French Canada. Here he grapples successfully with an unsolved problem: did immigrants from the distinctive culture of France respond to the New World environment as did the small farmers of the New England or Virginia back country of that day? His answers will both please and displease advocates of the theories of Frederick Jackson Turner. The *seigneurs* and *habitants* whose long, narrow farms fringed the St. Lawrence did develop some characteristics typical of Anglo-Americans subjected to the frontier's influence, he finds, but they failed to develop many others, while their institutions remained virtually unchanged.

The searching nature of these inquiries suggests that this is a sophisticated book, and one that will appeal to the learned investigator no less than to the serious student seeking the most authoritative word on the beginnings of French Canada's frontier. Professor Eccles makes few concessions to romanticism or popularization. Those who wish Parkmanesque descriptions of wilderness battles, complete with well-defined heroes and villains, will be advised to look elsewhere. But those who wish to read analytical history at its best, those who appreciate the truth above fiction, those who want the latest word on the expansion of a significant section of North American society, will find on the pages that follow a memorable intellectual experience. They will also be rewarded with more accurate knowledge of a century of Canadian history than is available in any other volume now in print.

This is one of the eighteen volumes in the Holt, Rinehart and Winston *Histories of the American Frontier* series. Like the others, it tells a complete story; it may also be read as part of the broader history of westward expansion told in connected form in these volumes. Each is written by an outstanding authority who brings to his task an intimate knowledge of the period he covers and a demonstrated skill in narration and interpretation. Each will provide the general reader with a sound but readable account of one phase of North America's frontiering past, and the specialized student with a documented narrative that is integrated into the broader story of the continent's growth.

The Huntington Library   **Ray Allen Billington**
April 1969

PREFACE

CANADA UNDER THE FRENCH REGIME was a small colony, seemingly of little importance in the greater world of European civilization in an age of imperial expansion. Its population at its conquest by Great Britain in 1760 was only some seventy thousand, yet the French in North America for over half a century dominated the larger part of the continent, from the sub-Arctic wastes to the Gulf of Mexico.

The frontier of this colony, for a variety of reasons, bore little resemblance to that of the English colonies. To a considerable extent the geography of the continent, the physical environment, accounted for this difference, but the marked disparity in social values and institutions was also an important factor. The Canadian frontier is deserving of study for itself, because it had many interesting aspects peculiar to it. It also serves, by way of contrast, to throw light in an oblique way on the frontier experience of the English colonies. These two European peoples, occupying adjacent areas, sharing much in common, in some respects reacted in the same way to their environment, but in others they reacted in markedly different ways.

This book does not attempt to confirm or refute the Turner thesis. It seeks to define the term frontier in the Canadian context, to discover the motives of those who peopled it, to define what they brought to the frontier and what effects the frontier experience had on them collectively. It has been quite impossible, given the imposed limitations on length, to provide a general history of New France as background; many important aspects had to be ignored or dealt with summarily, but an attempt was made to include enough to keep the events on, and the influence of, the frontier in a meaningful context. If the reader approaches the subject totally ignorant of the history of Canada, he will be at a disadvantage, but I do not consider that I can be held accountable for that.

A major problem is a dearth of source material on the early decades of the colony's history; for the subsequent periods the opposite holds true. In the period up to 1663 some significant questions cannot be answered; in the later years the great mass of material, and the increasing complexity of events, necessitate a careful selection of topics. For these reasons the study had to be confined to the Canadian frontier; the frontiers of Acadia and Louisiana were discussed only in so far as they affected Canada. Similarly, in the chapter dealing with the Seven Years' War, emphasis was placed on events in the west since they were more pertinent to the theme of the book, and, as the evidence revealed, this was one aspect of the war that seemed in need of reappraisal.

It remains to thank the individuals and institutions without whose help this book could not have been written. Research grants afforded by the Canada Council, the Ewart Foundation of the University of Manitoba, and the British American Oil Fellowship Fund at the University of Toronto made it possible to pursue the necessary research at the various archives. The staffs at the Public Archives of Canada, the Archives du Québec, and the Archives du Séminaire de Québec, could not have been more helpful. To the Centre d'Études Canadienne-Françaises at McGill University, where I spent a most agreeable year as visiting professor and was afforded every assistance while writing the book, I am very grateful. In particular I must thank the director of the Centre, Professor Laurier L. LaPierre, Madame O. Colmagne-Civitello, and Madame L. Stam for the help they so cheerfully afforded me in the preparation of the manuscript. To my research assistant at McGill, Mr. Peter Moogk, my thanks are also due, particularly for certain of the maps. My colleague at the University of Toronto, Colonel C. P. Stacey, kindly read the chapters dealing with military affairs; it was most reassuring to have the benefit of his critical appraisal. To the general editor of the series, Ray Allen Billington, go my sincere thanks for his invaluable comments and constructive criticism.

Montreal and Toronto W. J. Eccles
April 1969

GLOSSARY

CERTAIN TERMS used in the text have no exact English or modern equivalent. Rather than employ clumsy, contrived translations it was thought better to retain the original versions and provide a glossary.

The names Canada and New France require definition. In the seventeenth century the two were used indiscriminately for the colony in the St. Lawrence Valley. By the end of the century New France was understood to comprise all French possessions in North America—Canada, Acadia, Louisiana, and the western posts. *Pays d'en haut* was the Canadians' descriptive name for the far west, meaning literally up country, or the country upriver from Montreal.

The terms *habitant, coureur de bois, voyageur,* were peculiar to Canada. In legal documents *habitant* was used to signify a resident, but in common usage it meant anyone below seigneurial rank who held land in the colony. The Canadians were very conscious of the fact that their social and economic condition was above that of peasants in France, hence the term *habitant* was favored because it lacked any servile connotation. It is still used in rural Quebec today. In the seventeenth century the term *coureur de bois* meant anyone who voyaged into the wilderness to trade for furs. Until 1681 laws forbade the practice, hence the name had a pejorative sense, meaning virtually an outlaw. Early in the eighteenth century the term *voyageur* came into vogue. Essentially *voyageurs* were wage-earning canoe men who transported trade goods and supplies to the western posts.

In seventeenth-century France there were two types of nobles: the old aristocracy, claiming descent from the Franks, was referred to as the *noblesse d'épée*, nobility of the sword; and the new aristocracy, the *noblesse de robe*, deriving noble status from high judicial and administrative offices purchased from the crown, was known as nobility of the robe, signifying the long robe worn by members of the legal profession.

There were three separate military organizations in New France. The *milice*, militia, comprising all able-bodied men between sixteen and sixty, was organized in companies and commanded by *capitaines de milice* selected by the governor general from among the *habitants*. The Troupes de la Marine were independent companies of regular troops raised in France to serve in the naval ports and the colonies. They came under the minister of marine, not the minister of war. During the Seven Years' War several regiments of regular troops were sent to Canada. They were known as Troupes de Terre because many of the regiments derived their names from French provinces, for example Régiment de Languedoc and Régiment de Guyenne.

The old regime monetary system was based on the *livre tournois*. There were 12 *sols* in the *livre*, 20 *deniers* in the *sol*. The sterling exchange rate varied from one shilling to one and sixpence per *livre*. To find the value of the *livre* in today's currency is extremely difficult; too many factors have altered in conflicting ways. The closest approximation that I could make is that the *livre* had the buying power of roughly two 1968 Canadian dollars. This estimate, despite strange anomalies, is based on prices of essential goods and services, wages and salaries, and the assumption that money has depreciated since the late seventeenth century to one-fifth of its former value. The *livre* as a measurement of weight was equal to approximately three-quarters of an English pound.

The term *arpent* was both a linear and an area unit of measurement. Linearly, it equaled almost 200 English feet, and in area about five-sixths of an acre.

CONTENTS

MAPS

◁ **1** ▷

The Nature
of the Canadian Frontier

*B*efore beginning a study of any frontier, the question has to be asked: frontier of what? In Canada under the French regime, as in the other European colonies in the Americas, the frontier can be defined as the outer limits of European civilization. It was a manifestation of the so-called expansion of Europe that began in the fifteenth century and continued for over four hundred years, until European civilization succeeded in dominating the world—the first civilization to do so. Only in the past half century has the tide of this advance been turned. How far the retreat will go remains to be seen.

This great wave of European expansion is frequently attributed to the new spirit of individualism released by the forces that accompanied the epoch known as the Renaissance. It may well be that the movement was an outgrowth of this spirit, but to be more specific one has to examine the motives of the Europeans who were willing to venture across uncharted oceans to conquer unknown lands against incalculable odds. Their motives were fourfold. The European had, first, an avid desire for recognition and fame, to distinguish himself among his fellows and achieve a higher social

1

status, to acquire those intangible qualities that the French refer to as *la gloire;* second, an insatiable curiosity, a thirst for knowledge, to know what is on the other side of a mountain, around the next bend in a river, on the other planets; third, highly developed acquisitive and competitive instincts, a desire to acquire more of this world's goods than his neighbor, an inability to accept what he had, no matter how much, as enough; fourth, a marked intolerance in religious beliefs, the conviction that his particular branch of the Christian Church possessed the only true faith and that all peoples everywhere should be converted to it, that those who resisted thereby merited extermination, or, at best, a lifetime of servitude to further the aims of Christians.

These attitudes were clearly defined by Samuel de Champlain, one of the more intrepid agents of European expansion, when he wrote in the preface to his journal, published in 1613:

> Among all the most useful and admirable arts, that of navigation has al-ways seemed to me to hold the first place; for the more hazardous it is and the more attended by innumerable dangers and shipwrecks, so much the more is it esteemed and exalted above all others, being in no way suited to those who lack courage and resolution. Through this art we gain knowledge of different countries, regions and kingdoms; through it we attract and bring into our countries all kinds of riches; through it the idolatry of paganism is overthrown and Christianity proclaimed in all parts of the earth.[1]

Such then, were the dominant motives that brought the French to North America to establish, first commercial bases, then missionary outposts, and eventually permanent settlements.

In early Canada it is possible to distinguish four types of frontier: commercial, religious, settlement, and military. Yet they were all part of one frontier, and this one frontier embraced the entire area, not merely the outer fringes of the territory in North America controlled by France. Thus the Canadian frontier was markedly different, in nature and historical develop-ment, from that of the English colonies to the south. The frontier of these latter colonies, and of the republic that eventually developed out of them, was basically a settlement frontier that advanced steadily westward in a roughly distinguishable, if very irregular, line marked by cleared land—a frontier constantly in contact and usually in conflict with the original inhabitants, the Indians. The Canadian frontier, on the other hand, con-sisted of a main base on a river that gave easy access to the heart of the continent, and several smaller bases, or outposts, far in the interior but dependent on the main base, which in turn was dependent on the mother country, France. The settlements of the main base, along a stretch of the St. Lawrence River between Quebec and Montreal, were a relatively narrow ribbon backing onto uninhabited virgin wilderness. Unlike the situation in the English colonies, the back areas of these settlements could be regarded as a frontier in only a very limited sense, but they were part of the much larger Canadian frontier.

If the Anglo-American frontier is accepted as the norm, then Canada can hardly be said to have had a frontier at all. Rather, it can be said to have been a metropolis, dominating the hinterland around it, and with a few incipient metropolises beginning to develop in the west at such points as Detroit and Michilimackinac, and in the Illinois country.[2] When Louisiana was established at the beginning of the eighteenth century, it quickly became a metropolis in its own right, competing with Canada for control of the entire hinterland south of the Great Lakes. To the east, Acadia developed along somewhat different lines. It served, at one and the same time, as a border march in the defensive system of Canada, as a base for the French and Anglo-American fishing industries, as a French agricultural settlement, as a base for missionary and fur trade activities, and as a hinterland of the rival metropolises, Canada and New England. It was, in fact, an area of overlapping imperial systems. In 1713 the main settled region was ceded to England, and from then on the areas remaining to France served as little more than a buffer zone protecting the approaches to Canada.

Geography dictated the pace and nature of European expansion in North America, and accounts in no small degree for the differences in the frontiers of the colonizing powers. When the continent is approached from Europe, there are only four main entryways into the interior: Hudson Bay and the St. Lawrence, Hudson, and Mississippi rivers. France gained control of the St. Lawrence and Mississippi, England of Hudson Bay and the Hudson River. At Hudson Bay the English made no attempt to establish settlements or to move inland; they maintained only a few commercial posts, supplied from England, where they waited for the Indians to come to them to trade. Farther south, close behind the area settled by the English along the Atlantic seaboard, the rugged mass of the Appalachian mountain chain blocked river communications and easy access to the western interior. The only major gap in this barrier is the valley of the Hudson and Mohawk rivers leading to Lake Ontario, and by way of the Great Lakes to the western plains. This route was, however, effectively barred to the English by the confederacy of the five Iroquois nations, who formed the most powerful military force in the region until the eighteenth century. By the time the English were ready to expand to the southwest, the French had established themselves in their new colony of Louisiana, purposely to block them.

In the English colonies the frontier was perforce the line of settlement created by axe and plow as settlers moved steadily westward away from the seaboard. In their wake the forest was cut down, the animal and human life it sustained killed or driven farther west. In some areas Anglo-American fur traders served as an advance guard of this destructive movement, but their numbers were relatively few. In short, the Anglo-American frontiersman

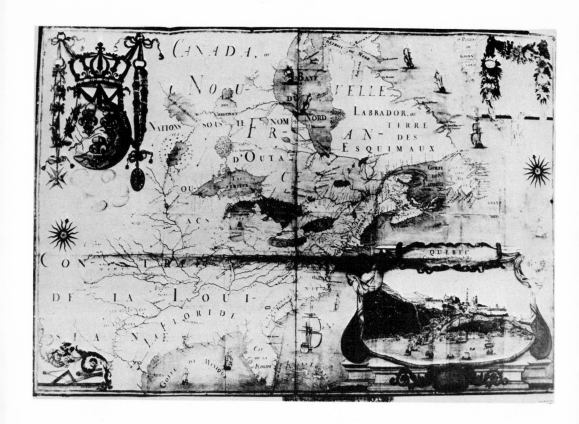

Map by J.-B.-L. Franquelin, 1688, indicating the extent of French penetration into the west in the seventeenth century. Lac de Buade is today called Lake of the Woods. Lac des Assinibouels and Lac des Christinaux represent Lakes Winnipeg, Manitoba, and Winnipegosis, drawn from reports of *coureurs de bois* and located some four hundred miles too far east. From this, and other evidence, it is clear that the French had reached the northwestern plains prior to 1688. (Public Archives of Canada)

was a potential settler, the enemy and destroyer of the frontier forestland and its denizens.

The development of the Canadian frontier and the relations of the Canadians to it were in marked contrast to this situation. The St. Lawrence and Ottawa rivers and the Great Lakes gave the Canadians easy and direct access to the interior of the continent. The Canadians could travel with relative ease from their base in the St. Lawrence Valley all the way to the Gulf of Mexico, north to Hudson Bay, or due west to the Rocky Mountains. Throughout the lands along these water routes, supplies of food were easily obtained. Game and fish abounded; corn-raising Indian tribes were eager to exchange food and furs for European goods in the southern half of the continent; and on the northern plains the great buffalo herds provided adequate food. Along these waterways, there was no barrier to westward progress of the Canadians until the Rocky Mountains were reached. They reached the shadow, at least, of the cordillera before the Anglo-Americans had managed to struggle across the Alleghenies.

Rivers by themselves, however, are not enough. A means of transportation is required; and here again the Canadians had a marked advantage over their Anglo-American and English rivals. The Indian's birchbark canoe was capable of carrying heavy loads, was light enough to be carried around river obstructions such as rapids by one or two men, and was manufactured entirely from materials readily available in the Canadian forest. The larger white birch trees that provided the essential sheets of bark for the outer shell of the canoe grew abundantly in the St. Lawrence Valley and the lands along the north shore of the Great Lakes, but to the south and north of this region the white birch of adequate size was scarce. The Iroquois and Anglo-Americans, when they could not obtain Canadian canoes, had to make do with canoes made of elm bark, or with dugouts, which were not nearly as serviceable. Similarly, the men at the Hudson's Bay Company posts were gravely handicapped by both the lack of canoes and skilled canoe men until well into the nineteenth century, when they devised a practical alternative, the York boat.[3]

Although the French had the physical means to penetrate into the interior, they could do so only with the agreement of the Indian nations. As long as the Indians received benefits and saw no threat to their own interests, they allowed the French to establish trading posts, and even a few settlements, on their lands. But to the end of the French regime, these posts and settlements were tiny islands, with a handful of men, amid a much larger population of Indians, who regarded the land as theirs. In some areas the French had much better relations with the Indians than did the Anglo-Americans, but this was by no means universal. For the French, good relations with the Indians were absolutely essential for commercial, religious, and political reasons; for the Anglo-Americans, however, these motives were not so dominant. Frequently the interests of the English settlers and the Indians were in direct conflict. This was particularly true on the eastern frontier, as the population of New England expanded and encroached upon the Indians' hunting grounds. In the west, the greed of the Anglo-Americans for land did not constitute a serious threat to the more powerful Indian nations until near the end of the French regime.

Ironically, French relations with the Indians were initially the same as were later to be those of the English. When, in the first half of the sixteenth century, the French attempted to establish settlements in the St. Lawrence Valley, the attitude of the resident Indian tribes changed rapidly from friendliness, to suspicion, to open hostility. This in no small measure contributed to the abandonment of the attempts by Jacques Cartier and Jean-François de la Rocque, sieur de Roberval, to found colonies in the St. Lawrence Valley in 1541.[4] By the beginning of the next century this relationship had changed radically for the better. In the intervening years the Iroquois tribes that had occupied the area between present-day Quebec and Montreal had departed, and no other sedentary tribes had settled in the vacant territory. It was, in fact, an unoccupied buffer zone between the Iroquois and Montagnais nations. Thus, when the French finally established their settlements in the St. Lawrence Valley, they did not have to dispossess the Indians. Moreover, the northern Algonkin nations welcomed the French, who were able to supply them with European weapons for use against their Iroquois foes to the south and the Sioux in the west. In exchange they gave furs, which had not been highly valued in Cartier's day, but which now enabled the French to realize substantial profits on the European market.

By the early seventeenth century the French had established a close commercial alliance with the Algonkin nations and their allies, the Huron. This led, inevitably, to a military alliance, and the French were obliged to commit themselves to the active military support of their commercial partners against the Iroquois. These in turn obtained European weapons from first the Dutch then the English, who by this time were established along the Hudson River. What had begun in the distant past as intermittent war between Indian nations, armed with weapons of wood, bone, and stone, waged in a fashion more akin to blood sport than to war as Europeans knew it, rapidly developed into a struggle between the rival imperial systems of the European powers. In the beginning the French had been drawn into the struggle between Algonkin and Iroquois as auxiliary troops, but the roles were soon reversed and the Indian nations became mere pawns in the larger European power struggle. Yet always they sought to play the French and English off against each other, supporting the side that seemed best to serve their interests and only for as long as this condition obtained.

Commerce was not the only motive the French had for maintaining good relations with the northern Indians. Religion was also an important factor. Within a few years of the establishment of a small commercial base at Quebec in 1608, French missionaries had begun their work far in the interior, among the Huron at Georgian Bay. These men, Recollets and Jesuits alike, had only one aim, to save the souls of the Indians by converting them to Christianity. To this end they lived among them, learned their languages, devoted themselves completely, and on occasion sacrificed their lives. Here was a unique type of frontier, a religious frontier of the mind, as these intellectuals, products of the highly civilized Baroque Age, heirs of Greece and Rome, medieval Christianity, the Renaissance, and the Catholic Reformation, struggled in a savage wilderness environment to impose their very sophisticated concepts and values on the North Americans of the Stone Age, who already had religious beliefs that sufficed very well for their needs. At first the missionaries sought to assimilate the Indians into French civilization, but failed. Too many of the Indians seemed to acquire only the worst traits of the French laymen they encountered; and conversely, too many of the French showed a marked aptitude for adopting Indian mores that were quite contrary to Christian teaching. The missionaries therefore strove to keep the Indians and French laymen apart in order to protect their charges from the debasing effects of too close contact with Europeans.[5]

Yet missionary activity, commerce, and imperialism inevitably became closely intertwined, as all three depended upon the Indians to achieve their aims. Among the western tribes, wherever the missionaries established their chapels, French fur traders also had their trading posts. So that control might be exercised over both the Indian allies and the French traders, military commanders with garrison troops were appointed to the main posts in the 1680s.[6] In this fashion French authority was extended over the interior of the continent. Policies were enunciated and orders issued by the king and the minister of marine at Versailles, sent to the governor general and the intendant at Quebec, and passed on by them to the officers commanding the western posts. The missionaries, too, were pressed into the service of the French crown, serving as liaison officers and intelligence agents, passing information back to Quebec and relaying orders to the post commanders.[7] By these means the writ of the king of France ran for thousands of miles into the far reaches of the North American wilderness.

But it could hardly be said that the French occupied the west. All they occupied west of the junction of the Ottawa and St. Lawrence rivers were trading and missionary posts, the closest being hundreds of miles away from the central colony. In between was virgin wilderness. By the eighteenth century a few of the posts, at Detroit and in the Illinois country, had developed to the point where some of the land was being settled to provide food for the men at the posts and the traders who traveled along the rivers to more distant tribes within the French fur trade empire. For the most part, however, the trading posts were a few long huts, perhaps surrounded by a stockade, with a small garden for growing vegetables, on a river bank near an Indian village.

Although the men who traveled to these western posts and beyond, referred to as *coureurs de bois* in the seventeenth century and as *voyageurs* in the eighteenth, are legendary figures in Canadian history, we do not know much about them. A great deal of research needs to be done to discover who they were, the true role they played in the history of the period, the changes wrought on them by their way of life, and the changes they wrought on Canadian society. Many of them, perhaps most, were illiterate, and only a very few committed anything to paper that has survived. We know them mainly from the comments of their contemporaries, for the most part in the reports of royal officials and missionaries, who deplored their way of life yet found them indispensable at times. We know that in 1714 there were reputed to be at least two hundred of them who did nothing else during their entire active lives,[8] returning to the settlements in the central colony only when age and rheumatism, to which their way of life made them all too prone, rendered them incapable of paddling from sunrise to sunset and carrying backbreaking loads over an infinity of portages. How many others in the colony made the occasional trip to the west for adventure, to amass a few hundred *livres*, or just to get away from their wives for a while, we do not know.

From the comments of contemporary observers, these men appear to have been a unique blend of French and Indian, wearing Indian dress, traveling like Indians, eating the same sort of food, speaking their languages, making war in the Indian manner, living off the land and enduring privation with the fortitude of the Indian. Many of them took Indian girls for wives, and, in the Indian fashion, changed them as fancy dictated; they gambled away their hard-earned profits as did the Indians and gloried in their physical prowess. In short, they embodied the antithesis of the middle-class virtues. What the Indians thought of them, we can only guess from negative evidence; most likely they accepted them as equals, for that they were. The missionaries, however, were aghast at their adoption alike of Indian virtues and vices, and some of the royal officials expressed alarm at the effect they had on colonial society.

In the late seventeenth century a French officer in the Troupes de la Marine described them in these terms:

> The Pedlers call'd *Coureurs de Bois*, export from hence every year several Canows full of Merchandise, which they dispose of among all the Savage Nations of the Continent, by way of exchange for Beaver-Skins. Seven or eight days ago, I saw twenty-five or thirty of these Canows return with heavy Cargoes; each Canow was manag'd by two or three Men, and carry'd twenty hundred weight, i.e. forty packs of Beaver Skins, which are worth an hundred Crowns a piece. These Canows had been a year and eighteen Months out. You would be amaz'd if you saw how lewd these Pedlers are when they return; how they Feast and Game, and how prodigal they are, not only in their Cloaths but upon Women. Such of 'em as are married, have the wisdom to retire to their own Houses; but the Batchelors act just as our *East-India-Men*, and Pirates are wont to do; for they Lavish, Eat, Drink, and Play all away as long as the Goods hold out; and when these are gone, they e'en sell their Embroidery, their Lace, and their Cloaths. This done, they are forc'd to go upon a New Voyage for Subsistence.[9]

The Canadian frontiersmen were an entirely different breed from the frontiersmen of the English colonies. They made no attempt to destroy the wilderness, because their way of life required its preservation. They were much more akin to the seamen of New England than to the Anglo-American frontier settlers. They voyaged in their frail vessels through the wilderness, carrying their goods to distant posts to exchange them for return cargoes of furs, just as New England seamen sailed to ports in Europe, Africa, and the West Indies, to exchange fish, rum, and timber for sugar, slaves, or manufactured goods. The New England men did not occupy the Atlantic, nor did the Canadians occupy the western wilderness; they merely established factories at remote points to collect the local produce and make it ready for the return journey to Montreal.

In contrast to the English colonies where the frontier became ever more remote from the settled areas along the seaboard, Canada was part and parcel of an all-pervasive frontier, for all the houses in the colony had the river at their doorstep and along it came the men of the wilderness, French and Indian alike, bringing the values and customs of the wilderness into the homes.

In the English colonies, as the frontier of settlement moved farther west, the restraints of civilized society weakened and the authority of the colonial governments became more difficult to maintain until it was almost nonexistent. Similarly, the absence of an educated clergy on this frontier did much to weaken the bonds of civilized behavior.[10] The frontier settlers, if they paid any heed to religion at all, depended on individual interpretation of the Bible, which in itself amounted to a rejection of authority. It was thus easy for them to reject all external authority. As long as they were able to control events, they needed to obey only the dictates of self-interest; but when they encountered hostile forces that they could not master, they immediately appealed for help to the colonial authorities. These authorities, remote from the dangers and problems of the frontier, frequently failed to respond, thereby creating hostility between the two sections.

Again the Canadian experience was different. The Canadian frontiersmen, although frequently out of the colony, many of them for years at a time, did make trips back to the central colony. They always retained some ties with civilization, and while they were in the west, the officers at the main posts and the missionaries exercised some degree of restraining influence over them. Although many of the *coureurs de bois* paid little heed to authority most of the time, all were aware of how they were expected to conduct themselves. They might honor the king's edicts and the canons of the Church in the breach rather than in the observance, but if their conduct became too notorious they had to reckon on the possibility of one day being brought to account.[11] Moreover, they were always a minority among the Indian nations and dependent on them to a large degree; in their own self-interest, they dared not behave in too offensive a manner. Any who did endangered not only themselves but other Canadians, perhaps the entire French position in a vast area.

The Anglo-American frontier settler, by comparison, felt no such restraint in his relations with the Indians. To him, they were merely savages whom he despised, feared, and wished removed from the lands he coveted.[12] The Canadian needed the Indians to provide goods and services, they were commercial partners; but the Anglo-American saw the Indian merely as an obstacle to progress to be exterminated as quickly as possible. On this point the nineteenth-century American historian Francis Parkman commented: "The English borderers regarded the Indians less as men than as vicious and dangerous wild animals. In fact, the benevolent and philanthropic view of the American savage is for those who are beyond his reach: it has never yet been held by any whose wives and children have lived in danger of his scalping-knife."[13] As with so much in Parkman's histories of New France, this was a half-truth. The Canadian attitude toward the Indian may not have been exactly "benevolent and philanthropic," but the Canadians had suffered heavily in their wars with the Iroquois, and they did manifest, in a variety of ways, considerable respect for these particular nations. The eighteenth-century Jesuit historian Father Charlevoix was closer to the truth when he wrote: "The British Americans . . . do not humour the Savages, because they see no need to do so. The French youth, on the contrary . . . get along well with the natives, whose esteem they easily win in war and whose friendship they always earn."[14]

Given this marked difference in frontier experience, what effect did the peculiarly Canadian conditions have on the central colony? In what ways did the Canadian frontier affect French culture and institutions in the settled communities? In studying this question one must begin with what the French brought with them from France, then note any departure from the culture and institutional practice of France. And here great care has to be exercised, for some quite radical changes were made by the French government in the institutions brought to Canada. This was particularly true in the administrative machinery and in the administration of justice. Reforms that the government could not make in France owing to the resistance of powerful vested interests were made in Canada. It would therefore be wrong to attribute these particular changes to Canadian conditions, that is, to the frontier environment. Little significant change occurred in the structure and working of the Church, only minor variations in methods to suit local conditions. In secular society, however, some marked changes occurred, setting the Canadian people apart as quite distinct from people of the same social class in France or in the English colonies. By the end of the seventeenth century a unique Canadian individual and a unique form of society had developed. To a large degree it was environment, the frontier experience, that brought this about.

One aspect of this development was made very plain in the military field. When the long-drawn-out struggle between England and France for imperial supremacy began in 1689, the Canadians were more than able to hold their own against the English colonies. They proved to be vastly superior to the Anglo-Americans in forest warfare, and the Indian nations, for the most part, favored the French. The devastating raids on the English border settlements bear witness to this. The attempts of the English colonies to conquer Canada all ended in failure; several large-scale expeditions had to be abandoned before they made contact with the foe owing to poor organization and general ineptitude. Only part of Acadia, very weakly defended, was lost by the French in all this time. In the mid-eighteenth century, the rapid growth of population in the English colonies, doubling every generation, caused the pressure of their westward movement to increase immeasurably. As long as the French had to contend only with Anglo-American fur traders they could more than hold their own, but in the 1750s a new element was introduced into the struggle, that of Anglo-American land speculators covetous of the Indians' lands in the Ohio Valley. Moreover, this time they could count on the full support of British military might. Thus began the final conflict between the two types of frontier, the fur trade and military frontier of the French, and the advancing land settlement frontier of the Anglo-Americans.

During the first three years after hostilities began in 1754, the French almost brought certain of the northern and central colonies to their knees; their governors were reduced to pleading with the imperial government to make peace at any price.[15] It was not the Anglo-American frontiersmen or the provincial troops that ultimately conquered Canada; rather, it was the frontiersmen who pleaded loudest for protection since they were bearing the brunt of the Canadian onslaught. Canada was finally conquered, after six long years of hostilities, by the Royal Navy and British regular soldiers. Although these troops initially suffered disastrous defeats, they eventually mastered the art of forest warfare. When the Indian allies of the French defected, the British were able to gain the upper hand in the west; and the tactical blunders of the French command enabled them to take Quebec. Once the French forts in the west and the colony's seaport were captured, the Canadian military and commercial empire collapsed. This made abundantly plain how tenuous French control of the interior had been.

After the conquest, the British found themselves obliged to adopt the old western policy of the French. They now sought to bar the area west of the Alleghenies to settlement by the Anglo-American frontiersmen and to preserve the Indian fur trade frontier. But eventually the British were swept aside by the Americans and their new-found allies, the French. The frontier of settlement then surged forward and the old Canadian frontier was finally submerged.

◁ **2** ▷

New France, 1524-1629: A Commercial Outpost

*T*he French were relative latecomers to the Americas. Hernando Cortes had conquered Mexico before Giovanni da Verrazano, a Florentine navigator financed by French and Italian bankers of Lyon, in 1524 sailed along and mapped the coast of North America from Florida to Maine. Ten years later, after Francisco Pizarro had conquered the Inca empire in Peru, the French again turned their attention to the New World. In 1534 the Breton sea captain Jacques Cartier made the first of his expeditions to North America. His fame rests on the fact that he was the first, not to discover the greatest entry of all into the interior of the continent, but to leave a detailed account that has survived of his voyages up the St. Lawrence.

At the end of May 1534, Cartier's two ships were in the straits of Belle Isle, between Newfoundland and Labrador, seeking a passage to Cathay. Labrador itself appeared to hold nothing of value, and Cartier dismissed it with the comment that he thought it must be the land that God gave to Cain. Continuing south into the Gulf, he skirted the shore of the Gaspé Peninsula, where he encountered a group of natives who obviously had had dealings with Europeans before. They held up furs and by signs indicated that they wanted to barter. Cartier's men gave them a few knives and other ironware, and a red cap for their chief—objects that delighted the natives. Farther along the coast, the impression that the native Canadians had previously encountered Europeans was confirmed. Cartier noted in his journal:

> This people may be called savage, for they are the sorriest folk there can be in the world, and the whole lot of them had not anything above the value of five sous, their canoes and fishing-nets excepted. . . . They made all the young women retire into the woods except two or three who remained.[1]

Clearly, at this time the French considered furs to be of very little value; and the removal of the women to a safe distance indicates that the Indians knew what to guard against when dealing with European sailors.

These particular Indians, members of the Iroquois nation that dominated the St. Lawrence Valley from Lake Ontario to Gaspé, were not wary enough. Cartier's men kidnapped two of the sons of their chief Donnacona and took them back to France. Cartier intended thereby to prove to the French authorities that he really had discovered new lands. He also expected, once these Indian youths had been taught to speak French, to gain invaluable knowledge of the country farther up the Gulf. As it was, who could tell what might lie beyond the most distant point their vision had penetrated? Asia might be reached by sailing only a little farther, or there might be lands like Mexico, inhabited by peoples rich in the things Europeans coveted most—gold, silver, copper, spices, precious stones.

This possibility sufficed for the Admiral of France, Philippe Chabot, to commission Cartier to undertake a second voyage the following year, and for Francis I to invest 3000 *livres* in the enterprise. This time Cartier had three ships and 110 men. By August 13 his expedition had sailed beyond the westernmost point reached in the first voyage, past Anticosti Island. Donnacona's sons, whom he had brought back with him, explained that the kingdom of the Saguenay was a little farther on, and beyond that again, the town of Canada. Tacking back and forth across the Gulf, Cartier proceeded southwest until he reached the village of Stadacona, near the present site of Quebec. There Donnacona was delighted to regain his sons and receive the gifts the French brought—knives, exotic clothing, and trinkets. On the banks of the St. Charles, near its mouth and beneath the high steep cliff, Cartier established his base.

After exploring the surrounding area in the heat of the late Canadian summer, Cartier made plans to continue up the river. But here he encountered difficulty; the natives of Stadacona were reluctant to allow him to proceed farther to the village called Hochelaga, where Montreal was later established. The French were to encounter opposition from the Indians for the same reason again and again during the next two centuries and more. The natives of Stadacona did not want those of Hochelaga to have the wondrous metal goods the French had brought, or if they were to have them, to receive them only through the medium of trade with the Iroquois of Stadacona. Commerce, with all its competitive devices, monopolies, forestalling, and profiteering, was by no means foreign to these men of the Stone Age.

Despite the Indians' resort to sorcery and their warnings that to proceed farther west would lead to a land of snow and ice where the group would surely freeze to death, Cartier persisted and with thirty men reached the village of Hochelaga at the foot of the mountain, that he named Mont Royal. Hochelaga was a typical Iroquois village. Surrounded by vast corn fields cleared from the oak forest, it was enclosed by a three-tiered palisade of tree trunks thirty feet high, with galleries at intervals on which were piled stones to be used in repelling enemy attacks. Within the palisade were some fifty bark huts. The Indians were not in the least timorous, which is hardly surprising in view of their great superiority in numbers, and the hairy, oddly clad strangers must have appeared to be weaklings compared to themselves. Several times in the French account of the trip mention is made of the robustness of the Indians, who during lengthy marches carried the French on their backs when they grew tired.

On the day of their arrival Cartier and his men climbed to the top of Mont Royal and there viewed the country in its autumn splendor for miles around. There were mountain chains in the distance to north and south, and the Indian guides indicated that farther up the river violent rapids barred the water route. They also indicated that up another great river flowing from the west was a land where the natives wore European clothing, lived in towns, and possessed great stores of metal similar to the silver of the captain's whistle chain and the copper of a sailor's knife handle.

And so the map of the interior of North America began to unfold. The great rapids, later to be mockingly named "La Chine," removed all hope of voyaging directly by boat to Cathay. But the "kingdom of the Saguenay," which was partly the product of the Indian's imagination and partly of wishful interpretation, was most intriguing. Here was something to raise the hopes of any European, perhaps enough to impress the king of France and persuade him that his investment had not been wasted—provided that it was continued. The next day Cartier and his men returned down river and by October 11 were back at their base, named Ste. Croix. By this time the French and Donnacona's tribesmen had become very suspicious of each other. Cartier's men therefore built a moated fort, armed with cannon. They did not yet know it, but a far worse danger than the hostility of the natives was approaching.

The site of their fort, present-day Quebec city, is approximately two degrees south of the latitude on which Paris lies. Cartier and his men had no way of knowing that there could be a great difference in the winter climate of the two places, particularly after the deceiving heat of the St. Lawrence

Valley summer. From mid-November until mid-April the fort and the ships were buried under several feet of snow and ice, and sub-zero winds howled across the frozen river. As though that were not enough, the men were stricken with scurvy. By mid-February only ten of the crew of 110 were even moderately healthy. Twenty-five died and far more would have succumbed had not the Iroquois shown the French a remedy, the bark and needles of white cedar boiled in water. This herbal tonic, rich in ascorbic acid, quickly revived the men. It also indicated that the Indians had some valuable knowledge hitherto denied Europeans.

Cartier, in true European fashion, began observing and interrogating them as best he could. He discovered that they believed in a God and life after death. When he somehow informed them that theirs was a false God, that a belief in the God of the French and the ceremony of baptism was necessary to attain heaven, the Iroquois asked that he baptize them. Cartier declared, quite erroneously, that he could not but he promised to administer the sacrament on a later occasion. He found the Indians' marriage customs deplorable, and that their system of communal holdings rather than private property had little to recommend it. The extent of their agricultural knowledge was quite impressive; they raised corn, melons, squash, and beans. They had no domestic animals except dogs, but wild game and fish provided them with an ample and seemingly well-balanced diet. That they were physically bigger and stronger than the French would seem to indicate that their diet was superior to that of Europeans. Much of their meat was eaten freshly killed, hence it would have retained its vitamin content. Only the surplus was smoked or dried to preserve it. Salt they did not use at all. One of their customs, the smoking of tobacco in pipes, proved to be too much for Cartier. He tried it and reported that his mouth seemed to be filled with flaming pepper.

Once the river was free of ice, Cartier made ready to return to France to obtain fresh supplies before beginning the search for the kingdom of the Saguenay and its stores of wealth. His relations with Donnacona left much to be desired, and it was imperative that he retain the amity of the tribe that controlled the entryway to the west. Therefore, before sailing, and in connivance with a rival of Donnacona for leadership in the tribe, Cartier and his men treacherously took Donnacona and several of his companions prisoner. Then, promising to bring them back after a year's sojourn in France, he sailed down river with two of his ships on May 6. Despite Cartier's promises, none of these Iroquois were ever to return to their homeland. From the Indian viewpoint these Europeans began by stealing the people from their land, and were to end by stealing the continent from the people.

Intriguing though the French Court found Cartier's account of his discoveries and what they implied, the troubled state of Europe in general and France in particular precluded another French venture in North America for the time being. The Protestant Reformation was making gains everywhere, but the renewal of hostilities between Francis I and the emperor, Charles V, prevented both rulers from devoting their attention to the suppression of heresy in their lands. In 1583, however, a truce was called in the war and within a year Francis I was entertaining schemes for sending another expedition to unlock the riches of the kingdom of the Saguenay, which were badly needed to restore his exhausted war chest. This time he sent not merely an exploratory expedition, but one to establish a permanent colony in Canada to serve as a base for the conquest of the farther kingdom.

To command this colonizing expedition, Francis selected a Protestant nobleman, Jean-François de la Rocque, sieur de Roberval. A soldier of some repute, a courtier, and a member of a powerful family, Roberval appeared to have the talents for an enterprise such as this, and Jacques Cartier, previously commissioned to command the expedition, now became Roberval's subordinate, his captain-general and master navigator. The king provided funds for 10 ships, 400 sailors, 300 soldiers, some skilled tradesmen, a few women, and all manner of livestock and supplies. By his commission, Roberval was empowered to grant land fiefs in seigneurial tenure; the prospect of such grants and of more portable riches was attractive to adventurous and penurious members of the lower nobility. It proved difficult, however, to recruit adequate numbers of artisans and laborers. Eventually, recourse was had to the royal prisons. Canada's first settlers appear to have consisted largely of gallows bait.

In Spain there was considerable alarm when reports of the preparations being made at St. Malo were received. Spies were ordered to learn of the expedition's intended destination. Grave fears were entertained that the French intended an assault on the Spanish settlements in the New World.[2] In any event, Spain claimed the lands previously visited by Cartier. It was even feared that the great river of Canada might give the French access to attack the southern Spanish colonies from the rear, but this was not seriously entertained for long. To strengthen his own case with the Papacy, Francis I declared in strong phrases that one of his chief aims in claiming lands in America was to establish the Christian religion among the heathen. During Cartier's previous expeditions no attempt had been made to convert the Indians.[3] Moreover, if the conversion of pagans to the Roman Catholic faith was a chief aim, it would appear odd that a Protestant should have been chosen as commander of the expedition and viceroy in the future French colony.

In May 1541 Cartier sailed with five ships. Roberval was delayed by the failure of his artillery and supplies to arrive and did not get away until the following year. Not until August 23 did Cartier reach Stadacona. The Iroquois village was still there. Five years had elapsed since Cartier's departure with his ten kidnapped Iroquois, and he had promised to bring them back safe and sound in ten months. All but one of them, a child, had died in France. When asked, Cartier admitted that Donnacona, an old man, was dead, but he declared that the others were alive and well, great lords now who preferred to remain in France. Although the Iroquois professed to accept this explanation, Cartier decided not to re-establish his old base on the St. Charles. Instead, he proceeded a few miles up river to Cap Rouge, where a small river cut a cleft in the cliffs on the north shore of the St. Lawrence. The surrounding area was rich forest land, obviously capable of bearing good crops once cleared. But far more important, along the cliffs, veins of rich iron and traces of silver, gold, and precious stones that appeared to be diamonds abounded. Cartier then sent two ships back to France to report on these exciting finds. Spain, it seemed, would not be the only country to tap the riches of a Mexico or a Peru.

Cartier soon discovered that the severity of the weather during the earlier expedition had not been a freak of nature; but scurvy was no problem this time. The Iroquois, however, were. Not without reason, they had come to distrust the French, and considering the sort of men in Cartier's band, it is quite likely that they gave the Iroquois good cause to wish themselves rid of the interlopers. At all events, the Indians harassed the French to such an extent that Cartier feared he and his men would be overwhelmed. In June they set sail for France. En route, they stopped at the harbor of St. John's in Newfoundland and there found, along with seventeen fishing vessels, Roberval with three tall ships. Cartier was ordered to return to Stadacona, but during the night, for reasons known only to himself, he and his ships stole out of the bay and set sail for Brittany.

Despite Cartier's defection, Roberval went on to Cap Rouge. He lacked Cartier's hard-gained knowledge and experience, and fifty of the men died of scurvy. In the spring Roberval tried unsuccessfully to get past the Lachine Rapids. Although the accounts do not mention Iroquois hostility, Roberval decided that another winter was beyond his resources. By September he and his men were back in France. The first attempt to found a permanent French colony in the New World had failed miserably, and the kingdom of the Saguenay was as remote as ever. Worse still, the gold brought back by Cartier proved to be iron pyrites, the diamonds common quartz.

The disappointment, combined with the turbulence of the wars of religion in France, put an end to the monarchy's interest in the new lands for the time being. Canada seemingly did not offer enough to warrant the great expense of colonizing expeditions. The land had been found to be fertile, but it produced only the same crops that would grow in Europe, and seemingly none of the exotic products of eastern and southern climes. No spices or dye woods had been found. The riches of the kingdom of the Saguenay, if they existed, were too remote, and the winters were enough to give any sensible man pause. Before the French would renew their attempts to claim and settle these regions, fresh inducements had to be found.

Meanwhile, European fishermen voyaged in increasing numbers to the shores of Newfoundland and the Gulf of St. Lawrence during the summer months. Before the end of the century some five hundred ships a year fished in what are now Canadian waters, and the Basques of Spain had established a whale fishery at Tadoussac, where the Saguenay River cuts deeply through the Laurentian shield to join the St. Lawrence. By this time too, the shape of the new continent was becoming clear. The cartographers of Europe had the benefit of more direct observation, less need to rely on wishful thinking and imagination. The French had done much here. They had found the main route to the interior of the continent and charted it from the open sea for some 1500 miles. French names, not Spanish, English, or Portuguese, were given to the rivers and islands along this route.

On the debit side, the French had alienated the Iroquois, who occupied the upper reaches of the river and dominated the neighboring tribes as far as the Gulf. There could be little hope that the French would successfully occupy the St. Lawrence Valley if this powerful nation opposed them; an army would have been needed for the task. But only by occupying the area from Stadacona to Hochelaga could any nation hope to push on into the interior, to the kingdom of the Saguenay or beyond to the western ocean and Cathay.

Disappointed in the north, the French turned their attention southward, to the lands claimed by Portugal and Spain. In 1555, under the auspices of Admiral Gaspard de Coligny, a Huguenot base for a colony was established at the mouth of the Rio de Janeiro. Five years later the Portuguese captured it. Next Coligny sought to establish a Protestant colony in Florida. It survived for three years, until in 1565 a Spanish expedition captured the French forts and put many of the would-be settlers to the sword. If the French were going to establish colonies in the New World, they would have to be well out of reach of the Spanish and Portuguese, which meant well to the north. In 1572 the massacre of St. Bartholomew's Day plunged France once again into civil war. Until peace and stability were re-established in the kingdom, colonial enterprises were out of the question.

Despite the anarchy of the fourth war of religion in France, French fishermen continued to garner wealth from the rich fishing grounds of the North Atlantic American coast. The cod of the Grand Banks was by this time one of the economic mainstays of northwestern France. As more ships engaged in the fishing, Normans and Bretons began to search for less crowded fishing grounds, pushing on into the Bay of Fundy and the Gulf of St. Lawrence. In the days of Cartier, French fishermen had traded European goods with the Indians for furs, but they had put little stock in this commerce. The Indians were avid for European knives, axes, pots, and trinkets, but the French fishermen had at first shown scant interest in exploiting the potential of this trade.

As each summer more and more Indians came to the coast with furs to exchange for European goods, the French seamen began to realize that profits to rival those obtained for fish could be made, and without the unpleasant labor of catching, drying, or salting the fish. Soon ships were going out from the northern ports of France for furs alone. Fur displaced fish as the economic motive for French penetration into the interior of the continent and was to remain the basis of the northern economy until the nineteenth century. The traders began pushing farther up the St. Lawrence, seeking out the Indians, striving to reach them before other ships arrived on the scene. It was no longer the lure of imagined stocks of bullion and jewels in mythical kingdoms that drew them on, but the tangible and rich profits of a readily available northern staple.

As a staple, fur had distinct advantages over many other commodities. First, it fulfilled the prime prerequisite of staples derived from overseas: it could not be produced in the mother country. Furs were light in weight, of a high value relative to bulk, easily packaged, easy to transport, and, in the early years at least, highly profitable. Perhaps most important, their production did not require a large labor supply; the Indians trapped the animals, processed the furs, and transported them to points along the Gulf that ships from Europe could easily reach. No special skills were required to engage in the trade; all that was needed was a ship and crew to cross the Atlantic and a supply of trade goods that appealed to the Indians. Some knowledge of the Indians' language and their tribal customs became a distinct advantage as competition between rival European traders increased. There was no need to capture and enslave Indians to process the staple, as was the case in the Spanish colonies; no need to import Negro slaves, at great expense, as was the case in the Spanish, the Portuguese, and subsequently in the southern English colonies. The fur trade, from the beginning to the end, was based on an economic partnership between Europeans and Indians. Thus, once the fur trade became well established in the St. Lawrence Valley, the French, who quickly came to dominate it, had to establish good relations with the Indians.

It was not, however, until the broadbrimmed beaver felt hat became fashionable in Europe in the latter part of the sixteenth century that the Canadian fur trade really came into its own.[4] The fur of the beaver was then by far the best material for the manufacture of hat felt. Each strand of the soft underfur on a beaver pelt has tiny barbs at the tip. When made into felt these barbs ensure that it will remain matted. As a result, beaver hats hold their shape better and wear longer than hats made of other materials. Beaver fur had been used for hat felt in the Middle Ages but by the late sixteenth century the animal was extinct in western Europe and only very limited supplies could be obtained from Scandinavia and Russia. Then Norman and Breton fishermen began to return from the North American fishing grounds with beaver pelts of excellent quality. The cold winters of the Canadian north caused the native animals to grow thick fur. Moreover, beaver pelts have two layers of fur, the soft, barbed underfur and long sleek outer guard hairs. The felting process required the removal of the outer hairs before the underfur was sheared off. The northern Indians fashioned beaver pelts into robes to wear and sleep in. The sweat and grease on their bodies and the smoke of their lodges made the pelts in these beaver robes soft and supple, and also loosened the guard hairs. Pelts so treated were easy to process in the making of felt, so they brought the highest prices in Europe. In the early days of the trade a knife, an axe, or a few cheap trinkets worth about a *livre* were all an Indian asked for a beaver robe that sold for over 200 *livres* in Paris. In one good trading season a man could make a small fortune. The market for beaver seemed limitless; beaver hats sold for over thirty *livres* and fashion decreed that all gentlemen wear them.

With huge profits to be made in the fur trade, the number of ships coming out each year to engage in it grew rapidly. The Indians, every bit as astute as Europeans, soon lost their initial awe of the bearded, pale little men in strange clothes who had marvelous goods to offer in exchange for a few sweaty furs. As the word spread, more and more of them gathered to trade. Tadoussac, where the Saguenay River flows into the St. Lawrence from the far north and with a wide bay offering safe anchorage, had become the customary meeting place by the end of the sixteenth century. Over a thousand Algonkin, Etchimin, and Montagnais gathered there every summer. They quickly learned never to trade with the first ship that appeared, but to wait until several arrived and competed with one another, thus driving up the prices.

It soon became obvious that the Europeans' end of the trade was being ruined. The number engaging in it had somehow to be reduced, and the only way seemed to be through an appeal to the crown for monopoly rights that would enable the recipient of the royal favor to exclude all others and stabilize prices at a profitable level. The king of France was quite willing to grant such a privilege, as it cost him nothing and could be made a vehicle for the extension of his territories and power overseas. But monopolies were no sooner granted than they were rescinded as those excluded brought pressure to have the charters canceled. Attempts by monopoly holders to establish colonies as year-round trading bases on Île de Sable in 1598 and at Tadoussac in 1600 ended in failure. It began to appear as though these northern lands were quite uninhabitable for Europeans and must remain merely a place where ships from France called to fish and trade furs during the summer months. Cruel experience seemed to prove that at the first snow flurries of autumn the land had to be relinquished to the Indians.

In 1603 Pierre Du Gua, sieur de Monts, obtained the title of Vice-Admiral and Lieutenant General of New France, along with a ten-year commercial monopoly, on condition that he establish sixty settlers. Partly for climatic reasons, partly to escape the competition of traders who refused to respect the rights of a monopoly holder, he chose to establish his colony on

Champlain Habitation, Port Royal, Acadia, 1605. Reconstructed on the original site. (Department of Indian Affairs and Northern Development, National and Historic Parks Branch, Ottawa)

the Atlantic seaboard well south of the St. Lawrence. When his expedition sailed from Le Havre in 1604, Samuel de Champlain accompanied it as cartographer. Both de Monts and Champlain had previously spent a summer at Tadoussac; Champlain had explored the St. Lawrence as far as Mont Royal, and its tributaries, the Saguenay and the Richelieu rivers. From the bases established in the Bay of Fundy, first at the mouth of the Ste. Croix River then across the Bay at Port Royal, Champlain now carefully charted the coast line as far south as Cape Cod.

It is sometimes asserted that had he gone a little farther he would have discovered the river Henry Hudson was to explore in 1609 and that he would surely have grasped the significance of this river, which gave access to the interior. It would then have been likely that the French rather than the Dutch would have established trading posts and settlements there and the whole history of North America would have been different. This is possible, but more than that cannot be said. The French were interested only in the fur trade and the search for a northwest passage. Some of the French were interested also in conversion of the Indians to Christianity. The Hudson River would soon have been found not to be the desired passage to the western ocean; moreover the lands to the north were far better suited to the fur trade. With their limited resources a choice between the Hudson River region and the St. Lawrence would have had to be made. It is unlikely that the southern entry would have been chosen when the St. Lawrence seemed to offer so much more.

As it was, de Monts' Acadian venture endured less than a decade. The amount of furs obtained from the Indians was insufficient to offset the costs of maintaining the settlement at Port Royal. Scurvy took a heavy toll and Cartier's remedy was no longer known. The religious quarrels of Europe accompanied the settlers, causing dissension among them. Merchants excluded from the North American trade by de Monts' charter paid it little heed. They continued to send out ships to barter with the Indians, and in 1607 they succeeded in having free trade restored. In 1611 the Society of Jesus stepped in to try to maintain the settlement in Acadia, thus making its entry into the North American missionary field.

By this time, the French were not the only Europeans to have established bases on the Atlantic coast. English fishermen had attempted to establish fishing posts on the Kennebec River but had been driven out by the Abenaki Indians. In Virginia, after initial failure a settlement had been established in 1607. Its governor, Sir Thomas Dale, upon hearing of the French settlement to the north was of the opinion that the continent was not sufficiently large to contain both French and English, despite the hundreds of miles of virgin wilderness that separated them. In 1613 he commissioned Samuel Argall to destroy the French settlements. That England and France were then not at war meant nothing. Argall and his men overwhelmed a French outpost near Mount Desert island, killed a Jesuit priest, wounded several of the settlers, took most of them prisoners, and then razed the buildings. Port Royal was next. Everything there that could not be carried off was burned to the ground. All but some twenty men who were away at the time were taken to Virginia or England as prisoners. Those who had escaped managed to eke out an existence until aid eventually came from France, but little remained of the missionary outpost and commercial establishment except a tenuous claim to title on the land. This raid set the pattern for the future of the region. Although blessed with rich natural resources the Acadian marches, owing to their geographic position, were doomed to remain a buffer zone between the rival empires until one or the other prevailed.

The French, in the early years of the seventeenth century, had returned to the St. Lawrence Valley in a fresh attempt to establish a commercial colony. What success they enjoyed they owed largely to the persistence and enterprise of one man, Samuel de Champlain. It was he who persuaded de Monts to try to recoup his Acadian losses by a trading venture far enough up the St. Lawrence to forestall the summer traders at Tadoussac. In July 1608 Champlain established his base at the narrows of Quebec, 130 miles upstream from Tadoussac. This marked the beginning of the westward movement in North America that was not to end until the Pacific was finally reached overland by Alexander Mackenzie, a Montreal fur trader, in 1793.

The Iroquois who in Cartier's day had dominated this part of the continent had long since moved to the south, to the Mohawk River and the lands south of Lake Ontario. There was no one to dispute French occupancy, as the entire valley of the St. Lawrence lay vacant, but for the ensuing quarter century there was no real attempt to establish much more than a trading factory and a warehouse for storing furs and trade goods—the furs to be shipped back to Europe and the trade goods transshipped for trade in the interior. No real attempt was made to settle the land. The merchants in France who provided the capital for the base would not invest a *sou* more than was absolutely necessary. All they wanted was a trading counter manned by salaried clerks.

This bastion of France's infant commercial empire, situated on the narrow strand between the steep cliff and the St. Lawrence with its seventeen-foot tide, consisted of three connected barracks, eighteen feet by fifteen feet, a large storehouse, and a pigeon loft, all surrounded by a palisade with a cannon mounted at the corners and a fifteen-foot moat complete with drawbridge. In the early years fewer than twenty men wintered at the base and no attempt was made to raise more than a few vegetables and salad greens. Food supplies were brought from France, and a large part of the men's time was consumed in cutting supplies of firewood to last through the five months of cruel winter.

Champlain made frequent trips back to France to plead for more aid, usually without success. When he returned to Quebec in the spring, more often than not he found that the men left behind to guard the base had done nothing—that they had made no improvements to the buildings or repairs, and had not planted any crops. In 1617 Champlain induced Louis Hébert, a one-time Paris apothecary of an adventurous disposition who had been at Port Royal for a time, to settle at Quebec. The company directors were induced to promise to support him and his family for two years and to pay him 200 crowns a year for three years. But when Hébert, having sold his assets, arrived at Honfleur to take ship for Canada, he was informed that he would be paid only 100 crowns and would have to serve the company as directed; only in his spare time would he be allowed to work his own land, and he had to sell any crops he raised to the company at current French prices. Hébert, having burned his bridges, had to accept, but with such treatment accorded an honest would-be colonist it is easy to see why no others followed him. Yet it is estimated that at this time upward of a thousand ships spent the summer on the Grand Banks, along the North Atlantic Coast, and in the St. Lawrence, fishing or trading for furs.[5]

To forestall the competition of the summer traders at Tadoussac, it was essential that the men at Quebec establish a commercial alliance with the Algonkin and Huron middlemen. These tribes, located north of the Great Lakes, garnered furs from the northern and western tribes in exchange for French goods. This was the main reason for maintaining the year-round base at Quebec. As soon as the ice went out of the river, Champlain's men could go up the St. Lawrence to meet the western tribes coming down with their furs and make sure they went no further than Quebec. Champlain was quick to realize that the Huron were the key to commercial success.[6] By establishing direct trade relations with the Huron, one middleman could be eliminated, an assured supply maintained, costs greatly reduced, and the rival traders undersold on the European fur markets.

The maintenance of good relations with the northern trading nations required that the French master their languages, understand their mores and values, show them respect, and pay court to them assiduously—treat them not as inferiors or subordinates but as commercial partners and social equals. The French were far more dependent on the Indians than the Indians were on them. Not only was there the gross disparity in numbers—prior to 1630 the number of French in Canada was less than a hundred[7]—but the colonists had to acquire all manner of specialized knowledge from the Indians, such as how to manufacture and use such essential things as snowshoes, toboggans, and canoes; in short, how to survive in the Canadian environment.

Within a year of establishing his fort, Champlain discovered that more than diplomacy was required to maintain trading relations with the northern tribes. In the summer of 1609 a war party of some sixty Huron and Algonkin came to solicit French aid in an attack on their ancient foe, the Iroquois.

Champlain had no choice but to comply. With two companions he accompanied them up the Richelieu River to the lake that came to bear his name. His account of what ensued provides a good glimpse of what war must have been like in that part of the world before the advent of Europeans. It resembled not so much war as then practiced in Europe but a form of savage blood sport that provided an opportunity for individuals to demonstrate their courage, fortitude, and skill.

The skirmish between the sixty odd northern Indians, the three Frenchmen, and some two hundred Mohawk was the first clash in a war between French and Iroquois that was to endure, off and on, for nearly a hundred years. For the Iroquois, it was their first encounter with firearms. The crude harquebuses of Champlain and his men suddenly belching flame, smoke, and thunder in the forest glade, three of the Iroquois falling mortally wounded, proved unnerving. The rest turned and fled. More were killed during the pursuit and ten or twelve taken prisoner. Champlain then had to witness another aspect of Indian warfare, one with which the French were to become all too familiar in the years ahead, the long-drawn-out, hideous torture of the captives.

It is sometimes asserted that Champlain's role in this brief clash was the direct cause of the ensuing long struggle between the French and the Iroquois. Although his role on this occasion did nothing to endear him to the Iroquois, too much must not be made of it. The French had established themselves in the St. Lawrence Valley and were allied commercially with the northern tribes, enemies of the Iroquois. Within a few years the Dutch established themselves on the Hudson River and provided the Iroquois with European weapons. Once this occurred the lines were irrevocably drawn; the ancient war between the Algonkin and Iroquois now became a war between two European powers and two economic regions for dominance in North America. The only way this could have been avoided would have been for both the St. Lawrence and Hudson rivers to have been colonized by a single European power. Champlain was merely an agent of existing forces; he did not create them.

For the first five years the returns from the fur trade were poor, barely enough to pay the costs of maintaining the base at Quebec with a staff of only seventeen or eighteen men. In an effort to persuade more of the northwestern tribesmen to bring their furs to Quebec, Champlain began the practice, much in vogue in North America today, of sending company field representatives to the Indian villages. Their first tasks were to learn the language of the Indians and as much as possible of their customs, the geography of their country, and to make maps of it for future use. In 1612 he sent Étienne Brulé to winter with the Huron. This young man demonstrated that the French could adapt themselves all too easily to the Indian way of life. During the ensuing quarter century he traveled through much of the interior of North America. He was finally killed and, according to the Recollet missionary, Sagard, eaten by the Indians, whose moral standards, indulgent though they were, he had succeeded in outraging.[8] He was the first Frenchman, but by no means the last, to be completely assimilated by the Indians.

By 1614 the trade in furs was proving so profitable that a new company was formed in France to ensure better backing for Champlain at Quebec. He was now able to make plans for a more stable settlement, bringing peasants to provide food for the trading staff so that the men at the post would not be totally dependent on food supplies brought from France. The hopes of the French crown to undertake missionary work among the Indians which would cement their commercial ties with the French as well as save them from eternal hell-fire in the next world, could now be realized. When the bishops of France gathered in Paris for the Estates-General of 1614, they quickly approved Champlain's suggestion that four of the Recollet order of the Minor Friars be sent to Canada to begin the stupendous task. In June 1615, Fathers Denis Jamay, Jean Dolbeau, and Joseph Le Caron and lay brother Pacifique du Plessis arrived at Quebec, where Champlain had already put men to work building a house and chapel for them. So eager were they to begin their work that two of their number left that year for Tadoussac and Georgian Bay.

This marked the beginning of the great missionary drive of the Counter Reformation French clergy to persuade the nomadic hunters of a vast continent to change their entire way of life, abandon their ancient customs, values, and religious beliefs, and live according to the precepts of a sophisticated European religion ill-adapted to their temperament and their needs. The efforts of these men of God, who sincerely believed that their ministrations were essential to save the Indians from an eternity of torment after death, to procure for them the bliss of a seventeenth-century European's concept of heaven were to contribute unwittingly to the final destruction of the North American Indian. Before they could have converted the Indian without debasing him they would somehow have had to persuade Europeans to live according to the tenets of their own religion.

During the first decade of this missionary endeavor it could not have appeared to the Indians that the Recollets posed any serious threat to their way of life. There were never more than four missionaries in New France at one time, and fewer than fifty Indians were baptized, most of them when they were at the point of death. In 1616 Father Le Caron returned to Quebec after spending one winter in Huronia. Not until 1623 did the Recollets go back to the Huron mission field, when Fathers Joseph Le Caron and Nicolas Viel and Brother Gabriel Sagard established a mission at the village of Quienonascaran. The following year Le Caron and Sagard returned to Quebec, leaving Father Viel to attempt the conversion of the Huron nation, estimated to number some 30,000 souls. The mere task of traveling to

Huronia in the company of the Indians almost broke the spirit of the early missionaries. Sagard, with deep feeling born of experience, commented:

> In order to practise patience in good earnest and to endure hardships beyond the limit of human strength, it is only necessary to make journeys with the savages, and long ones especially, such as we did; because besides the danger of death on the way, one must make up one's mind to endure and suffer more than could be imagined, from hunger, from sleeping always on the bare ground in the open country, from walking with great labour in water and bogs, and in some places over rocks, and through dark thick woods, from rain on one's back and all the evils that the season and weather can inflict, and from being bitten by a countless swarm of mosquitoes, and midges, together with difficulties of language in explaining clearly and showing them one's needs, and having no Christian beside one for communication and consolation in the midst of one's toil.[9]

Like most of the missionaries, Sagard found Indian food hard to stomach. Between Montreal and Huronia the Indians had supplies of corn cached at intervals of two-days travel. En route they existed on two meals a day of sagamité, corn ground between two stones and boiled into mush in a kettle; mixed in with it were any dirt and insects that happened to be on the stones. If fish or birds were caught, they were just thrown into a pot and boiled without being drawn; small animals had their fur seared off in the fire before they were tossed in. As the stew came to the boil, the feathery, furry scum was scooped off the top; then everyone dipped in. If a war party returning home with prisoners ran short of food, one of the captives was knocked on the head, quickly butchered, and boiled in the kettle. This technique of making one's food supply walk had distinct military advantages, but the French were appalled by the practice. And when an Indian, while paddling in a canoe, felt the need to urinate, he merely used the same birch bark bowl that served him to scoop his share of the sagamité out of the pot.

Given that there were so few of them and that it required years to master the Indians' languages, it is no wonder that the Recollets enjoyed little success. It has to be noted, however, that they found it difficult to adjust to the strange environment. They were, in fact, ill suited to the task by training and by temperament; but if nothing else, they did make a beginning in establishing good relations with the Indians. This in no small measure aided the French fur traders, for whom the missionaries served as public relations officers.

While the Recollets were establishing their mission in Huronia, Champlain was forced to accede to the demands of the Huron and Algonkin that he again provide them with military aid in their war with the Iroquois. The economic struggle between the rival commercial metropolises on the St. Lawrence and the Hudson rivers was now fully engaged. The Iroquois, provided with weapons by the recently established Dutch at Fort Orange, where Albany stands today, and paid high prices in trade goods for furs, were becoming increasingly bold, ambushing the northern tribes en route to trade at Quebec and pillaging them of their furs or goods. To maintain his commercial alliance, Champlain had to agree to his allies' demands. He also hoped, after the campaign, to continue on to discover the western ocean that the Indians spoke of with tantalizing vagueness.[10]

With two French companions and ten Indians, he set off for Huronia in July 1615, traveling by way of the Ottawa and Mattawa rivers, Lake Nipissing, and French River. On the way they were met by a party of 300 Ottawa, naked and grotesquely tattooed, with elaborate coiffures, master canoe men and great traders, who were soon to become the chief partners of the French in the fur trade. On birch bark with a piece of charcoal, one of them drew a map for Champlain of his country to the west for future reference. Taking leave of the Ottawa at the mouth of the French River, Champlain and his companions paddled swiftly south, over thirty miles a day. On August 1 they reached Huronia, landing near present-day Penetanguishene. Here Champlain found himself in pleasant country, with rolling hills and meadows intersected by shallow rivers and streams, and towering hardwood forests—oak, elm, and maple—with here and there heavy growth of poplar and spruce where forest fires had burned off the hardwoods. Running crisscross through this land were well-worn trails connecting the many Huron villages, which contained some thirty to thirty-five thousand people.

The villages, containing upward of two thousand people each, were for security reasons usually built on a hill and surrounded by as many as three palisades some twenty-five feet high. Galleries provided a place for bowmen to fire on attackers and for boulders and boiling water to be dropped on an enemy attempting to hack through the palisades. Inside were the long houses, some eighty feet by thirty feet, shaped like latter-day Quonset huts, the framework of supple branches lashed together with twisted strands of elm bark and the whole covered with sheets of elm or birch bark. Within the huts two racks extended along each side, one some three or four feet off the ground, the other a few feet above it, like double-deck bunks. Covered with fur robes, these were the sleeping quarters; children above, their elders below. Each long house held several families. Down the center were fires for warmth and cooking; two families usually shared a fire. Some of the smoke from these fires found its way out through the covered doorways at each end; most of it remained in the hut keeping mosquitoes at bay but frequently causing serious eye problems for the occupants, sometimes resulting in blindness later in life. There was no privacy in the long house, and property rights were almost nonexistent.

Scattered among the long houses were smaller sod and bark structures, smoke houses for meat, drying racks for fish, a sweat house used in the treatment of certain ailments. Here and there elevated racks held the bodies

Huron village, reconstructed at Midland, Ontario.

of the recently departed, awaiting the great feast of the dead for final interment. All around the long houses, paving the area between them, were garbage, bones, and offal, which were tossed casually to the half-wild dogs who swarmed about. The filth and stench, the swarms of biting insects, winged and crawling, were almost more than the more gently nurtured of the seventeenth-century French could stomach; but for those from the lower elements of European society it could not have been much worse than what they had known in the crowded sections of Europe's cities. Surrounding the village were the stump-ridden fields where the squaws cultivated the indigenous corn, squash, and beans, and the peas recently acquired from the French. Despite primitive methods the yield was adequate, and, unlike the Montagnais, the Huron were singularly provident, storing enough food for months or even years ahead. They appear to have eaten little meat; fish and vegetables were their staple foods. This was probably because, with such a large population in the area, little game remained. Yet that their food supply was sufficient and their diet adequate, is attested to by their hardihood.

Champlain spent a month in Huron villages such as these while his commercial allies, in what seemed to him desultory fashion, gathered their forces for an invasion of the Iroquois country. Not until September 1, after nights of feasting and dancing, was the war party, made up of some five hundred warriors, ready to depart. With him, Champlain took twelve French *engagés* who had accompanied Father Le Caron to build and maintain the Recollet mission post. By way of Lake Simcoe, the Kawartha Lakes, and the Otonabee and Trent river systems, they reached Lake Ontario, crossed it at the eastern narrows, and landed on what is today American soil. By October 10 they had reached their objective, the fortified village of the Onondaga. From the moment they arrived, the plans of the attackers miscarried. The Iroquois village had fortifications far stronger than those of Huron villages, and the firearms of the French had little effect on the stout long palisade. After a futile, disorganized assault, during which the Hurons suffered several casualties and Champlain was twice wounded, the attacking force beat a rapid retreat to Huronia.[11]

This minor battle was to have considerable significance. It marks a turning point in Iroquois history. When Jacques Cartier first sailed up the St. Lawrence, the Iroquois had dominated that water route to the sea. By the time Champlain reached Quebec, they had been driven back and confined to the area south of the St. Lawrence and Lake Ontario, west of the Hudson, and east of the Niagara River. On all sides they were beleaguered, by enemy tribes, to the east were the Mohegan, to the south the Andastes, to the north the Huron and Algonkin tribes. Only to the west where lay the lands of the Neutral were they relatively secure; and now the French had begun moving southwestward from Quebec up the St. Lawrence to its junction with the Ottawa, to trade with the foes of the Iroquois, providing them with ample supplies of steel weapons. The Iroquois had retreated as far as they could go; they now had to stand or die. In 1687, at the onset of fresh hostilities with the French, the Mohawk chiefs were to declare, "we intend to stay here and to live here and die here, for where can we run?"[12] They probably said the same prior to the abortive assault by Champlain and the Huron on the Onondaga village.

Afterward things must have looked different. The French with their firearms had been shown not to be invincible. Their prestige declined accordingly. The invading army had been beaten back and was not likely to return. If the Iroquois were to obtain supplies of firearms, they could retaliate, perhaps regain the lands they had lost. With the Dutch on the Hudson River willing to give almost anything to trade for furs, arms could be had. After 1615 the Iroquois took the offensive. To the end of the century the French found themselves engaged in a desperate struggle to defend their fur trade empire against the assaults of the Iroquois, who were seeking to divert the trade from Montreal to Albany, ultimately from Paris to London, with themselves playing the lucrative role of middlemen.

In 1623 word came to Quebec of developments in the west that were to become all too familiar throughout the ensuing history of New France. That summer a delegation of western Indians came to Quebec to trade and complained that the Huron and some Algonkin had held them up en route, seeking to prevent them from going to trade at Quebec and robbing them of much of their cargo. The Huron and their Algonkin associates were determined to maintain their profitable middlemen role. The following summer a delegation of Iroquois came to trade and to make peace with their Huron and Algonkin foes. Champlain agreed to act as mediary, but when the company directors in France learned of this development they were quick to see the danger. Peace between the Huron, the Algonkin, the French, and the Iroquois might enable the latter to divert the western fur trade to the Dutch. This would have destroyed the French commercial base on the St. Lawrence and ended all hope of a French colony in that part of the world.

Even at this early date the relationship of the Iroquois to the French was a paradoxical one. Their enmity threatened the survival of the French fur trade empire by either severing its communications with the western tribes or by destroying the base at Quebec in an open assault. Yet their friendship was equally dangerous, for were they to make a firm peace with the western tribes that traded with the French, they might grant these tribes access to the Dutch trading post on the Hudson or serve as middlemen for them. French control of the trade of the interior of North America was dependent on the Iroquois to serve as a barrier between the western tribes and the traders of whatever nationality on the Hudson. But the French really had little cause for concern on this score. The Huron, whose lands were now stripped of beaver and who would not allow the western tribes to trade with the French directly, were no more willing to allow the

Iroquois to interpose themselves as middlemen. Moreover, the Iroquois, whose own territories were rapidly becoming denuded of fur-bearing animals, either had to seize new trapping grounds from other tribes or force those tribes to trade furs to them for European goods obtained from the traders on the Hudson or at Quebec. Economic factors alone made the Iroquois enemies of the Huron and northern Algonkin tribes.

In 1625 the French base at Quebec was made somewhat more secure when five Jesuits arrived at the solicitation of the Recollets to aid in the missionary field.[13] These members of the powerful Society of Jesus, men of heroic character, highly trained and disciplined, were to have much greater success in Christianizing the Indians than had the Recollets. Moreover, they were to be of inestimable value in the extension of French power in North America. Willing to endure incredible hardship, even torture and slow death, to achieve their ends, they quickly came to have great influence in the councils of the Indian nations. Although primarily servants of their God and the Roman Church, they were also loyal subjects of the French king, for it was only by furthering the secular aims of the crown that they could maintain their missionary posts.

When they first arrived, the French at Quebec still numbered less than seventy. The land had not been touched by a plow; only small patches of ground had been cleared. In all, not more than fifteen acres were under cultivation. The chartered company persisted in putting obstacles in the path of settlement. Brother Gabriel Sagard wrote:

> . . . the country is almost uninhabited and uncultivated, and this through the negligence and lack of interest of the merchants who hitherto have been satisfied to get furs and profit out of it without having been willing to make any outlay for cultivation, settlement, or progress of the country. This is the reason they have done little more for it than at the first day, for fear they say, lest the Spaniards should turn them out if they had made it a more valuable land. But this is a very feeble excuse, by no means admissible by persons of sense and experience, who know very well that establishments could be made and fortified, if there was any willingness to incur the necessary expense, so that they could not be driven out of them by any enemy. But if they will do nothing more than in the past Antarctic [sic] France will always be a name of fancy, and ourselves an imaginary possession in other's hands.[14]

Eventually reports of the bleak state of affairs reached the Cardinal-minister Richelieu. The result was swift action. By April 1627 a new vehicle for colonization had been formed by the energetic cardinal, the Company of New France. This new company, with over one hundred shareholders each subscribing 3000 *livres*, was composed of men and women who, for the most part, were moved more by religious and patriotic motives than by the hope of enrichment, although the twelve titles of nobility granted by the king for distribution among the shareholders were also powerful incentives to invest in the enterprise. The company was given the title to all lands claimed by France, from Newfoundland to Lake Huron, with the usual monopoly on trade and the obligation to establish settlers in the colony, at least two hundred a year and a total of 4000 by 1643. To end the continual religious squabbling, Richelieu wisely ordered that only Roman Catholics could settle in New France.

At long last it appeared that the French foothold in North America was to be firmly established and expanded sufficiently to ward off the ever-present threat of its destruction by the Dutch or English. It would, however, have been far better had the founding of this ambitious undertaking been delayed a year or two, for England and France were on the verge of war. While the company's ships at Dieppe were being loaded with colonists, provisions, building materials, and livestock, in England the government was issuing letters of marque to privateers. One recipient was Jarvis Kirke, a long-time resident of Dieppe and now a merchant of London, who had good knowledge of the trading possibilities in the St. Lawrence area. With the financial support of other London merchants, he outfitted three ships manned by two hundred men and sailed in March 1628, a few weeks before the ships of the Company of New France left Dieppe. With this time advantage Kirke reached the St. Lawrence first, captured the French ships he encountered en route and the trading post at Tadoussac. He then sent his brother David Kirke up river to Quebec, where he presented a demand for its surrender, couched in quite polite terms, to Champlain who as politely rejected it. David Kirke, confident of intercepting the French supply ships, forbore launching an assault. He assured Champlain that he would return in good time to allow him to reconsider. This was no idle threat; a few weeks later the French supply ships were captured in the Gulf after they had suffered two casualties and used up their ammunition. Eleven ships and 600 prisoners were taken, the latter being sent back to France. The Kirkes then returned to England, confident that they could seize the post at Quebec the following year before the French were likely to take effective measures for its defense.

Meanwhile, Acadia, too, had been assaulted by the British. After the destruction of Port Royal by Argall in 1613, de Monts' lieutenant, Jean de Biencourt de Poutrincourt de Saint-Just and his son Charles had re-established the base. For a few years they derived a profitable trade both there and at a fort on the St. John River, but little was done to increase settlement. As the trade in furs declined, the base was allowed to fall into desuetude, this at a time when to the south the English and Dutch settlements were steadily growing. At this juncture of events a Scot, Sir William Alexander, remarking that a New France, a New England, and a New

Amsterdam had been established in North America, decided it was time a New Scotland was founded. He obtained from the English king a grant of the lands stretching from the Ste. Croix to the St. Lawrence. Using the Ulster plantation as a model, where baronetcies had been established by Englishmen of means, he offered titles in his grant for a sizable fee. In 1627 four ships with seventy colonists seized Port Royal and the following year Alexander and the Kirke brothers joined forces to form the Scottish and English Company to exploit the trade in Acadia and the St. Lawrence Valley. This Company, like the French companies that had preceded it, was interested not so much in colonization as in the quick profits of the fur trade and fisheries.

In the spring of 1629 the Anglo-Scottish company sent ships to both Port Royal and Quebec, while a French relief expedition waited too long in port for a naval escort. For want of supplies, Champlain had sent as many of his men as he could spare to winter in the Indian villages. The little plots of land cultivated by the apothecary Hébert and by the Recollets and the Jesuits produced enough to feed only a few of the residents. By the time the Kirkes arrived in three ships with two hundred men the handful of French who remained at Quebec had been reduced to grubbing for roots and the charity of the Indians to avert starvation. Champlain had no choice but to capitulate.

At the time of the capitulation the French had been laboring for some three decades to establish a commercial colony in North America. They had very little to show for it. Yet it is difficult to see how, at that juncture of events, they could have done more. With French energies fully occupied by the Thirty Years' War, it is a wonder that Richelieu had paid any attention at all to New France. Certainly the crown could spare neither men nor capital for colonizing ventures. The task had perforce to be left to private enterprise, and French capitalists were interested only in obtaining the maximum profit with the minimum investment. They could not be expected to provide troops for the colony's defense or to invest large sums for settlement, even if competent settlers could have been induced to take up land in the wilderness, where it took a year's hard labor to clear an acre or two for seeding. These companies were formed for commerce, not to establish basic industries, and the only viable commercial enterprise in Canada was the fur trade. All that was needed for this trade was a warehouse, a plentiful supply of trade goods, and the maintenance of communications between France and Quebec on the one hand, the trading post and the western Indians on the other. For this purpose there was no need for large numbers of French to be stationed at Quebec; in fact, the fewer there were the lower the costs and the higher the profits. The private companies were not rigorously opposed to settlement as such, only to its interference with trade or to any attempts to make them subsidize it.

Commerce and Evangelism, 1632-1662

*W*hen Champlain arrived back in Europe, he discovered that an agreement to end hostilities had been signed by the rulers of England and France the previous April 29, 1629, nearly three months before his capitulation at Quebec. After much haggling, France regained title to its lands in North America by the terms of the Treaty of St.-Germain-en-Laye. On July 13 Thomas Kirke handed over the fort at Quebec to Emery de Caen, but not before he had garnered the spring trade in prime winter pelts. Nor did he leave much else. Some of the buildings had burned to the ground, and from the others the English stripped the furniture, the doors, even the window frames. The French had to begin over again, almost from scratch.

Meanwhile, the Company of New France was reorganized. Enough capital was found to maintain the Quebec base for a few years; efforts were made to recruit settlers; and Champlain was commissioned Lieutenant of New France by both the crown and the company. On May 23, 1633, he arrived at Quebec with three ships loaded with supplies, workmen, a few soldiers, even some women and children. Three Jesuits had returned the preceding year; they set to work building a chapel and making plans to re-establish the mission in the Huron country. In May, eighteen Montagnais canoes came to trade. The following month several Algonkin and Nipissing arrived. This was a promising beginning, no more.

Then, at the end of July, a great flotilla, 500 Huron in 150 canoes, came down from the west loaded with prime furs. In January a member of the Company in France reported cheerfully, "The ships from New France arrived on 21 December at La Rochelle. They were richly laden, the Indian allies of the French having this year brought down an extraordinary quantity of furs. That colony is in a very fine state."[1] The success of the commercial colony appeared to be assured, at least temporarily. As long as the furs reached the company's warehouses, all seemed to be well.

Yet this tiny French colony in the interior of North America, containing few more than a hundred people, rested on shaky foundations. It served only two purposes, the trade in furs and the garnering of heathen souls for the Church of Rome. Both these activities were completely dependent on the Indians, hence both inevitably drew the French farther into the wilderness, thereby weakening the main base at Quebec. Recent events had demonstrated the need to strengthen this base, for when it was lost, fur trade, missionary work, everything was lost. As the French were soon to discover, the external threats to their incipient colony were greater than ever.

The Dutch were now well established on the Hudson River. At Fort Orange the Iroquois could obtain European goods, including firearms. In 1626 they had traded over 8000 beaver and other furs; it is estimated that by 1633 they were bringing nearly 30,000 pelts a year to the Dutch.[2] This exhausted the supply of fur in Iroquois territory. The attempts of the Iroquois to obtain furs through trade from the Huron and Algonkin tribes came to naught. There was, then, no alternative, now that they were dependent on European manufactured goods to maintain their recently improved standard of living, but to wage war to divert the flow of northwestern furs from the French at Quebec to the Dutch on the Hudson, with themselves reaping the middleman's profit. As early as 1633 they attacked a party of Champlain's men on the St. Lawrence above Quebec, killing two and wounding four others. For the next sixty years and more the French were to have little respite from the attacks of this relentless foe.

In 1634 a fort was built at Trois-Rivières, at the mouth of the St. Maurice River, one of the main river routes to the north. Not only did this fort serve to deter the Iroquois, it quickly became, as intended, a main base for the fur trade. Within a few years the Jesuits established a mission there, and settlers began clearing the adjacent land. But the intervening forest land between Quebec and Trois-Rivières remained wilderness for several years. This new settlement was, in effect, a satellite trading and missionary post of Quebec, and communications between the two along the St.

Lawrence were constantly threatened by marauding Iroquois war parties. Had the aim of the French been purely a colonizing one, it would have been far better for them to concentrate their meager resources in one consolidated colony at Quebec. But commerce and evangelism dictated westward expansion by leaps and bounds; consolidation had to come later.

In 1638 Jean Nicolet, an agent of the Company of New France, voyaged to Lake Michigan, then down Green Bay to the Fox River to establish trade relations with the Winnebago and arrange a peace between them and their old foes the Huron. A vast and distant new region was thus opened to commercial exploration. This was the pattern that eventually brought most of the continent under nominal French control, and led to its destruction.

The Company of New France, by the terms of its charter, was obligated to bring out two to three hundred colonists a year and to settle 4000 people on the land by 1643. It never paid more than lip service to this commitment. In 1634, to avoid having to raise more capital or to diminish its trading profits, the company began the practice of granting large tracts of virgin wilderness as seigneuries to individuals on condition that the grantees bring out settlers and get the land cleared. That year Robert Giffard, a company servant, obtained a large fief at Beauport, a few miles below Quebec. He brought a goodly number of settlers from France and got them established in his seigneury. During the next few years some members of the French gentry, Jean Juchereau de Meur, Pierre Legardeur de Repentigny and his brother Charles Legardeur de Tilly, and the Leneuf brothers, Jacques Leneuf de la Poterie and Michel Leneuf du Hérisson, obtained large seigneurial grants along the river near Quebec, brought their families, laborers, and servants, and began clearing the land. The Jesuits also brought workmen, laborers, and settlers to bring their lands into production.

In the early seventeenth century land was regarded as the basis of all real wealth, and there were not many avenues for the safe investment of capital, let alone its acquisition. In the hierarchical society of the age, social status was all-important and was measured to no small degree by the amount of land a family owned. A landless peasant or workman settling in Canada could have land for the asking and could enjoy privileges denied his class in France, privileges such as hunting and fishing as well as freedom from taxes and all manner of restrictions that bedeviled the lower classes in Europe.

Granted all these attractive features and more, the fact remained that beginning life afresh in the Canadian wilderness was a daunting proposition. There were, first of all, the dangers of the Atlantic crossing. The voyage could take anywhere from three weeks to more than three months. In the early seventeenth century, the carrying of passengers was a new thing. The ships of the day were not built for it, and the crews had little experience in coping with the problems it entailed. Food supplies sometimes ran out if headwinds endured too long; then scurvy took its toll. As late as the mid-eighteenth century, if fewer than 10 percent of the ship's company died during a crossing, it was considered a good trip.[3] French peasants and artisans, who had likely never seen the sea, must have thought twice before deciding to take their chances in the Canadian wilderness.

Those who did, once arrived in the colony, were faced with the back-breaking task of clearing the land to plant a crop. The arable land in the St. Lawrence Valley was covered with dense hardwood forests, mainly oak, birch, elm, and maple, interspersed with stands of pine. Cutting down these trees, clearing away the trunks and slash, usually by burning, was no task for the lazy or the feeble. Two acres were as much as a man could hope to clear in a year. Then a few years had to elapse to allow the stumps and roots to rot sufficiently for them to be removed and the field cleared for the plow. Much of this labor had to be performed during the summer months, while dense clouds of mosquitoes and black flies made life almost unbearable for newcomers from Europe. But these insects were as nothing compared to the menace of marauding Iroquois, waiting to cut down the unwary. Little wonder, then, that the population of New France increased slowly; by 1640 it numbered only 359, and ten years later it was estimated to be 675.[4]

In order to stimulate interest in their work in New France, the Jesuits began the publication of their annual *Relations*. These carefully edited accounts of their activities in the mission field, combined with appeals for aid, were almost paradoxical. On the one hand they described the hardships that the missionaries had to endure, the immensity of their task, the constant danger from the Iroquois, and on the other they stressed the need for more settlers to consolidate the colony, pointing out all the advantages that the country could offer to workmen and peasants in France, who too frequently did not know where their next meal was coming from. The *Relation* of 1636, for example, contained much sound advice to prospective immigrants, but accounts of the devastation wrought by the Iroquois, the constant state of terror they engendered, and the horrible tortures they inflicted on any so unfortunate as to be taken alive were not well calculated to cause an exodus from France to Canada.

The religious orders, principally the Jesuits, were responsible for what little development there was in the colony. The Ursulines and the *Soeurs Hospitalières* of Dieppe, encouraged by the Jesuits, in 1639 established a school for girls and a hospital at Quebec. Originally, they had intended to devote themselves principally to the Indians and by serving them to win them over to the Christian faith. In this aim they failed. The Indians resisted their best efforts, but they remained to afford future colonists their services. All these religious institutions were completely dependent on funds provided by the parent order or by devout individuals in France. Existing as they did in this hand-to-mouth fashion, they were frequently on the verge of being forced to give up and return to France. Only blind faith and a very profound sense of commitment kept them going.

One of the chief agencies for strengthening the colony was the powerful, very wealthy, and very influential secret lay society, the Compagnie de St. Sacrement, formed between 1627 and 1630 by the then Viceroy of New France, the Duc de Ventadour, to promote the aims of extreme right-wing Catholicism.[5] As early as 1636 the Jesuits in New France had proposed founding a missionary settlement at Montreal. Three years later with Father Charles Lalemant, until recently Superior of the Jesuits in New France, acting as intermediary, the Compagnie de St. Sacrement was instrumental in bringing it about. This clandestine organization, dedicated to increasing the authority of the Church, its membership made up of men of great piety and either great wealth or political power, was persuaded to support the Société de Notre Dame de Montréal, established in 1640 by Jean-Jacques Olier, the founder of the Messieurs de St. Sulpice.

This society, sometimes known as Messieurs les associés pour la conversion des Sauvages de la Nouvelle France en l'Ile de Montréal, was able to raise a large amount of money, to obtain a grant of the larger part of the island of Montreal (they obtained the remainder in 1659), and to recruit a party of some fifty devout colonists under the command of Paul de Chomedey, sieur de Maisonneuve, a thirty-three-year-old army veteran whose piety had greatly impressed the members of the society. Late in 1641 they arrived at Quebec, to the great joy of the settlers there. A few months earlier the Iroquois had renewed their assaults on the French and their allies, ambushing them along the waterways and in their fields. These reinforcements from France seemed providential. Governor Charles Huault de Montmagny, who had succeeded Champlain after his death in 1635, and the people at Quebec were therefore dismayed to learn that Maisonneuve intended to take his party to Montreal where they would be exposed to the full fury of the Iroquois. They did their best to persuade him to abandon this suicidal scheme and settle near Quebec. But Maisonneuve, imbued with the spirit of the crusaders, declared that were every tree on the island to be changed into an Iroquois, his honor would still oblige him to go there and found a colony.

The following spring the group departed from Quebec and established their post of Ville Marie, on a site once selected as suitable by Champlain and partially cleared. Champlain had chosen this particular spot with an eye to the fur trade. The island of Montreal itself, some thirty miles long and ten miles across, stands at the junction of the two great waterways to the interior, the St. Lawrence and the Ottawa. The latter was the main route of the Huron and Algonkin, bringing their cargoes of furs to trade with the French. A trading post at this point spared them the long paddle to

Trois-Rivières or Quebec, and exposure to ambush by the Mohawk who traveled by way of the Richelieu to the St. Lawrence, downstream from Montreal. In fact, the western nations had suggested to Champlain that he establish a post there. The land on and about the island was very fertile, and being some fifty miles south of Quebec's position, it was hoped that the winters would be less severe.

That the site was so advantageous for the fur trade indicated that it was equally well suited for missionary work, since both activities were dependent on the Indians. There is no gainsaying that Montreal was established, not for commercial reasons, but solely for religious purposes. It can claim to be the only great metropolis in North America so founded. Father Vimont, who accompanied the colonists to Montreal in 1642, explained that the site was chosen because it ". . . gives access and an admirable approach to all the Nations of this vast country . . . so that, if peace prevailed among these peoples they would land thereon from all sides." The motives of the colonists, he made clear, were purely altruistic: "Their intention is to have houses built in which to lodge the savages, to till the soil in order to feed them; to establish seminaries for their instruction and an Hôtel-Dieu for succoring their sick."[6]

The infant colony was able to maintain itself on this high religious plane for only a few years. The commercial opportunities latent in the site were too obvious to be neglected. Many of the original settlers, and certainly their governor Maisonneuve, preserved their religious fervor intact, spurning commerce; others did not. The society in France encountered great difficulty in recruiting colonists in subsequent years and had to enlist any who offered themselves. Men such as Jacques Le Ber and Charles Le Moyne, although they lived exemplary lives, made fortunes as merchant fur traders. Others were quick to follow their example. Dollier de Casson, the Superior of the Sulpicians at Montreal, in 1672–1673 commented not only on the religious aspects of the establishment but also on its commercial assets, stating "there is no doubt that the spot is one of the best in the country for the inhabitants, because of the trade they can do there with the savages who come down the river in canoes thereto from all the nations living higher up the river."[7]

For the first twenty years after its establishment, while Maisonneuve was in command, piety, indeed, puritanism, dominated in Montreal, albeit its ardor dwindled as the population increased. As late as 1663, a Montreal resident was fined 10 *livres* for plowing "in plain view" on a Sunday, but fifty years later the intendant had to issue an ordonnance forbidding the bachelors of Montreal to maintain their mistresses in the town in so flagrant a manner.[8]

That the handful of colonists at Montreal was able to survive during those early years was little short of a miracle. Thirty years later Dollier de Casson remarked: "Truly, God showed His favour to these new colonists by

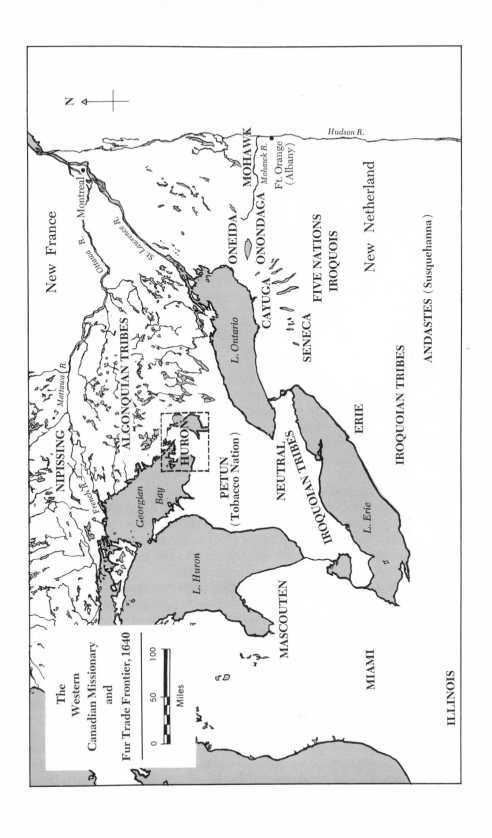

The
Western
Canadian Missionary
and
Fur Trade Frontier, 1640

Miles

0   50   100

Hudson R.

MOHAWK

Mohawk R. Ft. Orange
(Albany)

New France

Montreal
Ottawa R.
St. Lawrence R.

ONEIDA

ONONDAGA

CAYUGA

SENECA

FIVE NATIONS
IROQUOIS

New Netherland

ANDASTES (Susquehanna)

ALGONQUIAN TRIBES

Mattawa R.

NIPISSING

French R.

L. Ontario

HURON

PETUN
(Tobacco Nation)

Georgian
Bay

NEUTRAL

IROQUOIAN TRIBES

ERIE

IROQUOIAN TRIBES

L. Erie

L. Huron

MASCOUTEN

MIAMI

ILLINOIS

not letting the Iroquois discover them too soon." Had the Iroquois known that a settlement was to be established on territory they claimed, doubtless they would have been there in force to oppose it, but their war parties were concentrated that year along the Ottawa and in the Georgian Bay area. For the ensuing two years communications between Huronia and Quebec were severed as the Iroquois attacked the French settlements in earnest; Montreal, Trois-Rivières, and even the area around Quebec, were besieged. During these years no furs came down from the west, and the colony's meager strength, some three to four hundred colonists all told, was steadily reduced as the casualties mounted. Only with great difficulty, and by offering extravagant terms, was the Society of Montreal able to induce enough men to reinforce its missionary outpost. In 1644 Father d'Endemare wrote to a friend at Dijon, describing conditions in the colony:

> It is almost impossible to make either peace or war with these barbarians; not peace because war is their life, their amusement, and their source of profit all in one; not war because they make themselves invisible to those who seek them and only show themselves when they have heavy odds in their favour. Go to hunt them in their villages and they fade into the forest. Short of levelling all the forests in the country, it is impossible to trap them or to halt the destruction of these thieves. This is why one can travel in the settlements only in armed bands or in barques armed with cannon and soldiers. Fishing and hunting is forbidden to the French; the fish and the birds have a truce with the fishers and hunters. The beauty of the country is now only to be looked at from afar. One can hardly gather greens in a garden for a salad in safety, and in order to get any supplies of wood everyone has to go in battle order or stand guard. It is not that these thieves are always all around us, but that one is never sure either that they are there or that they are not hence we have to beware of them all the time. Were it not that we hope God will eventually deliver us the country would have to be abandoned, for we are well aware that human strength and wisdom alone cannot save us.[9]

In 1644 the queen mother, Anne of Austria, responded to urgent appeals from the Society of Montreal and had a further reinforcement of sixty soldiers dispatched to New France, forty having been sent in 1642. The Jesuits obtained donations from wealthy individuals amounting to 90,000 *livres* to help defray the costs of defending the settlements. Without this assistance the tenuous French hold on the St. Lawrence Valley could not have been maintained. It barely survived from one year to the next. The role of the mercantile company as a colonizing agent and its influence in colonial affairs had shrunk almost to nothing. Power had been transferred, by default, to the religious and the military men in the colony.

It was under these circumstances that a group of the leading settlers proposed the formation of a purely Canadian company to take over the fur trade monopoly and administer the colony's affairs. The Jesuits gave them their strong support. The directors of the Company of New France, plagued by the loss of revenue when no furs were shipped, heavily indebted as a result of dishonest operations by certain employees, and under pressure from the court where the queen had hearkened to Jesuit counsel, were quite willing to cede their privileges to the Canadian group. In March 1645, the terms of the agreement were ratified whereby the Community of the Habitants of New France was empowered to grant lands under seigneurial tenure and received a monopoly on the marketing of all furs in New France—that is, the settlers were free to trap or trade with the Indians as before but they had to sell their furs to the Community of the Habitants. In return it was required to pay the costs of the colonial administration—salaries and upkeep of the governor, the clergy, and the military—and, inevitably, to bring at least twenty immigrants to the colony each year. The Company of New France retained its title to the land and the right to appoint the governor and officers of justice.

This Community of the Habitants was composed of all heads of families in the colony and divided into three classes, principal, middle, and lower. The profits of the fur trade were to be divided into three equal shares, one to each class, then divided among the members. It has been argued that the half dozen leading men in the colony who organized the Community diverted most of the profits of the fur trade into their own pockets and obtained official posts for themselves with generous emoluments attached.[10] They did have themselves appointed directors, but with such a small population in the colony, it is likely that there were no others capable of organizing, or directing, the Company. Since the colonial budget was fixed at 49,000 *livres* a year, to pay the salaries of the governor and junior officials, the military garrison, and grants to the religious orders, it did not leave much for the directors. Yet quarrels quickly ensued over the allocation of funds. The Jesuits, in 1646, declared that the directors were a bunch of thieves who had used their posts to line their own pockets. It is virtually impossible to discover how much credence should be given such accusations. The evidence is very scanty, and what there is derives from parties who were anything but disinterested, or else were retelling hearsay accounts of years earlier. Perhaps the soundest judgment was that rendered a few years later by a royal commissioner, Louis Gaudet-Dufont, who was sent to investigate conditions in the colony and declared that the accused were all men without education or experience and nearly all of them were incapable of resolving problems of any consequence.[11]

In any event, in 1647 the crown established a form of representative government in the colony. A Council was constituted comprising the governor general, the superior of the Jesuits, and the governor of Montreal. A local official with the imposing title of Admiral of the Fleet and three syndics elected by the people of the three districts, Quebec, Trois-Rivières, and Montreal, were to attend the council but with a deliberative voice only.

One piece of evidence that has survived suggests that this Council was not unmindful of the interests of the humbler settlers. In order to pay the administrative costs of the Community of the Habitants and to discharge its debts, a tax of 50 percent had been levied on beaver pelts. In 1653 one of the syndics informed the Council that the price of goods in the colony was so high—the markup charged by the La Rochelle merchants being 60 percent for dry goods and 100 percent for wines and spirits—that the settlers could not realize a reasonable profit on their trade with the Indians. The syndic asked that the tax be reduced to 25 percent and the Council granted the request.[12] In 1657 the membership of the Council was altered by royal decree to include four members elected by the settlers, thus giving them a greater voice in the direction of the colony's affairs.

But no matter what form the administrative framework might take, the colony was dependent on agriculture for subsistence and the fur trade to provide the goods that had to be imported from France, and both activities were at the mercy of the Iroquois rather than of the Council. When, in 1645, the Iroquois made peace, the Huron brigades brought vast quantities of furs to the Community's warehouses. In 1646 a profit of close to 100,000 *livres* was realized, and in 1648, 250,000 *livres*. Then, in 1649, the Iroquois onslaught against the Huron began in earnest. This great trading nation, and its intricate commercial empire upon which the French fur trade had in a large measure come to depend, was shattered. The Jesuit *Relation* for 1652–1653 bleakly stated: "For a year the warehouse at Montreal has not bought a single beaver from the Indians." Destroyed too were the Jesuit missions in Huronia. The fur trade and religious frontier had suddenly been driven back some four hundred miles to Montreal.

The destruction of Huronia made very plain how closely intertwined were the fur trade and missionary work, both being entirely dependent on the Indians for their essential ingredients, furs and heathen souls. Although begun by the Recollets, the Huronia mission had made very few converts prior to the arrival of the Jesuits in 1626.[13] In 1632 the Recollets were excluded from the Canadian mission field by order of Cardinal Richelieu. From this time on the Jesuits dominated it, and within the colony proper they came to wield influence that, in some circles, came to seem sinister. There can be little doubt, however, that they were better qualified to undertake the task. The fervor of the Catholic Reformation was still strong, and no group was more ardent to establish the Roman faith among pagans and heretics alike than the Jesuits. They were all intelligent men, of exceptionally strong character, militant, and highly disciplined. Their zeal for missionary work verged on the fanatical; death in the pursuance of their task held no fears for them. They regarded martyrdom as a most sublime end, one to be coveted; indeed they became convinced that martyrs were essential to accomplish their mission.[14]

At first the Jesuits, like the Recollets, the Ursulines, and the Soeurs

Hospitalières, acted on the assumption that the Indians had to be civilized and assimilated into French civilization before they could properly be converted to Christianity;[15] that is, comprehend the religion and live by it. In this these missionaries all had very little success. The Indians they encountered at Quebec were for the most part Montagnais, nomads who lived an extremely primitive existence. When they were persuaded to leave their children with the religious to be educated, it was only for the summer. In the autumn when they returned to the northern forests, they took their children with them; more often than not the children, once the novelty wore off, refused to submit to discipline or stay cooped up in the classroom and ran away to rejoin their families. Eventually the clergy had to admit defeat. The Ursulines then devoted their considerable talents to educating the children of the colonists and an occasional Indian girl. The Jesuits established their college for boys at Quebec in 1635, the first institution of higher learning to come into existence in America north of Mexico. The following year it had all of twenty registered students studying under Father Charles Lalemant, Canada's first professor. The sons of Canadian settlers were now able to obtain as good an education at Quebec as could be obtained in a French provincial town.

At the same time the Jesuits did not relinquish their main aim of converting the Indian nations to Christianity. Refusing to be discouraged by the seeming impossibility of the task and supplied with ample funds by the wealthy and devout in France, they maintained a mission among the Montagnais on the north shore of the Gulf of St. Lawrence, one at Miscou at the mouth of the Baie de Chaleur, and another on Cape Breton. The missionaries who served the northern Montagnais had by far the worst of it. This primitive people had not learned to store food, let alone grow it. Their entire lives were spent in hunting and collecting, living hand-to-mouth. In winter they moved constantly through the dense forest in search of game, their only shelter a lodge made of saplings and bark, hardly deeper than the snow, and not high enough for a man to stand in erect. Men, women, children, and dogs with their fleas crowded in until there was no room to move, and in the center a fire filled the cramped space with smoke. There they huddled, roasted on one side, clothing scorched, and frozen on the other side as icy blasts whistled through cracks in the bark. Sometimes the smoke was so dense inside that the occupants could breath only by placing their faces against the ground. "I have," wrote Father Le Jeune, "sometimes remained several hours in that position, especially during the most severe cold and when it snowed; for it was then the smoke assailed us with the greatest fury."[16] Semistarvation was normal for these nomads, interspersed with brief periods of gross gluttony when game was killed, followed by days when the choice was to eat putrid meat or starve.

These physical tortures were not the worst that the missionaries had to endure. The problem of mastering the Indian language, finding some way to communicate the concepts of Christianity to these barbarians, and gaining some ascendancy over them in order to induce them to accept the tenets and live by them were the hardest, particularly when the Indian medicine men feared that they would lose their power and status were their people to hearken to the intruder. Father Le Jeune remarked:

> The cold, heat, annoyance of the dogs, sleeping in the open air and upon the bare ground; the position I had to assume in their cabins, rolling myself up in a ball or crouching down . . . hunger, thirst, the poverty and filth of their smoked meats, sickness—all these things were merely play to me in comparison to the smoke and the malice of the Sorceror.

The missionaries persevered in their heartbreaking task until the end of the century, then, with new mission fields opening in the far west among tribes giving promise of better results, the Tadoussac mission was reluctantly abandoned. During those years, however, the Jesuits among the Montagnais, in their rovings, acquired much knowledge of the topography of the area between the St. Lawrence and James Bay and established a valid claim to the territory for France.

It was in the west, in Huronia, a vast area bounded by Georgian Bay, Lakes Huron, Erie, Ontario, and Simcoe, that the Jesuits concentrated their major effort. The Huron, estimated to number some thirty to thirty-five thousand, had attained a more advanced culture than the Algonkin nations. Living in semipermanent villages, they depended on agriculture for their main food supplies and traded their surplus corn with the northern and western tribes for furs. In 1634 the Jesuits established St. Joseph mission in the village of Ihonatiria and three years later a second mission at nearby Ossossané. Then, in 1639, a much more ambitious establishment, named Ste. Marie, was set up near the mouth of the Wye River. It consisted of a chapel, hospital, mill, stables, barns, a residence for the priests and another for the lay workers, all surrounded by a log palisade with stone bastions. As many as sixty-six French resided there at one time, priests, lay brothers, servants, a surgeon, an apothecary, and a number of artisans. Cattle, pigs, and poultry were brought by canoe from Quebec, and fields were cleared to grow wheat, corn, and vegetables sufficient to feed the hundreds of Indian converts who eventually came to settle nearby. Rarely, however, were there more than three priests at Ste. Marie at any one time; the rest, some eight or ten, were usually away serving the missions in outlying villages, or traveling by canoe and along woodland trails to the more remote Petun, or Tobacco, nation, the Neutral to the southwest, and the northern Algonquian tribes. These tiny outposts of French and Christian civilization, separated from the settlements on the St. Lawrence by hundreds of miles of wilderness, formed a unique frontier, a frontier of the intellect. There the products of the highly sophisticated Baroque civilization confronted the Stone Age.

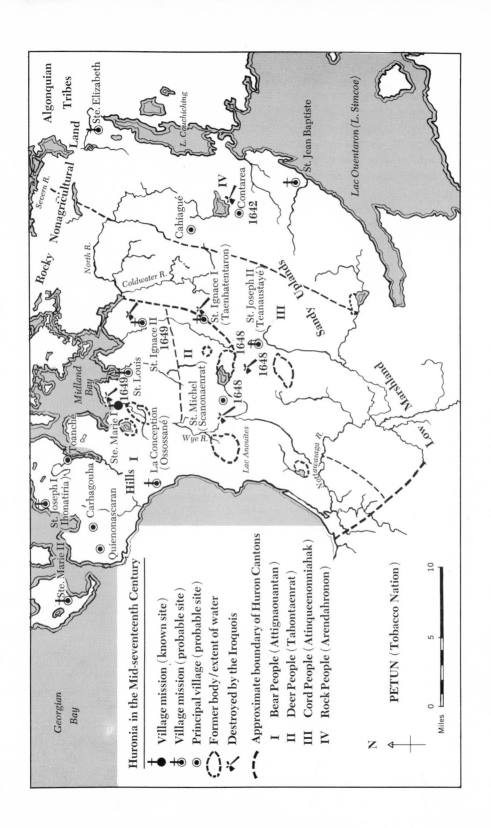

Huronia in the Mid-seventeenth Century

Village mission (known site)	
Village mission (probable site)	
Principal village (probable site)	
Former body / extent of water	
Destroyed by the Iroquois	
Approximate boundary of Huron Cantons	
I Bear People (Attignaouantan)	
II Deer People (Tahontaenrat)	
III Cord People (Atinqueenonmiahak)	
IV Rock People (Arendahronon)	

PETUN (Tobacco Nation)

N

Miles

0   5   10

Georgian
Bay

Ste. Marie II

St. Joseph I
(Ihonatiria)

Carhagouha

Quienonascaran

Quieunonaca

Rocky   Nonagricultural   Land

Algonquian
Tribes

Ste. Elizabeth

Severn R.

Troanche

Midland
Bay

Hills   I

La Conception
(Ossossané)

Ste. Marie I

1649

St. Louis

St. Ignace II
1649

II

St. Michel
(Scanonaenrat)

Wye R.

Lac Anouites

Nottawasaga R.

Marshland

Low

Coldwater R.

North R.

Cahiagué

L. Couchiching

IV

Contarea
1642

St. Ignace I
(Taenhatentaron)

1648

1648

St. Joseph II
Teanaustayé

1648

1648

III

Sandy
Uplands

Uplands

St. Jean Baptiste

Lac Ouentaron (L. Simcoe)

The Indians, although curious about the strange religious practices and beliefs of these Europeans, had a religion of their own which sufficed for their needs and which they showed a great reluctance to abandon. Theirs was a cruel world in which sudden death could come at any time. In seeking to explain chance events and the phenomena of nature that affected their lives at every turn, they had developed a deep-rooted set of mystic beliefs. For them, the natural world, inanimate objects as well as animals, was inhabited by spirits; some were benevolent, some malevolent, all had to be placated, appeased, or at least acknowledged. They believed that in their dreams they were in communication with the spirit world; thus, to dream of success in the hunt ensured it; to dream of disaster caused plans to be abandoned. Some among them were able to induce conditions of hysteria in themselves and in this way communicate with the spirits. These were the shamans, the wise men, who healed the sick with simple remedies or magic, and gave advice on what action to take to cope with major problems. They were the priests of the Indian culture. Others possessed supernatural powers, but used them malevolently; these were the sorcerers, and they had to be appeased.

One great difficulty in any attempt to understand the religious beliefs of the Indians at the time of their first contact with Europeans is that these beliefs were passed from one generation to the next orally. The Indians had developed a large body of myths and legends to account for the inexplicable in nature, and although some of the Jesuits sought to understand these beliefs, the language barrier and the desire to impose their own alien beliefs made real understanding virtually impossible. Yet this primitive religion was intricately interwoven into the whole of Indian life and society. The early Recollets and Jesuits discovered that the Indians appeared to believe in a supreme being and in an after life, hence in the immortality of the soul. The problem thus became whether these beliefs could be accepted in essence and amended to accord with Christian beliefs, or whether they had to be destroyed, eradicated, then replaced by a pure Christian creed. For many years opinions were divided on this issue. At first the Jesuits, appalled by the strange mores and incomprehensible practices of the Indians, wished to eradicate everything and impose a completely European scale of values, way of life, and religion; but as they came to understand the Indians better and to discover how impossible such a task was, they came to accept much and to seek to build on it.

In 1647 Father Ragueneau wrote:

> One must be very careful before condemning a thousand things among their customs, which greatly offend minds brought up and nourished in another world. It is easy to call irreligion what is merely stupidity, and to take for diabolical working something that is nothing more than human; and then, one thinks he is obliged to forbid as impious certain things that are done in all innocence, or, at most, are silly but not criminal customs . . . I have no hesitation in saying that we have been too severe in this point.[17]

Jesuit mission of Ste. Marie des Hurons, reconstructed on the original site. (Huronia Historical Development Council, Province of Ontario)

Hospital, reconstructed, at Ste. Marie des Hurons. (Huronia Historical Development Council, Province of Ontario)

This statement has to be regarded as one man's opinion. Others of the Jesuits were not so tolerant. Some found the trials of everyday life among the Huron almost unendurable and the complexity of their self-imposed task heartbreaking, but at the same time these very factors gave them a deep sense of personal satisfaction. The greater the obstacles, the greater the challenge and the more worthwhile the achievement in meeting it. Although in some ways very humble, these Jesuits were not without pride.

Indeed, in the humbling of their own flesh there was an element of pride. In the Huron long houses the filth, smoke, squalor, fleas, and stench, the constant sight of what appeared to the Jesuits to be lewdness, were bad enough; the constant awareness that death could come at any moment was harder still on even the most steely nerved. Father Le Jeune, after describing these physical vicissitudes remarked:

> Add to all this, that our lives depend upon a single thread; and if, wherever we are in the world, we are to expect death every hour, and to be prepared for it that is particularly the case here. For not to mention that your cabin is only, as it were, chaff and that it might be burned at any moment, despite all your care to prevent accidents, the malice of the Savages gives especial cause for almost perpetual fear; a malcontent may burn you down, or cleave your head open in some lonely spot. And then you are responsible for the sterility or fecundity of the earth, under penalty of your life; you are the cause of draughts; if you cannot make rain, they speak of nothing less than making away with you.[18]

In the face of all this the Jesuits persisted.

Their first task was to master the Indian language. Fortunately, Huron was the *lingua franca* of the Indian nations north of the Great Lakes, but to acquire fluency in it was extremely difficult. Words and phrases had to be noted, checked, and revised to establish a definite meaning, and many of the abstract concepts of the Christian religion were completely novel to the Huron; hence there were no words with which to explain them. In addition, the Jesuits had little opportunity to pursue this task. As Father Charles Garnier noted:

> Frequently I do not have a quarter of an hour in the day to study owing to the frequent visits one must make and the horde of Indians who interrupt us in our cabin whenever we are there . . . before I arrived here all that it had proved possible to do was to acquire a smattering of the language . . . those who think that one has only to show a crucifix to an Indian to convert him deceive themselves. The difficulties are far greater than one thinks. The conversion of the Indians takes time. The first six or seven years will appear sterile to some; and if I should say ten or twelve, I would possibly not be far from the truth.[19]

The Jesuits were very conscious of the fact that they were in Huronia only on sufferance. In 1636 there were only six Jesuits, their servants, and lay assistants in the area. Five years later there were still only thirteen priests and seventeen laymen in the whole of Huronia.[20] Compulsion was out of the question, converts could only be made by persuasion or by subterfuge, and persuasion proved to be extremely difficult. The Indians found little that appealed to them in the Christian way of life, certainly not enough to cause them to abandon their old beliefs, which had sufficed for so long. Moreover, attempts by the Jesuits to make them change many of their established customs did not sit well. The Indians lived without laws and with very few restraints; every man was free to live as he thought best, and crimes were punished by the victim or his kin, not by the collectivity. The only restraint on action was the normal desire to be held in esteem by his fellows.

Women were the masters of their own bodies and from puberty until pregnancy they gave themselves to any male who pleased them. To the Jesuits this was carnal sin. They learned to overlook the Indian girls' total lack of modesty, their habit of divesting themselves of all clothing whenever it impeded their actions, but they could not tolerate their seeming lewdness.[21] Some others of the French, the men sent by the fur trade companies to establish good trade relations, found the Indian moral standards very acceptable and took full advantage of the Indian girls' total lack of sexual inhibitions. Thus, when the Jesuits tried to persuade the Indians to live chaste lives, they met a cool reception. The Indians saw no merit in such an innovation and pointedly asked why, if chastity were such a fine thing, all the French Christians did not practice it. To this the missionaries were hard put to find a convincing answer.

They found that before they could hope to enjoy any real success, they had to undermine the old beliefs of the Indians, and in so doing, they helped to destroy their culture. One approach to this was to demonstrate that the Indians' reliance on dreams to govern their future actions was inefficacious. Once a few of the Huron had been converted and openly rejected the belief in dreams as a means to communicate with the spirit world, this task became easier, for when these converts had as much success at the hunt as the pagans, the latter began to doubt their old beliefs. When the prayers of the Jesuits for a good hunt, a catch of fish, for rain after drought, or for good crops were answered, the Indians were impressed and admitted that the Jesuits were greater shamans than their own. Another weapon in the Jesuit armory totally new to the Indians was the concept of hell. Father Le Jeune commented "many of them are very glad to die Christians, not in truth, so much through love as through fear of falling into the fires with which they are threatened."[22]

If the Huron were occasionally impressed by the efficacy of Jesuit prayers, they were quick to blame them for anything that went amiss. In the 1630s they had ample reason for this, when a European disease against which they had no resistance struck their villages. Although only a guess can be made of the total number of deaths, it appears that about half the Huron nation, or over 15,000, died in the decade.[23] The losses were particularly heavy among the children. The Jesuits saw in this, as in other hindrances to their endeavors, the work of Satan. It did, however, offer opportunities hitherto lacking and they quickly seized them. One problem had always been that they feared to baptize an Indian unless reasonably certain that he would henceforth lead a Christian life; but with the moribund this precaution was unnecessary. The missionaries were now able to baptize the dying by the hundred, but they were forced in most instances to do it surreptitiously, for the Indians, remarking that death almost always followed swiftly on the priest's ministrations, associated cause with effect. Also because the Jesuits were blamed for the disease, they encountered more resistance than ever to their missionary work, but they took satisfaction from the fact that the thousands whom they had somehow managed to baptize had gone to a heaven that otherwise would have been barred to them. What was lost to this world was gained for the next.

No sooner had this plague run its course and begun to abate than another, and even worse, disaster struck the Huron. The Iroquois had warred with them intermittently for a long time, but they had also sought to negotiate a commercial alliance in order to obtain furs, no longer obtainable in their own territories, to trade at Albany for the European goods they were now dependent on. Between 1640 and 1645 they concentrated their attacks on the French settlements between Quebec and Montreal, and blockaded the Ottawa River route. They gained some furs from their ambushes along this river but not enough; and when, in 1645, they succeeded in negotiating a commercial alliance and peace treaty with the Huron and French, they gained nothing. The Huron took a huge store of furs to the French and none to the Iroquois. The Iroquois thereupon embarked on a war of extermination against the Huron preparatory to taking over their middleman role with the northern and western nations. In 1647 their sudden assaults forced the Huron to abandon some of their outlying villages and withdraw to the more populous villages near Ste. Marie for protection. No canoes traveled to or from Montreal all that year for fear of ambush. Huronia was isolated. Attempts were made to renew the peace treaty with the Onondaga and to arrange a military alliance with the Andastes, an Iroquois nation occupying lands in the Susquehanna Valley and hostile to the Five Nations Confederacy. For some months the Jesuits were confident that the Iroquois assaults would be curbed, and in their *Relations* they dwelt on the success the mission was at last beginning to enjoy.

At or near the main mission post of Ste. Marie there were some thirteen Huron villages, and the mission itself was a sizable establishment. During the year over 3000 persons had been given shelter and food. The converts now numbered in the hundreds, and over two thousand in all had been baptized, although the majority of these last had been moribund. In 1648 a Huron party, 250 strong, made the twenty-day journey to the French settlements and routed an Iroquois war party near Trois-Rivières. Some thirty French accompanied them back to Huronia, taking with them a heifer and a small cannon. Since three young boys were among this party, it is evident that the French were confident the Iroquois threat would be contained.[24]

In their absence, however, a large Iroquois war party had made its stealthy way to the borders of Huronia. No watch was kept at the two frontier villages of St. Joseph mission, and many of the men were away hunting. Suddenly, at sunrise, the Iroquois debouched from the cover of the forest near one of the villages. Rushing through the surrounding corn fields, they quickly hacked a breach in the palissade. Within there was terror and panic at the first triumphant Iroquois war cries. Some of the warriors tried to make a stand, but it was futile. They were quickly hacked down. Neither women nor children were spared as the Iroquois swept through the village. Father Antoine Daniel hurriedly baptized all he could before he too was butchered. It was all over very quickly. The bark long houses were set ablaze, with terrified or wounded Huron cowering inside to be consumed in the flames. The neighboring village was served in the same fashion. The survivors fled to Ste. Marie. Of a total population in the two villages of some three thousand, it was estimated that seven hundred, mostly women and children, had been killed or captured. The destruction of these villages spread terror throughout Huronia. For the Jesuits, however, there was the consolation that many of the slain had been baptized during the assault who otherwise might not have been. Indeed, nearly 1300 were baptized that year.[25]

After this Iroquois army had withdrawn, the death toll continued to mount. The Huron usually stored enough food to last them through at least one winter, but the supplies at St. Joseph had gone up in flames. Some fifteen outlying villages were abandoned. Over 6000 persons took refuge at Ste. Marie. The Jesuits did what they could to feed the multitude, but starvation stared them all in the face. By spring Huron morale was at a low ebb. In mid-March the Iroquois struck again, far sooner than could have been expected, for the Indian nations usually made war only when the trees were in full leaf to provide cover for surprise, ambush, and swift retreat. This Iroquois army, Seneca and Mohawk, one thousand strong, well armed with Dutch muskets, had wintered on the borders of Huronia. The mission villages of St. Louis and St. Ignace met the same fate as St. Joseph. Fathers Brébeuf and Gabriel Lalemant were less fortunate than had been Father Daniel. They were taken alive and for hours had to endure the most hideous tortures before they expired at the stake.

At Ste. Marie the smoke rising from the burning villages had been visible. The terror-stricken survivors soon began to arrive. Next day the Iroquois moved against Ste. Marie but a Huron counterattack drove them off with heavy losses. They retired to St. Ignace, devoted their attention to burning their prisoners for a while, then began the long march back to their own country with a rich harvest of scalps and plundered furs. The surviving Jesuits and the French laymen at Ste. Marie now took council what to do.

Although the Huron warriors still greatly outnumbered the Iroquois invaders, their will to resist was broken. To them it seemed that nothing could withstand the Iroquois with their muskets. Flight out of their reach seemed the only salvation. Some sought refuge with the Neutral nation, others with the Petun and the Erie. One entire Huron village surrendered to the Iroquois, its occupants were spared and incorporated into the ranks of the Seneca, greatly reinforcing them.[26]

To the Jesuits, there seemed little point in remaining in Huronia. The only reason for being there had vanished with the destruction of the Huron villages. In the hopes of salvaging something, they decided to withdraw to St. Joseph Island in Georgian Bay with a large body of the Huron and there begin again. On May 15, 1649, the extensive buildings at Ste. Marie, constructed at great cost, were burned to prevent their desecration by the pagan foe. Some three hundred families, most of them Christians, removed with the Jesuits to the ill-chosen island. There was not enough food to feed a fraction of this number and by the following spring only a few hundred remained alive. Gathering what little food they could, the survivors abandoned the island. Some went to Quebec with the Jesuits to eke out a wretched existence at Lorette, a few miles from the settlement; others struck south to join the Andastes on the Susquehannah River. The Huron nation and trading empire was no more. Only piles of ashes, charred human bones, clearings in the forest where vast corn fields had once stood, marked its extent.

The French fur trade and missionary frontier had been driven back, but only temporarily. Five years before the destruction of Huronia a Jesuit commented:

> We are only at the entrance of a land which on the side of the west, as far as China, is full of Nations more populous than the Huron. Toward the South, we see other Peoples beyond number, to whom we can have access only by means of this door at which we now stand.

In April 1649 Father Charles Garnier stated that the ruin of the Huron would force the Jesuits to work among the more distant nations. This, he believed, was clearly part of God's grand design.[27] The French fur traders, too, were now obliged to voyage to the western Great Lakes to trade with the "far Indians" and persuade these Algonquian nations and the remnants of the Huron to take their furs to the French settlements. In 1656 alone over thirty Frenchmen, Pierre Esprit Radisson and Médart Chouart de Groseilliers among them, voyaged to the far west to establish commercial relations with the distant tribes. Rumors were soon circulating of a great river that ran south to Mexico.

The Iroquois, meanwhile, had suffered heavy losses in their assaults on the Erie and Neutral nations. But the intended destruction of these nations, along with the Huron, had not been an end in itself. It was control of the western fur trade that the Iroquois desired. In 1653 they succeeded in negotiating a peace treaty with the French, and Jesuit missionaries were allowed to establish themselves in the villages of the Five Nations. The Iroquois were now free to trade at both Montreal and Albany, to play off one against the other. All they had to do was to step into the middleman's role vacated by the Huron. This, however, eluded them. The Ottawa and the remnants of the Huron who had fled westward took over. The Ottawa were well-qualified for this task. They were expert canoemen and they now began garnering furs from all the tribes, except the Sioux their ancient foes, in the western Great Lakes area.

By 1660 the French had established a trading post near Chagouamigon Bay, on the south shore of Lake Superior, and in 1665 a Jesuit was resident there, seeking to convert the large mixed population driven out of the eastern Great Lakes region by the Iroquois assault. After being interrupted for only a few years the flow of western furs once again began to reach Montreal and Trois-Rivières. Significantly, none of the furs came in Iroquois canoes. It appeared that all their campaigning had been for nothing. The basis of their peace with the French was thus removed—indeed, had never been operative. Once again Iroquois war parties began blockading the Ottawa. Their devastating assaults on the French settlements were renewed. By 1658 the Jesuit mission at Onondaga had to be abandoned. The fifty-three men who had comprised it managed to escape a few hours before their slow death at the stake was to occur.[28]

While all this blood was being spilled in the west, the central colony was racked by internal dissension and suffered heavy losses from constant Iroquois assaults. The Iroquois blockaded the river routes, stopping the transport of furs from the west. When the settlers went out in the morning to tend their crops, they could never be sure of living to see their families at the end of the day. In the fields, behind any bush, stone, stump, or hillock, an Iroquois could conceal himself and lie patiently for hours on end, waiting for an unwary settler to come within reach of his tomahawk. In addition to individual forays, war parties of a hundred or more Iroquois warriors were ravaging the settlements from Montreal to below Quebec, destroying crops, burning homes and barns, slaughtering the unwary. In 1661 alone sixty-eight men were lost out of a total population of little more than twenty-five hundred. Those who died fighting were fortunate compared to those taken prisoner to the Iroquois cantons. More often than not they were slowly tortured to death to provide sport, and to strike fear into the hearts of all the Iroquois' foes, a form of primitive *Schrechlichkeit*.[29] Needless to say, the Indian foes of the Iroquois responded in kind.

Despite this terrible external menace, bitter wrangling between the clerical and secular authorities, and even among the clergy themselves, grew steadily worse. In 1658 a bishop had been appointed to New France but without the colony being made a bishopric. The first appointee, Abbé François de Laval de Montigny, was made Bishop of Petraea—*in partibus infidelium*—and Apostolic Vicar in Canada. This meant that legally he came under the direct authority of the Papacy and not, as in the case of the Gallican bishops, under the French crown, but in practice this distinction made little difference. Eventually, in 1674, Canada was made a see and Laval then became Bishop of Quebec. What made things difficult at the outset was that in 1657 the Sulpicians had taken over the parish of Montreal and became seigneurs of the island. Within a few months they were feuding bitterly with the Jesuits, and with Laval after his arrival in 1659, over ecclesiastical jurisdiction.[30]

The disputes between the clergy and the secular authorities centered about the sale of brandy to the Indians. The clergy were bitterly opposed to this traffic because of the debasing effects it had on the natives, who used liquor only to get drunk; once in that condition they frequently went berserk and perpetrated the most hideous outrages. The Indians believed that when intoxicated they were transported to the dream world of their pagan gods, and there was little they would not do to achieve this.[31] They would gladly trade their winter's catch of furs for enough brandy to make them drunk, particularly after an unscrupulous trader had given them a dram or two. With a few kegs of brandy the fur traders could realize far greater profits than with other goods. When the clergy demanded that the sale of liquor to the Indians be banned by the authorities, the fur traders objected strongly. The bishop responded by declaring that anyone known to have traded liquor to the natives would be excommunicated. At first the governor, Pierre de Voyer d'Argenson, supported this stand but he subsequently took offense and sanctioned the liquor trade. The bishop and the governor were immediately in bitter opposition to each other.

Finally, with no hope of a surcease to this travail, both the civil and religious leaders of the colony appealed to the only agency that seemed likely to be able to help, the French crown. If aid had not come it is doubtful that New France could have survived much longer. As it was, some settlers were giving up and returning to France. One thing was very clear; as a colonizing agency private enterprise had been tried for over half a century, and found wanting.

Yet by 1660 a good deal had been accomplished. The colony was now more than a mere fur trade depot. The population had passed the two thousand mark, and a good deal of land was under cultivation, enough to feed the people in normal times. The towns of Trois-Rivières and Montreal had been founded, and a generation of colonists, albeit few in number, had grown up whose roots were in Canada. The basic institutions had been established—schools, hospitals, law courts, and a representative colonial council of sorts. If anything, the colony was over-institutionalized, and the institutions were too dependent on financial support from outside sources. But the greatest achievement was that the French had learned how to live, and live quite well, in the strange Canadian environment. They had mastered the technical skills of the Indian and had learned how to live

Jesuit map of Huronia and surrounding lands, 1657. (Public Archives of Canada)

among them on at least equal terms. They had voyaged far into the interior and could go anywhere on their own; they were no longer dependent on the Indians to transport or even guide them. The maps drawn by the Jesuits of this period, based on information gained from members of the order and from fur traders, indicate a fairly exact knowledge of the St. Lawrence Valley and the area around the Great Lakes Basin. The basis of future French colonial enterprise had been established: the garnering of furs and savage souls.

For the Indians, the first half of the seventeenth century was far more crucial than they could possibly have imagined. During those years many thousands of them in the eastern half of North America had direct dealings with Europeans for the first time. Prior to this epoch they had lived with varying efficiency in an easy balance with nature. Hunting, and in the case of some primitive agriculture, had sufficed for their physical, social, and spiritual needs. With the advent of the French in the St. Lawrence Valley the whole way of life of the Algonkin and Iroquois nations suffered a technological and cultural revolution. Within a few years old skills were lost as the Indians became dependent on European goods and technology. Metal replaced flint and bone; the musket replaced the lance and the bow. They now had to have knives, axes, muskets, and ammunition to hunt and for self-defense. They had to have steel needles, awls, and European trinkets to maintain individual status. They were no longer as free as they had been, for they had become dependent on these external agents over whom they had only limited influence and control.

Their standard of living indubitably rose, but they had to pay an exorbitant price. Part of the price was the destruction of old cultural, social, and spiritual values. Their old religious beliefs were undermined, where they were not destroyed. The nature of war also underwent a revolution. Before the coming of the Europeans, the Indians' wars had been limited; their motivation and their primitive weapons had precluded too heavy casualties. Afterward their wars became wars of extermination—total war, fought for economic ends, and increasingly for ends sought by Europeans. European diseases, to which the Indians had no resistance, decimated them; and alcohol, which affected them the way narcotics affect civilized peoples today, degraded and debilitated them, weakening their resistance to the physical and moral encroachments of Europeans. The great Huron nation was virtually destroyed during these years, but it was only the first to go.

Politically, lines that were to endure for a century and a half were clearly drawn by the 1660s. The French, in commercial and military alliance with the Algonquian tribes of the north, were locked in a bitter struggle between rival metropolises, that of the French and that of the European nation dominating the Hudson River. The accident of geography whereby the St. Lawrence gave easy access to the heart of the continent enabled the French to dominate the interior of North America with a mere handful of men. But to maintain this dominance close ties with the Indians were essential.

◁ 4 ▷

Institutions and Environment

*T*he urgent appeal to the crown for aid by the civil and religious authorities in Canada could not have come at a more propitious moment. In 1663 France was at peace and in a dominant position in Europe. Louis XIV had recently taken complete power into his own hands upon the death of Cardinal Mazarin. Within a few years, under the able direction of Jean-Baptiste Colbert, France had the most efficient administration of all the countries in Europe. Colbert was responsible for internal affairs in the realm and had charge of the French colonies. His main aim was to strengthen and greatly expand the French economy—increase exports, reduce imports, achieve a favorable balance of trade and a budgetary surplus.

In the attainment of these aims the French overseas colonies were intended to play an important part. They were to provide France with raw materials that the kingdom would otherwise have had to import from foreign countries, and with a market for French manufactured goods. Colbert wanted to obtain far more than intermittent shipments of furs from the French possessions on the mainland of North America, but he was fully cognizant of the value of this commodity and wished to see the trade increase. In addition to furs he wanted New France to provide the mother country with timber, ship masts, and naval stores, which were then being

Louis XIV, by Robert Nanteuil. (Public Archives of Canada)

imported from Russia and Scandinavia. He also wanted it to produce an agricultural surplus and to ship foodstuffs to the French West Indies plantations. Fish, wheat, peas, and barrel staves were to be exported from Quebec to the Caribbean, and rum, molasses, and sugar were to be shipped to France; French manufactured goods were to be carried back to Canada. In other words, he wished to emulate the triangular trade of the English with their American colonies.

But before any of this could be done, New France had to be made much more self-sufficient, able to stand on its own feet, and no longer dependent on France for its basic needs. A new framework of government had to be installed; capital, labor, and administrative talent had to be invested; and before these factors could be brought properly into play, the Iroquois had to be subdued to give the colony security. Within the short space of five years, Colbert accomplished all these initial steps. Indeed, he accomplished far more in that time than all the private companies had done in the preceding six decades, and thereby laid the foundations for a vast expansion of French power in North America.

Colbert began his colonial reorganization by revoking the charter of the Company of New France. The outstanding debts of the Community of the Habitants were subsequently liquidated, in the same way as was done at this time with the debts of many bankrupt municipalities and societies in France. The colony's financial slate was wiped clean, but to implement Colbert's plans for Canada a great deal of capital was needed. To raise it, he formed a new commercial corporation, copied from the Dutch and English East India companies, which were enjoying success. He encountered great difficulty, however, in persuading Frenchmen, let alone foreigners, to invest in the Compagnie de l'Occident, and much of its capital had to be provided by the crown.[1] It was in fact a crown corporation directed by Colbert, and Canada was now a royal province governed by royal officials.

To make the colony secure from the external threat of the Iroquois, four companies of regular troops were shipped to Quebec, followed by the Carignan Salières regiment comprising nearly eleven hundred men under veteran officers. In three campaigns these regular soldiers learned a great deal, the hard way, about campaigning in the North American forest against expert guerrilla fighters such as the Mohawk. In one campaign launched, foolhardily, in January 1666, the French suffered more casualties than they inflicted on the Iroquois. Several of their wounded survived only because the Dutch at Albany offered them sanctuary, for which the French were most grateful. The following autumn the recently appointed viceroy, Alexandre de Prouville, seigneur de Tracy, led the Carignan Salières regiment and 400 Canadian militia once again into the Mohawk country. The enemy declined to stand and fight this army that came marching through their lands with drums beating and matchlock fuses glowing. They faded into the depths of the forest.

Jean-Baptiste Colbert, by Geille. (Public Archives of Canada)

The four villages with all their winter food supplies were burned to the ground; a cross was planted bearing the arms of Louis XIV; and to cries of *"Vive le Roy"* the Mohawk lands were claimed for France by right of conquest. This done, nothing remained but to march back to Quebec. No Mohawk were killed or captured, but they had been dealt a severe blow none the less. More particularly so since they were at this time being hard pressed by their ancient foes the Mohegan. They therefore decided to sue for peace. At the same time the other four nations of the Confederacy made overtures for a peace treaty. They had recently suffered heavy losses in their war against the western Algonquian nations. A large Mohawk and Onondaga war party had been almost annihilated by the Ottawa, and the Seneca and Cayuga had been severely mauled by the Andastes. In addition smallpox had swept through their villages. As a result of these disasters, and on receiving news of the arrival of large French military reinforcements, in July 1667 the Five Nations sent an embassy to Quebec to accept Tracy's terms. They agreed to end their hostilities with the French and their Algonquian allies.

Unknown to the French, while they were subduing the Iroquois, England and France were at war. When the authorities in New York learned of this, and being greatly perturbed by the French incursions into lands they claimed, they were eager to raise a force among the northern colonies for an attack on Canada, but New England refused to cooperate. In 1667 news came that the Treaty of Breda had ended Anglo-French hostilities. Then, as later, English colonial disunity was one of the main safeguards of New France.

With the Iroquois threat removed, peace restored in Europe, and initial administrative reforms in France well under way, Colbert began implementing his colonial program. The Dutch commercial threat to the French West Indies was eliminated and order restored in these valuable possessions. Acadia, ceded back to France by the Treaty of Breda, was regained in 1670 despite the spirited opposition of its governor, William Temple, who then made overtures to obtain French citizenship in a futile attempt to retain a grip on the potential resources of the area. The Chevalier de Grand Fontaine was appointed governor; a company of regular troops was sent out to garrison Port Royal, and was accompanied by some thirty settlers to augment the province's meager population, which numbered fewer than four hundred.

It was, however, Canada, the colony in the St. Lawrence Valley, to which Colbert devoted his main effort. In addition to the viceroy Tracy, who returned to France in 1667, Colbert sent a tough professional soldier, Daniel de Remy, Sieur de Courcelle, to Quebec as governor general. From this time on, all the colony's governors, with one exception, Le Febvre de la Barre, were professional soldiers or naval officers. Of perhaps greater

Alexandre de Prouville, seigneur de Tracy, lieutenant general of all French territories in North and South America, 1663–1667, by Lenfant. (Public Archives of Canada)

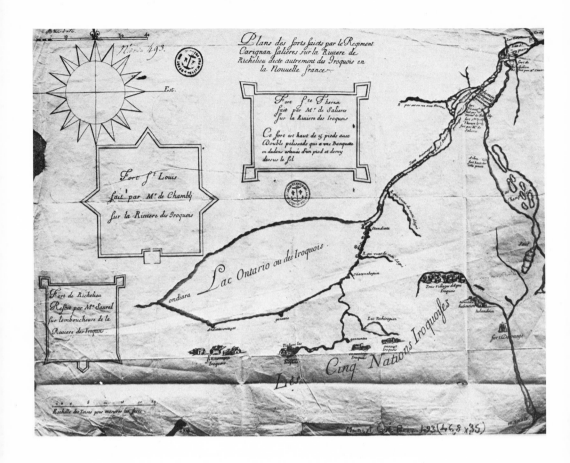

Iroquois cantons and newly constructed forts in the Montreal region,
1666. (Public Archives of Canada)

significance was the appointment of an intendant, Jean Talon, to the colony. This official was responsible for the administration of justice, colonial finances, and civil administration. The governor general retained control of military matters and Indian relations, but the general well-being of the colony was mainly the responsibility of the intendant.

The officers and men of the Carignan Salières regiment, who had been sent to the colony on the understanding that they would return to France after eighteen months, were given every encouragement to remain. Several officers accepted seigneuries along the Richelieu River and settled there with the men of their companies, some 400 in all, as their *censitaires*. They were granted half pay for the first few years and the essential farm implements. It was intended that these new seigneuries along the Richelieu River would bar that main route, used by Mohawk war parties so frequently in the past to ravage the colony. The inspiration for this military settlement was the *praedia militaria* of ancient Rome[2]—a frontier settlement by veterans who could be called upon to defend the frontier at any time.

It is frequently stated that the institutions of New France were feudal in origin. This is a term that obscures more than it explains, particularly when used in a pejorative sense. In fact, the word feudal was not coined until the late eighteenth century, after New France had ceased to exist. Certainly the term can hardly be applied to the seigneurial system of land tenure in Canada. As it is generally used, feudalism implies military obligation. In New France the seigneurial system was not based on military service; it was merely a method of apportioning land, bringing it into production, and obviating the evils of speculation.

Title to all land rested with the king, who granted concessions to seigneurs on the condition that they get their grants cleared and make them productive. They were required to establish settlers on part of their lands, to build a mill for their use, and to maintain a court of law to settle minor disputes. For their part these settlers, or *censitaires*, as they were known, were required to clear the lands they had been granted and to pay modest dues, *cens et rentes*, to their seigneur, which amounted to less than 10 percent of their income. The *censitaires* did not owe military service to their seigneurs, but to the crown as members of the militia, and their militia officers were not the seigneurs but men chosen by the governor general from among their own ranks. Except in rare instances, they did not perform *corvées*, labor service, for their seigneurs; but they were required to serve on a crown *corvée* for a day or two a year, repairing roads or bridges, or doing maintenance work on the common.

Any dispute between a seigneur and his *censitaires* was adjudicated by the intendant. Were either party to fail to fulfill his obligation, that is, to bring the land into production with a reasonable time, the intendant could, and frequently did, revoke his concession. A seigneur was not a landlord in the same way that an English colonial landowner was; he had obligations and responsibilities both to the crown and to his *censitaires,* and the intendants saw to it that he fulfilled them. They also saw to it that the *censitaires* fulfilled their obligations.

The seigneurs were little more than land settlement agents and their financial rewards were not great. What they did gain, and what made men eager to become seigneurs, was the greatly enhanced social status, made manifest in a variety of ways. Under the old regime, social status was to no small degree independent of a man's wealth, and was eagerly sought after. If a *censitaire* sold his land to anyone other than a direct heir, he had to pay one-twelfth of the sale price to the seigneur, who also had the right to buy the land at the price offered by a would-be purchaser within forty days of the sale. When land was sold, what the seller received was, in essence, not the worth of the land but compensation for the improvements he had made on it. One of the main aims here was, of course, to curb speculation. Under pioneer conditions such a system had much to recommend it for the simple reason that it was skillfully devised to operate under those particular conditions. Rather than being feudal, it was very modern, that is, mid-seventeenth century.

In the early years of royal government, as a result of the influx of military and civilian settlers, there was a vexing shortage of women in the colony. Colbert quickly took this problem in hand. Orphanages were scoured for robust girls of good character. The prospect of a husband, free land, tools, and other essentials, plus a crown dowry of 20 *livres* for those willing to cross the Atlantic proved quite appealing. Orphan girls of good family were induced to emigrate, at the crown's expense, to provide wives for the officers who had chosen to stay in the colony. Each year the ships carried hundreds of the *filles du Roi* to Quebec, where they were cared for by the Ursulines and Hospital sisters until they found husbands. This rarely took more than a fortnight.[3]

Each year families of settlers also were sent at the king's expense, in addition to several hundred *engagés,* indentured laborers. As many as 500 persons were sent in a year. The indentured men were bound over to the established settlers for three years, at a modest but reasonable wage, and at the expiry of their contract were given land. In this way they gained valuable experience of local conditions, without which they would not have been able to cope on their own, and the seigneurs got more of their land cleared. Besides men and women, enough cattle, sheep, goats, and horses were shipped by the crown to make the colony self-sufficient within a few years. During these first seven or eight years of royal government, the crown invested nearly a quarter of a million *livres* a year in the colony.

Every summer, when the ships reached Quebec there was great excitement as they unloaded their cargoes of supplies and immigrants. Bachelors eager to take a wife studied the "king's girls" with an appraising eye; seigneurs looked over the *engagés* for men with sturdy frames, or for one with a trade; and the visiting Indians stared in amazement at the first horses sent to the colony—"French moose without horns"—and asked how they had been made so tractable. Despite all Colbert's instructions and precautions, some of the immigrants proved to be lazy, feeble, or debauched, but on the whole there appears to have been surprisingly few of these. Apparently some of the girls sent out were most unprepossessing, and tl.e officials at Quebec were obliged to impose restrictions on all bachelors untii the last of these had been married off.

A far more serious problem was the incidence of disease on the ships. Often the immigrants who survived a crossing, when ship fever had taken its toll, were more dead than alive upon arrival. Nursing them back to health was, on occasion, a large item in the colony's administrative budget of 36,000 *livres* a year. Fortunately, the colony had hospitals, the Hôtel-Dieu at Quebec and at Montreal, and although very hard pressed they managed somehow to cope with the sudden influx of grievously ill. As the population expanded, other institutions had to be established to care for those who were unable to care for themselves and who had no family to assume the responsibility. Every family was not only expected but was required by law to care for its indigent members. When parents became too old to provide for themselves, the children had to make provision for them. If they failed to do so, the intendant, by *ordonnance*, convened them and saw to it that this was done.

In the final decades of the seventeenth century war conditions reduced numbers in the colony to the point where many had no family to aid them, or their families were unable to provide assistance. The crown then accepted the responsibility. In 1685 *bureaux des pauvres* were established in the three towns and the country districts. Their purpose was to assist the deserving poor to get back on their feet, and to prevent the undeserving poor, those who preferred mendicancy to honest toil, from becoming an economic liability and a social nuisance. Before the end of the century alms houses, the *Hôpitals Généraux*, were founded in Quebec and Montreal to care for the indigent, aged, incurable, and orphans, the latter being apprenticed to acquire a useful trade. Foundlings were a particular charge of the crown and were well cared for. Great care was taken that none of these unfortunates should be exploited or made to suffer unduly because of their circumstances. This undoubtedly was paternalism; it was also humanitarian. Poverty was not regarded as a sin or a crime, but as a fault in the fabric of society that had to be mended.[4]

Despite heavy losses from disease, during these first years of royal government the population increased from some 2500 in 1663 to more than 6500 by 1668. By 1672 the crown had sent to Canada at least five to six thousand men and women, and there is no evidence that any of them were dragooned into going. After that date, however, government-subsidized emigration was reduced to a trickle. Some skilled tradesmen and artisans were sent, but under contracts that guaranteed them high wages and return passage to France once their work was completed. In addition large numbers of regular soldiers were subsequently sent; most of these settled in the colony upon being discharged. Apart from this, after 1672 the colony's population was augmented mainly by natural increase and little by immigration.

When compared to the great waves of immigration that flooded into the English colonies during the hundred years between 1660 and 1760, the French effort appears meager indeed. But the circumstances of the two mother countries were very different. New France represented only one small part of Colbert's plans for French economic expansion. In France itself he was faced with a shortage of skilled labor for the new industries that he was establishing, and the vast increase in the size of the army with the onset of Louis XIV's wars drained the available supply of able-bodied men.

Owing to the peculiarities of the French social system, there was a chronic shortage of investment capital for economic development. The chief aim of the newly rich middle class was to purchase a government post and then rise in the royal service and recoup the investment by means of fees or grants for faithful service. Thus the crown absorbed much of the nation's limited supplies of talent and capital. The capitalist notion that money should be invested in an industrial or commercial enterprise purely to make profit and the bulk of the profits plowed back to expand the enterprise, was quite alien to the dominant social values. It was chiefly for this reason that the economy of both France and New France expanded under the stimulus of the state, and why New France became, under royal government, a military bureaucracy.

The geography of France and of Britain was also a major factor in their differing social and economic development, as well as in their colonial policies. Britain, being an island, was relatively secure from attack by foreign powers—as long as it maintained a navy stronger than that of its potential foes—and had no great need for a large standing army. This had several consequences. Britain could afford to export surplus manpower to its colonies, and its need for ships to defend its shores provided the means to do so. Lacking a large army, the British crown was unable to withstand the assault on its power by the aristocracy, allied with the gentry and rising capitalist class. In this way parliament rather than the crown became sovereign. France, on the other hand, surrounded by other land powers, all potentially hostile, had to maintain a large army to defend its frontiers. With such an army, a monarch could impose his will on the people, and had no need to consult them before imposing taxes. Therein lies one reason for the difference between Louis XIV's reign in France and that of the Stuarts in England. Without the English Channel, it is highly unlikely that parliamentary government would have developed in the form that it did, or that England would have become the great colonizing power that it became in the seventeenth and eighteenth centuries. More likely, it would have been another Netherlands.

Given the need in France for an army and the outbreak of war with the Dutch Republic in 1672, it is not surprising that French colonial activity was somewhat curtailed. What is surprising is that despite these wars and the drive to expand the nation's economy, the crown was able to devote as much attention as it did to New France. In 1669 Colbert had declared that the colony should now be able to stand on its own feet. This it certainly did, and within five years the minister was desperately striving, without success, to restrain its proclivity for expansion. To the people in New France the future, at long last, looked very promising. In 1668 the Jesuits at Quebec reported:

> It is pleasant to see now almost the entire extent of the shores of our River St. Lawrence settled by new colonies, which continue to spread over more than eighty leagues of territory along the shores of this great River, where new hamlets are seen springing up here and there, which facilitate navigation—rendering it more agreeable by the sight of numerous houses, and more convenient by frequent resting places. . . .
>
> Fear of the enemy no longer prevents our laborers from causing the forests to recede and from sowing their fields with all sorts of grain. . . . The Savages our allies, no longer fearing that they will be surprised on the road, come in quest of us from all directions, from a distance of five and six hundred leagues—either to re-establish their trade, interrupted by the wars; or to open new commercial dealings, as some very remote tribes claim to do, who had never before made their appearance here, and who came last Summer for that purpose. . . .
>
> Moreover since a country cannot be built up entirely without the help of manufactures, we already see that of shoes and hats begun, and those of linen and leather planned; and it is expected that the steady increase in sheep will produce sufficient wool to introduce that of woolen goods. That is what we are hoping for in a little while, since animals are becoming abundant here, especially horses, which are beginning to spread throughout the entire country.[5]

All of this could not have been done under the old colonial institutions. To implement Colbert's policies in New France a new administrative framework, modeled on that of a French province but with significant differences, was established. Some of the innovations were deliberate on Colbert's part; such as attempts to introduce improvements or reforms that he would have liked to introduce in France but could not owing to the opposition of powerful vested interests. Other modifications were introduced more gradually in response to the North American environment. The theory of government was, of course, that sovereignty lay with the divine-right monarch. After the turbulence of the Fronde, the acceleration of the earlier trend toward a centralized government was accepted by the vast majority of the people as a very desirable step, conducive to law, order, and personal security. In New France the immediate benefits conferred by the crown were so great that no one could envisage a better system. When abuses crept in, those who suffered looked to the crown for redress, and this was accorded in enough instances that no one thought of looking elsewhere.

The king delegated authority to his ministers, reserving for himself supervision over foreign affairs. Colbert was, to a much greater extent than the other ministers, given a free hand; only major decisions were referred to the king and then only to give the minister's decision the added weight of the monarch's support. Thus the government of New France resided in the cabinet of the minister of marine, assisted by his *commis,* akin to deputy ministers in the present-day parliamentary system. It was the minister who made policy, on the expert advice of these *commis* and the senior administrators in the colony.

Of these last, the governor general enjoyed the highest status, and in the final resort exercised the greatest power. The position of this official was rather anomalous. He was not a viceroy yet he represented the king. No visible check to the power of the throne could be allowed, particularly after the experience of the Fronde and the example of recent events in England. Unlike the provinces in France, where the powers of the local governors had been reduced to almost nothing, New France, owing to its remoteness from the metropolis, had to have a governor who could exercise the royal power in times of crisis and symbolize it always.

It is a commonly held assumption that a major weakness of this autocratic, highly centralized administrative system was that the governor and intendant frequently were unable to use their initiative when swift action was needed because all decisions had to be referred to the minister, which meant that at least a year would elapse before action could be taken. In fact, the local officials were expected to use their own initiative on such occasions, and they did. They had much more latitude to act than did the officials of the provinces of France and precisely because the situation demanded it. In 1713 Governor Philippe de Rigaud de Vaudreuil stated in a dispatch to the minister that Michel Bégon, the newly appointed intendant who previously had been intendant at Rochefort, "has a lot to learn about many things here, in time he will come to understand that there is a great difference between Rochefort and Quebec; at Rochefort one receives your orders every week and here only annually, which means that often something is begun and finished before we have had the time to inform you about it."[6]

The greatest strength of the Canadian administrative system was the swiftness with which the governor and intendant could mobilize the entire resources of the colony. In time of war this gave the French a great advantage over the English colonies and explains in no small measure why they were able more than to hold their own against them for so long.[7] Yet this same remoteness from the direct supervision of the crown made it necessary to prevent the governor from abusing the authority delegated to him by the king. The concept of checks and balances was as yet unknown and would have been instantly rejected as unworkable and positively dangerous; but the problem was a very vexing one, made more so by the fact that the nature of the governor general's position necessitated the appointment of a senior officer who by definition had to be a member of the *noblesse d'épée*. And it was this class that had recently challenged the power of the throne, albeit unsuccessfully, in the uprising of the Fronde, but not before reducing the kingdom to chaos and opening it to invasion by foreign armies.

It is frequently said that the French, unlike the pragmatic Anglo-Saxons, proceed from theory to practice. In the government of New France, however, a viable administrative system was arrived at by the pragmatic method. One of its chief agents was the office of intendant. A great deal has been written on the origins of this office.[8] Suffice it to say that by 1660 the intendants had become one of the vital elements of the central government. The office had become powerful because it had proved its worth. It was not venal, and it was eagerly sought after by the burgeoning *noblesse de robe;* thus only officials of proven ability acceded, and their retention of office was at the king's pleasure. Any intendant who proved to be incompetent, dishonest, or disloyal could expect to be dismissed from the royal service, his own career finished, and his sons' careers jeopardized.

Given the presence in a colony as remote as was New France of a governor general who was a member of the old nobility and a senior military officer accustomed to exercising arbitrary authority, to giving orders and having them carried out without question; and of the intendant, a career man of the *noblesse de robe* which was despised by the feudal nobility whose power was in decline; with their respective spheres of authority ill defined, it would have required men of great tolerance and wisdom to avoid conflicts. Since such men were in as short supply then as now, during the first quarter century of royal government the administration of the colony was disrupted on occasion by disputes between these senior officials. Consequently, the minister of marine and the king were obliged to define the powers and responsibilities of these officials more closely, and this resulted in the powers of the governor general being stringently restricted. In this way New France, like other countries, developed a form of constitutional government. It was not the environment—that is, frontier conditions—which brought this about. The changes that were made resulted from the minister's reaction to conflicts in the colony, which in turn arose out of social stresses that had originated in France rather than in Canada.[9]

Similarly, safeguards had to be enacted to protect the individual against the arbitrary acts of officialdom. Colbert, in a dispatch to the governor general in 1674, made it plain that the right of the people to move freely in the colony and to attend to their own affairs without interference was not to be transgressed. Some of the senior officials, however, held the view that their private interests were synonymous with those of the crown; hence to oppose them was akin to treason. The king quickly disabused them of that notion. When it was brought to his attention that the governor of Montreal was behaving in a despotic manner, imprisoning people who refused to submit to his arbitrary demands, he issued an *ordonnance* forbidding the colonial governors to imprison anyone without immediately charging him and bringing him to trial before the courts. Only in cases of treason or sedition, which Colbert pointedly remarked "hardly ever happen," could the governors take the law into their own hands.[10] This royal *ordonnance* was enacted in 1679, the same year Parliament in England passed a measure to serve the same purpose, the act known as *habeas corpus*.

Despite these limitations on his power, the governor general retained his authority in military affairs and in negotiations with the Indian nations. He also retained the right to exercise the royal authority and countermand the orders of any of the other officials, but he could only do this when he was convinced that he would be held accountable by the minister were he not to do so. When he did, he had to be able to justify his actions to the king or expect to be severely reprimanded, if not dismissed from his post. The early governors and intendants were continually instructed by the minister that they had to cooperate in all things, and the governor general in particular was ordered that only in the most extraordinary circumstances could he interfere with the work of the other officials, particularly of the officers of law. After one governor general, the Comte de Frontenac, the governor of Montreal, François-Marie Perrot, and two intendants, Jacques Duchesneau and Jacques de Meulles had been summarily dismissed from office for their failure to heed these instructions, the colonial administration functioned with relative tranquillity.

It was the intendant, however, who was responsible for the general administration of the colony, the administration of justice, and the disbursement of the colony's finances. As the population increased, deputy intendants answerable to the intendant at Quebec had to be appointed at Montreal, Trois-Rivières, and Detroit. Beneath them were a host of lesser officials who superintended roads, harbors, shipping, and municipal affairs, most of them were necessary, some were not. A few sinecure posts were created to provide pensions for men who had given long service to the crown and in their declining years lacked the means to live honorably. The towns of Montreal and Trois-Rivières also had local governors and town majors who were answerable to the governor general, but their functions were chiefly military.

It was accepted as axiomatic that the function of the government—that is, the crown—was to govern, to maintain law and order, and to protect the proper interests of all segments of society. The concept that society consists of free and equal individuals was not given credence, since it was clearly not in accord with the facts. It seemed obvious that in a civilized society no man is completely free, that every man must relinquish a degree of freedom of action for the common good, and that all men are not equal. It also appeared obvious that society consisted of groups of individuals having common interests, functions, duties, responsibilities, rights, and privileges. Thus, the function of the crown was to ensure that each group in society performed its proper function, discharged its responsibilities, and was maintained in the enjoyment of its time-honored privileges.

The concept that if every individual pursued his private advantage to the best of his ability the general good would somehow result, would have been rejected. This meant that in economic affairs it was taken for granted that the best interests of the consumer, that is, society as a whole, and not those of the individual producer, must prevail. Therefore no merchant, habitant, or artisan was permitted to charge all that the traffic would bear. At the same time it was recognized that merchants and artisans perform their functions best when allowed the maximum of freedom, but human frailty being what it is, the government was expected to intervene to maintain quality, fair prices, good measure, and also proper reward to the producer or merchant for his goods or services. This concept of an organic society obliged the intendant to issue a great number of *ordonnances* regulating the economic life of the colony. The weights and measures of the shopkeepers had to be inspected regularly; the quality and weight of the bakers' bread had to be checked; and the number of tradesmen allowed to keep shop had to be regulated so that they could gain a proper living and the needs of the people could be met. When, for example, it was suggested that there were not enough butchers in one of the towns, an assembly was held to discover the views of the people and to decide whether another butcher should be allowed to function. In times of shortage the intendant had to allocate supplies and regulate prices.

All of these regulations were regarded as necessary, and had the royal officials not enacted them the people would have complained. Many, if not most, of the intendant's *ordonnances* were enacted in response to complaints or requests from the people. Undoubtedly some of the people chafed under these restrictions much of the time, but the intendant's *ordonnances* were not regarded as the dictates of a despotic government interfering with the freedom of the individual, but as necessary measures to prevent, curb, or remove abuses.[11]

In the country districts a uniquely Canadian official emerged early in the royal regime and quickly became indispensable. This was the *capitaine de milice*. In 1669 Governor Rémy de Courcelles had received orders from the king to organize the Canadian settlers into militia companies and to see to it that they received military training.[12] Companies of militia, each with a captain in command and subordinate officers, were established in both the towns and the country parishes, and proved their worth in all the colony's wars. These captains of militia were appointed by the governor general and of necessity had to be men respected by the *habitants* of their respective parishes, but their main function in peacetime was to act as sub-delegates of the intendant and as local police officers. They served as the vital link between the administration and the people, making the desires or complaints of the people known to the officials, who were usually responsive. In this ingenious way the seigneurs were prevented from becoming too powerful; they were neatly bypassed in the chain of authority, and when certain of the seigneurs attempted to have the militia captains made subordinate to them, the minister immediately instructed the governor to order them to desist. Like the English justice of the peace, the militia captain received no pay or emoluments; the prestige and status of the office sufficed. As in England, where the administration could not have functioned effectively without the justice of the peace, so in New France the office of *capitaine de milice* was an essential cog in the administrative machinery.

Prior to 1663 there had been a Council at Quebec, presided over by the governor, which had enacted legislation. Colbert reorganized it, making it the Sovereign Council for the colony. It was now made up of the governor, the bishop, the intendant, an attorney general, a recording clerk and five councilors. The number of these last was soon found to be insufficient and in 1675 two more were added; then in 1703 their number was raised to twelve. In 1675 their power and prestige was considerably enhanced by their being given royal commissions to serve during the king's pleasure. Previously they had been appointed and dismissed at will by the governor and bishop jointly, which had led to serious disputes and abuses. The king further restricted the power of the governor by decreeing that the intendant would preside over the meetings of the Council. This body thus became sovereign in fact as well as in name.

In France the concept of separation of powers was not in vogue. It was thought that those best qualified to judge in law were those who had enacted it; therefore the Sovereign Council had both judicial and legislative powers. It registered and promulgated the laws as they were enacted by the king, legislated to meet the needs of the colony, and heard some cases in first instance for the district of Quebec and criminal cases on appeal for the entire colony. Over the years, as the amount of litigation increased, the Council restricted itself increasingly to its judicial function, leaving legislation to be enacted by the intendant.

Beneath the Sovereign Council were the lower courts in Quebec, Montreal, and Trois-Rivières. The judges of these courts were responsible for enacting a good deal of municipal legislation, governing such things as street traffic, road maintenance, garbage disposal, and fire regulations. In the countryside some of the more populous seigneuries had seigneurial courts, but these appear to have been few in number and heard only minor civil disputes. All of these courts were governed by the *Coutume de Paris* and by the body of customary law enacted in the colony. A thorough study of the administration of justice in New France has yet to be made, but it appears that it compares quite favorably with the systems in vogue in both France and England in the seventeenth and eighteenth centuries. Close examination of a few criminal cases gives reason to doubt that the highly regarded Anglo-Saxon adversary system was superior to the inquisitorial system employed in New France.

Unlike in England, the death penalty was rarely invoked and only for serious crimes. All told only sixty-seven persons were executed under the French regime. Although torture could be used to obtain evidence, its use was restricted to persons accused of crimes meriting the death penalty and whose guilt was manifest. In all, under the royal regime, the *question extraordinaire* was employed nineteen times, and as a consequence in four cases the accused, who would otherwise have been hanged, was acquitted, and in five cases the punishment was reduced.[13] Imprisonment for debt appears not to have been in vogue; the absence of this quaint practice was probably due to the fact that under French law the person committing a debtor to jail had to furnish him with adequate food; if he failed to do so, the debtor had to be freed and could not be reimprisoned for the same debt.[14] Another factor may well have had some bearing on the matter; no one could have survived long in a Canadian prison, particularly in winter.[15]

One vexing problem that the Sovereign Council had to face shortly after its establishment was whether or not Indians in the colony were subject to French law. The whole question of French relations with the Indians was here shown in clear relief; for if the Indians who committed what were crimes under French law could be held accountable to the officers of that law, it could be said that the French were truly sovereign. If they could not, if the Indians considered themselves as subject only to their own rudimentary laws for crimes committed against French subjects, then clearly they were free, independent, and sovereign in their own right within the confines of the French colony; and this could only mean that New France, in effect, had divided sovereignty, French and Indian.

In 1664 the Attorney General of the Sovereign Council found himself faced with this knotty problem. In March of that year an Algonkin Indian, most likely drunk, had raped the wife of an *habitant* of the Île d'Orléans. He was arrested and charged with the crime but escaped before his trial was completed. The attorney general then asked the Sovereign Council to determine not only whether or not this case should be pursued further, but also for guidance in all such cases involving Indians: whether, in fact, the Indians could be regarded as subject to French law. The Sovereign Council, like today's academics faced with a tricky problem, responded by appointing a committee to study the question and report back. This committee was composed of the Jesuit fathers in charge of the nearby mission Indians and a number of *habitants*. Their advice appears to have been to discuss the issue with the chiefs of all the nearby tribes since the Indians could not be expected to be conversant with French law in such cases.

On April 21 the Sovereign Council, with the governor general and the bishop in attendance, met with the chiefs of six tribes from the environs of the colony and explained to them that the Algonkin accused of the crime in question, under French law, would have been sentenced to be hanged if found guilty. The Indian spokesman, Noel Tek8erimat,* chief of the Algonkin of Quebec, proudly replied that they had maintained friendly relations with the French for a number of years, and if the behavior of their young braves had given grounds for complaint on occasion, so too had that of some Frenchmen while among the Indians. He declared that they were not aware that the death penalty could be imposed for rape, only for murder; therefore in this case it must not be invoked. In the future, however, they would accept this law. The chief then profited from the occasion to demand that certain abuses suffered by his tribe at the hands of the French, namely the seizure of an Indian debtor's goods by French creditors when hunting was poor, be stopped so that the French and Indians could continue to live in amity. The Council agreed to see that justice was done in these matters in the light of each particular case.[16] The Indians had thereby agreed to accept French law governing cases of rape when an Indian was the accused and a French subject the plaintiff; but that was all.

Fifty years later the principal issue was still not resolved in favor of the French. In 1714 the governor and intendant asked the crown for a ruling, since Indians who became drunk in the colony or caused damage or bodily injury and were put in jail for breach of the peace declared that no one had the right to imprison them without their consent and that they were not subject to the laws of the colony. The King's reply was, "the matter is extremely delicate"; that the colonial authorities must begin by striving to accustom the Indians to submit to military justice and gradually bring them to accept the laws that govern the French.[17] The Indians still regarded themselves as individually free and collectively sovereign.

Eventually the French had to admit defeat. They evaded the basic principle involved by tacitly granting the Indians in the colony something akin to diplomatic immunity. The Indians claimed that no one was accountable for his actions while drunk; the liquor not the imbiber was responsible. The French had to accept this concept, and when a crime was committed by an intoxicated Indian, the French subject who had provided the liquor to excess was prosecuted for breaking the king's Ordonnance of May 24, 1679. If found guilty the accused also had to pay damages to the victim of the crime, or to his or her heirs, parents, or legal guardians.[18] The French were unable to impose their law on the Indians, and for one good reason; to have

---

*The symbol 8 was used by the Canadians to signify a sound in the Algonkin tongue not found in French. The closest approximation to it in French appears to have been "oua," or in English a guttural "wha."

attempted to do so with any degree of vigor would have alienated the Indians, and this the French could not afford to do.

Much of the credit for the seeming equity and efficacy of the Canadian judicial system must be given to Colbert and Louis XIV. They were painfully aware of the gross abuses rampant in the courts of law in France, but the vested interest of the legal fraternity was too powerful to allow effective reforms. In New France this did not obtain, and sweeping departures from custom were made at the outset. One of the most effective of these reforms was Colbert's refusal to allow any lawyers to practise in the colony. The drawing up of contracts and work of that sort was done by notaries, who also received copies of the intendant's *ordonnances* and promulgated them; but in court every man pleaded his own case, and the judges interrogated both litigants and witnesses under oath, then rendered their verdict.

Another reform was the tariff of legal fees, strictly regulating all fees that a legal officer, from a lowly clerk or bailiff to a royal judge, could charge for every conceivable service.[19] This scale of fees was surprisingly low, and it was rigidly enforced. Moreover, in cases heard by the Sovereign Council there were no fees at all. All disputes between a seigneur and his *censitaires* were settled by the intendant, and the intendant could hear, without costs or fees, petty civil suits involving less than 100 *livres*. In more serious civil suits, if both parties agreed, the intendant could adjudicate again without charges of any kind, but without the right of appeal. In 1706, the intendant stated that he had adjudicated over 2000 such cases without costs.

It would, of course, be too much to expect that abuses did not creep in, or that there were never miscarriages of justice. Some of the intendants upon first assuming office declared that the administration of justice was in a shocking state, but always added that they had been quick to rectify matters. Certainly the intention of the king and his senior officials was that justice must be swift, impartial, and available to all. It paid, however, to be a member of the establishment. The records of the Sovereign Council indicate that on occasion the court was more lenient with members of their own class, bearers of "*un beau nom*" (a good name), than with accused from the lower orders. This may be why, in 1712, Louis XIV instructed the governor and intendant at Quebec: "Justice must be rendered alike to rich and poor, strong and weak, to the *habitant* as to the seigneur";[20] and in 1717 a royal edict declared that poverty must never bar a subject from seeking justice in the courts.[21] There is good reason to believe that it rarely did.

Again, there is no evidence whatsoever that the departures made from legal practices in France were brought about by the influence of the frontier. They represented reforms imposed by the central government and reflected the humanitarian attitude of Louis XIV and his ministers.[22] Further evidence of this last is to be found in the swift action taken by the minister upon the receipt of petitions from the humblest of the king's subjects, and in the granting of half pay to ordinary soldiers serving in the colony who were discharged on grounds of age and enfeeblement. All of this was only one aspect of the general attitude of the king. Louis and his ministers firmly believed that they were required to govern in the interests of all the king's subjects, rich and poor alike; that the time-honored rights and privileges of each subject and social group had to be protected by the crown.[23] Unlike in England and its colonies, property was not sacred; it was human rights, not property rights, that were paramount. Here again, the frontier environment had no influence whatsoever. These were values imported from the mother country.

For a few years after the inauguration of the royal regime, the existing element of representative government, the office of syndics, was retained. Colbert, however, was very suspicious of any such device and gave orders to suppress it quietly, "it being a good thing that each man speak for himself and that no one speaks for all."[24] This was not as retrograde a step as it might seem today. The *capitaines de milice* were able to perform the function of the syndics more effectively, and one of the intendant's principal duties was to discover the needs of the people and seek to aid them in every way.[25] That both the intendants and the governors took this seriously is made manifest by the institution of public assemblies to discover the views of the people on specific issues before important legislation was enacted. Such assemblies eventually came to be annual events, held at Quebec when the ships arrived from France, that being the occasion for large numbers of residents throughout the colony to come to the main town.

These meetings resembled a latter-day university faculty meeting chaired by a strong-minded dean more than they did a New England town meeting. The governor and intendant determined the agenda and delegated someone to act as *rapporteur* to explain the issues to be discussed. All in attendance were free to speak their minds on the questions before the assembly, and the governor and intendant gave their views last to avoid inhibiting the meeting. When all had had their say, the intendant "collected the voices," that is asked each person in turn to give his opinion, then, guided by the consensus, he gave his decision. The *rapporteur* then drew up minutes of the meeting which were signed by him, the governor, the intendant, and five members of the assembly, two from Quebec, two from Montreal, and one from Trois-Rivières. In this way the ordinary people did have some say in the administration of their affairs and were required to accept a degree of responsibility for the legislation enacted. Significantly, when in 1706 Louis XIV was informed that this was the practice, he gave instructions that it should be formalized and the procedure drawn up in judicial form to ensure that future assemblies would be held in the proper manner.[26] And in 1710 Vaudreuil and the intendant Raudot were ordered by the king to convene a colonial council to determine what measures should be taken for the security of the colony; a report had to be drawn up and its recommendations strictly adhered to, with a copy going to the king.[27]

The principle of consultative government was further extended in 1708 when the merchants of Quebec, and in 1717 those of Montreal, were permitted to establish chambers of commerce to concert together and to nominate, in each town, one of their number to make representations to the governor and intendant on measures they considered would assist them in the conduct of their business affairs. In the country parishes, too, the *habitants* held frequent assemblies to decide local matters, usually, if not as a rule, at the behest of the intendant or his deputy.[28] But the people at large were not permitted, under any circumstances, to call assemblies on their own to discuss public issues. They could make their views known to the *capitaine de milice* who would pass the information on to the intendant. It then rested with him to decide what action to take. Although every subject had the right to present a petition to the king, and some at least had their requests granted, the circulation of petititons to gather signatures was strictly forbidden. Such petitions, and unsanctioned public meetings, were regarded as seditious.

What is particularly significant about the type of assemblies that were held is the fact that the institution was imposed from above, as a means to aid the royal officials in their administration of the colony. There is no evidence of "frontier democracy" at work here. Given that there was adequate consultation between governors and governed, it is not surprising that the Canadians failed to manifest the Anglo-Saxon proclivity to exercise control over those who enacted legislation. There were, however, additional reasons why this tendency was markedly lacking; the main one being that no direct taxes were levied in the colony. With the exception of very occasional taxes levied for special purposes and after discussion in an assembly,[29] the only taxes the Canadians paid were the *quart*, a 25 percent export tax on all beaver pelts they sold to the agent of the company which had the marketing monopoly, a similar 10 percent on moose hides (both these taxes were removed in 1717), and a 10 percent import tax on wines and liquor.

In 1714, when the French Government was extremely hard pressed financially, the minister suggested imposing a tax on the Canadians to defray the administrative costs of the colony. The governor and intendant strongly opposed the suggestion, claiming that the *habitants* had suffered great hardship during the war just ended, that they were the first line of defense against the English to the south and it would not do to make them discontented.[30] That ended it. In comparison with the lower classes in France the Canadians were very well off indeed, particularly in the years after 1714, but no governor or intendant in his right mind would have supported the imposition of taxes; to have done so would have made his task more difficult. No tax, no trouble; and no administrator asks for trouble; it was as simple as that.

It might be argued that the authorities feared that any such measures would cause an exodus to the west, or to the English colonies. This was highly unlikely; the number that could hope to survive in the west was limited by the economics of the fur trade, and as for desertion to the English colonies, language and religion were major barriers. Indeed, it would appear likely that a greater number from the English colonies settled permanently in New France than went the other way.[31]

On the whole the institutions imposed on the colony by the crown worked well. This was largely because the senior officials sent from France were, with a few notable exceptions, experienced, competent, and relatively honest. It is extremely doubtful that the colony could have provided from among its own population a steady succession of administrators of this caliber. In fact, a recurrent problem in the colony was to find men with the necessary education and capacity to perform administrative and judicial functions competently. There is no evidence that the colonials had any serious complaint against the system or desired any radical changes.

In the final analysis, as with any system of government, everything depended on the competence of the senior administrators, particularly the governor and intendant. When these officials abused their authority, the only recourse the people had was to complain to the minister, which they did on occasion most vociferously; if his orders to desist were not obeyed and the complaints continued, the officials were eventually recalled. Meanwhile, the people had to submit. It was, in short, military government; but interposed between these officials and the people, acting as a buffer and a check on despotic rule, were the courts of law, particularly the Sovereign Council, made up of local notables who took their duties very seriously. Until the closing years of the regime when the intendant François Bigot made a mockery of established institutions, and too-complaisant governors failed to call a halt to his activities, the administrative institutions of New France served the needs of the people tolerably well.

◁ 5 ▷

Society and the Frontier

*O*f the more tangible factors that influenced Canadian society there can be no doubt that geography was very important. The St. Lawrence River and certain of its tributaries dominated life in the colony. The land suitable for agricultural settlement stretched in a narrow band along the St. Lawrence, wider on the south shore than on the north. Near Quebec the Laurentian Shield, scraped nearly bare long ago by an advancing ice age, meets the river. Below this point only small pockets of land at river mouths were suitable for agriculture. Above Quebec, on the north shore, the Shield draws away from the river to a distance of some forty miles at Montreal. On the south shore the belt of fertile land is quite wide between Quebec and Montreal but becomes a narrow ribbon along the river toward Gaspé. West of Montreal there is also good land but on both the St. Lawrence and Ottawa rivers, rapids make communications difficult. Consequently throughout the French regime land settlement was concentrated in the St. Lawrence Valley from a point a few miles west of Montreal to a little below Quebec, with pockets of settlement on both sides lower down the river.

Prior to 1663 the number of settlers and the amount of land cleared

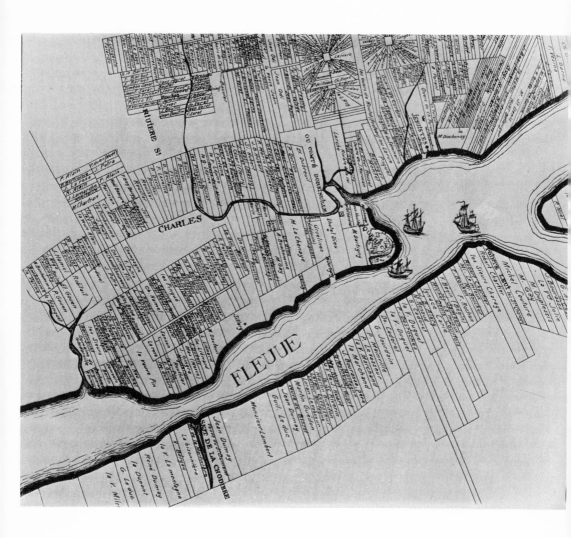

Section of Gédéon de Catalogne's map of the settlements on the St. Lawrence, 1709. The radial-spoked concessions, top center, were an attempt by the French government to have the settlers concentrated at the hubs in villages, rather than dispersed, each family on its own strip of land. The scheme met with very little success and was quickly abandoned. (Public Archives of Canada)

grew very slowly. In 1634 the first seigneurial grant was made to Robert Giffard by Richelieu's Company of New France. During the ensuing thirty years some seventy other seigneuries were granted. The company sent a few settlers to the colony but in the main let this responsibility fall to the seigneurs who, for the most part, lacked the means to engage in a large-scale immigration program. The religious orders did bring out a goodly number of servants, laborers, and settlers; and the crown from time to time sent detachments of soldiers to aid in the colony's defense. By these means the population slowly grew, and stretches of forest near the three areas of settlement, Quebec, Trois-Rivières, and Montreal, were cleared back from the shores of the river. In 1640 the total French population in the colony—settlers, soldiers, clergy, fur trade company employees—numbered only about 240; by 1663, largely as a result of the efforts of the religious orders, this number had increased to some 2500. After the latter date, under the stimulus of the crown, settlement increased very rapidly; by 1669 the population had increased by two thirds, and by the end of the century it was at approximately the 15,000 mark, doubling thereafter each generation to a total of some 70,000 at the Conquest.[1]

The St. Lawrence dictated the pattern of settlement in another way. It was the main means of communication in the colony, in summer by canoe or sailing barque, in winter by sleigh on the ice. The need for roads was thus obviated until the eighteenth century. Every settler desired land on the river, and the land holdings early took on the peculiar pattern that has endured to the present day, that of narrow strips running back from the river. Survey lines separating seigneuries ran at right angles to the river and as the generations succeeded each other the individual holdings became increasingly narrow. According to the law of the land, the *Coutume de Paris,* a seigneur's eldest son inherited the manor house and half the domain land; the rest was divided among the remaining children. The children of the humbler settlers, the *censitaires,* inherited equal parts of the parental land. After a few generations many of the individual holdings became too narrow to be worked efficiently, and in 1745 the intendant forbade anyone to build a house or barn on land narrower than one and a half arpents (approximately 100 yards) by thirty or forty linear arpents in depth. Those who contravened the *ordonnance* were fined 100 *livres* and their buildings were torn down at their expense.

By the eighteenth century the pattern was well established. Along both banks of the St. Lawrence from Quebec to Montreal the farms stretched back from the river, the houses and barns on the river bank spaced a few hundred yards apart. Every few miles there was a seigneurial manor house and a mill, and eventually a steep-roofed stone church. Later in the century concessions were taken up in the second range and another row of narrow strip farms stretched back from the rear of the first, with a roadway between the two. To anyone traveling by river up to Montreal nearly all of New France passed in review.

Habitant's house, Île d'Orléans, *ca.* 1700.

This pattern of land settlement was not without its disadvantages. Until the end of the seventeenth century the Iroquois were an almost constant menace, and with the homes spaced in this fashion mutual aid in times of attack was almost impossible. Individual farms and their occupants could be destroyed all too easily before aid could be mustered. While the Iroquois assaults were at their height stockaded forts had to be built in the exposed seigneuries where the people could take refuge with their livestock, abandoning their homes to the depredations of the enemy. Attempts by some of the royal officials to have the settlers live in villages with their concessions radiating out like spokes of a wheel, were not very successful. The Canadians insisted on having river frontage and living apart, lords of their own little domains, with access to the wider world beyond by way of the river.

By the mid-eighteenth century the farm houses in the first range and the churches, were nearly all of stone, thick-walled, substantial; steep Norman roofs were modified by a graceful curving wide eave, to afford shade in the hot Canadian summers. Peter Kalm, a Swedish professor of natural history who visited Canada in 1749, going by boat from Montreal to Quebec remarked:

> The country on both sides was very delightful to-day, and the fine state of its cultivation added to the beauty of the scene. It could really be called a village, beginning at Montreal and ending at Quebec, which is a distance of more than one hundred and eighty miles, for the farmhouses are never above five arpents and sometimes but three apart, a few places excepted. The prospect is exceedingly beautiful when the river flows on for several miles in a straight line, because it then shortens the distance between the houses, and makes them form one continued village. . . . We sometimes saw *windmills* near the farms. They were generally built of stone, with a roof of boards, which together with its wings could be turned to the wind.[2]

The principal crop grown was wheat but the climate of the St. Lawrence Valley was not particularly suitable for this cereal. Heavy rains sometimes caused serious loss from smut; early frosts were a constant menace; and plagues of caterpillars occasionally destroyed everything growing. Yet crop failures appear to have been no more frequent than in France, where they were anticipated, on an average, once in five years.[3] In the early years the yield was high, the natural result of rich virgin soil. By the mid-eighteenth century it had declined considerably, despite the increase in the number of cattle and the consequent increased use of manure.

Peter Kalm was very critical of the inefficient agricultural methods he had observed in the English colonies. He was not less critical of those in New France; they both compared unfavorably with farming methods that he had studied in England, which he stated were the most advanced in Europe. One factor that militated against efficient agricultural production, in New France as in the English colonies, was the chronic shortage of labor. When able-bodied men could obtain land very cheaply, they were not inclined to work for others, except at excessively high wages. The wages paid skilled tradesmen were also high, resulting in a drift from the country to the three towns, which contained 25 percent of the colonial population. A much more important factor, however, was the large number of men, of necessity the young and physically fit, who were continually out of the colony on voyages to the west.

All the evidence indicates that the Canadian *habitants* and the laboring class in the towns enjoyed a higher standard of living and much more personal freedom than did their counterparts in Europe. This undoubtedly accounts, to some degree, for the difference in their attitudes and character that visitors from Europe all remarked on. But what seems to have had an even greater influence was their frequent contact, on terms of equality, with the Indian nations. Nor did they have to voyage far for this contact. Within the confines of the colony, or close by, were several resident Indian bands. Near Quebec, at Lorette, resided a band of Huron, survivors of the 1649 diaspora. A few miles south of Quebec was the Abenaki village of St. François, removed from Acadia to protect the colony's southern approaches from Anglo-American incursions up the Connecticut River. Near Montreal were two Indian settlements: the Mission Iroquois at Sault St. Louis and the Sulpician mission that had first been established on the lower slopes of Mount Royal, then, as the town grew, had been moved first to the north side of the island, later to the western tip, and finally across the Lake of Two Mountains to Oka. The Mission Iroquois at Sault St. Louis (Caugnawaga to the Iroquois) were originally Mohawks who had been converted to Christianity by the Jesuits and had then removed to New France the better to preserve their new faith.[4] Members of other of the Iroquois nations, after conversion, subsequently moved to Caugnawaga to spare themselves the constant taunts of their fellow tribesmen who had remained pagan.

Another reason for this Iroquois defection to Canada was the desire to avoid the Albany rum traders. Not all the Indians were incapable of resisting the temporary delights that intoxication brought; the authorities of both New France and New York were frequently asked by the chiefs of Iroquois and Algonkin nations to keep liquor away from their villages. The governors of New France, for the most part, did their best to comply and managed to curb the abuse to a considerable degree. The same could not be said of the authorities at Albany. There, rum and whiskey of such appalling quality that it was little better than poison was the main item of trade, used to get the Indians drunk before they traded their furs and then defraud them. This practice was so common that the Dutch traders at Albany were little more than Canada's secret weapon, for although many of the western Indians would bypass the French posts to go to Albany where they were given all the liquor they could drink,[5] they were not so besotted that they did not later realize the consequences. This is not to say that there were no Canadian traders willing to use liquor in the same way in their commercial dealings with the Indians. The Jesuit missionaries at Sault St. Louis waged a constant struggle to keep such traders away from their charges, and the Oka mission had removed to this site largely to keep the converts away from the taverns and unscrupulous purveyors.

The members of this latter mission were a mixture of Iroquois and northern Algonkin; the common factor was their conversion to Christianity. During the colonial wars these warriors, particularly those of Sault St. Louis, performed valiant service; indeed, the authorities at Albany were greatly concerned lest most of the Five Nations should remove to Canada. Had this occurred Albany and all the northern settlements would have had to be abandoned. Although in expeditions against the villages of the Five Nations the Mission Iroquois could not be depended on—they frequently gave their kinsmen warning—the devastating raids on the settlements of New England were carried out by war parties composed largely of these domiciled tribesmen, combined with Canadian militia, and led by officers in the colonial regulars, the Troupes de la Marine. Thus the Canadians were closely associated with the Indians, waging war after their fashion, using their techniques and becoming as adept in the harsh, cruel methods as any Iroquois or Abenaki. There was therefore a demonstrable degree of truth in the opinion of the Canadians expressed by one French officer: "They make war only by swift attacks and almost always with success against the English who are not as vigorous nor as adroit in the use of fire arms as they, nor as practiced in forest warfare."[6]

In peacetime, too, the Canadians were in constant association with the Indians. The Indians were frequent visitors to Montreal, and to prevent constant blood baths, the intendant had to set aside certain taverns for the Indian trade, allocated by nation, and strictly regulated. It is, therefore, hardly surprising that the Canadians early adopted much of the Indian way of life and became imbued with some of their character traits. Native foods such as corn, squash, and pumpkins found ready acceptance. Indian means of travel—the snowshoe, toboggan, and canoe—were quickly mastered. Many of the Canadians, who were inveterate pipe smokers, preferred to mix their locally grown tobacco with the inner bark of the cherry or dogwood tree, a custom borrowed from the Indians. In their mode of dress the *habitants* copied the Indians, with an effect rather startling to European eyes. The women, except when dressed up fine for Sunday mass, wore a short jacket or blouse and a short skirt which, Peter Kalm several times observed "does not reach to the middle of their legs."

It was during their frequent trips to the west that the Canadians were most exposed to the Indian way of life. Immediately following the establishment of royal government in 1663 the population of the colony expanded rapidly, from approximately 2500 to an estimated 15,000 by the end of the century. Of the latter number as many as five hundred of the active males were always off in the west on trading expeditions. It was during these years that senior officials, newly arrived from France, began to comment on the striking difference between the Canadians and their peers in France. Inevitably, these officials were first struck by what seemed to them the deleterious social and economic effects of the metamorphosis.

The Marquis de Denonville, governor general from 1685 to 1689, was appalled by certain attitudes and habits of the Canadians. Instead of laboring on the land, they preferred to spend their lives in the bush, trading with the Indians, where their parents, the *curés*, and the officials could not govern them, and where they lived like savages. Even when they returned to the colony these youths showed a shocking proclivity for going about half naked in the hot weather, as did the Indians. "I cannot emphasize enough, my lord, the attraction that this Indian way of life has for all these youths," Denonville wrote to the minister. But he then went on to say, "The Canadians are all big, well built, and firmly planted on their legs, accustomed when necessary to live on little, robust and vigorous, very self willed and inclined to dissoluteness; but they are witty and vivacious."[7] The intendant Jean Bochart de Champigny in 1691 wrote in much the same vein, stating, "It is most unfortunate that Canadian youths, who are vigorous and tough, have no inclination for anything but these voyages where they live in the forest like Indians for two or three years at a time, without benefit of any of the sacraments."[8]

Peter Kalm in 1749 was also much impressed by the martial qualities of the Canadians, acquired through their frequent sojourns in the west. He noted that they were exceptional marksmen: "I have seldom seen any people shoot with such dexterity as these. . . . There was scarcely one of them who was not a clever marksman and who did not own a rifle." He then went on:

> It is inconceivable what hardships the people of Canada must undergo on their hunting journeys. Sometimes they must carry their goods a great way by land. Frequently they are abused by the Indians, and sometimes they are killed by them. They often suffer hunger, thirst, heat, and cold, and are bitten by gnats, and exposed to the bites of snakes and other dangerous animals and insects. These (hunting expeditions) [*sic*] destroy a great part of the youth in Canada, and prevent the people from growing old. By this means, however, they become such brave soldiers, and so inured to fatigue that none of them fears danger or hardships. Many of them settle among the Indians far from Canada, marry Indian women, and never come back again.[9]

Some of the Jesuit missionaries in the west took a much more jaundiced view of the effects of the close relations between the Canadians and the Indians. Fathers St. Cosme and Carheil at Michilimackinac made that post appear, from their description, a veritable Sodom or Gomorrah, where the only occupations of the Canadians, apart from trading furs, were drinking, gambling, and lechery. Things had come to such a pass that the *coureurs de bois* took Indian women with them rather than men on their trading expeditions. The men claimed that these women worked for lower wages than men demanded, and were willing to perform such chores as cutting firewood and cooking. The missionaries refused to be persuaded that other fringe benefits were not involved.[10] The governor general Vaudreuil, although he did not support the Jesuit proposal to keep the Canadians and Indians as far apart as possible, was strongly opposed to mixed marriages. He claimed that the children of mixed blood incorporated the worst character traits of both races and were a constant source of trouble. He therefore issued orders forbidding such marriages at Detroit, the main French post in the west at that time (1709).[11]

These complaints on the part of the missionaries have to be taken with a pinch of salt. To them chastity, or failing this monogamy with the benefit of the marriage sacrament, was the ideal. They expected these *voyageurs* who, if married, had left their wives in the colony to live like monks while in the west. The Indians had different moral values and chastity was not among them. Father Charlevoix, who was not a missionary, took a more tolerant view of Canadian society in the 1740s. He commented:

> Our Creoles are accused of great avidity in amassing, and indeed they do things with this in view, which could hardly be believed if they were not seen. The journeys they undertake; the fatigues they undergo; the dangers to which they expose themselves, and the efforts they make surpass all imagination. There are, however, few less interested, who dissipate with greater facility what has cost them so much pains to acquire, or who testify less regret at having lost it. Thus there is some room to imagine that they commonly undertake such painful and dangerous journeys out of a taste they have contracted for them. They love to breathe a free air, they are early accustomed to a wandering life; it has charms for them, which make them forget past dangers and fatigues, and they place their glory in encountering them often. . . . I know not whether I ought to reckon amongst the defects of our Canadians the good opinion they entertain of themselves. It is at least certain that it inspires them with a confidence, which leads them to undertake and execute what would appear impossible to many others. . . . It is alleged they make bad servants, which is owing to their great haughtiness of spirit, and to their loving liberty too much to subject themselves willingly to servitude.[12]

These observations on the cupidity of the Canadians, coupled with their spendthrift attitude, are significant for these same traits were quite pronounced among the Indians. Like the Indian, the Canadian did not see any merit in storing up worldly goods; both looked down on those who did, and up to those who spent their money ostentiously on good living. The Canadians, too, became proud, independent, and improvident, glorying in their physical strength, their hardihood, and their contempt for danger, caring little for the morrow. One French officer commented, in 1757:

> "They are not thrifty and take no care for the future, being too fond of their freedom and their independence. They want to be well thought of

and they know how to make the most of themselves. They endure hunger and thirst patiently, many of them having been trained from infancy to imitate the Indians, whom, with reason, they hold in high regard. They strive to gain their esteem and to please them. Many of them speak their language, having passed part of their life amongst them at the trading posts."[13]

It would seem an obvious conclusion that the Canadians had acquired this attitude from the Indians, and were able to do so because the necessities of life were relatively easily come by in Canada. In other words, this character trait was a product of relative affluence and the frontier environment. It was to no small degree the fact that the Canadians did come to share this attitude with the Indians that their individual relations with them were usually better than were those of the Anglo-Americans. Ruette D'Auteuil, the attorney general at Quebec, spoke the truth for his day when he claimed that, the price of trade goods being equal, the Indians preferred to have dealings with the French rather than with the English.[14] This view was later corroborated by a British commentator who stated that, "the French have found some secret of conciliating the affections of the savages, which our traders seem stranger to, or at least take no care to put it in practice."[15]

Not only did the Canadians travel to the far west, they also voyaged northeastward, serving as crews on fishing boats in the Gulf and in the seal- and whale-hunting expeditions along the coast of Labrador. There, too, they came in frequent contact with Indians, and also with the Eskimo. In wartime they served on privateers, preying on shipping along the New England coast. French privateer captains frequently called at Quebec to take on crews, Canadians being very highly regarded for their toughness and bellicosity.

Canadians in all sections of the colony were accustomed to make trips to distant parts of the continent and to live among peoples of an entirely different culture. The whole continent from Labrador and Hudson Bay to the Rocky Mountains and the Gulf of Mexico was their world. Unlike their counterparts in Europe who rarely moved beyond the confines of their native parish, there was nothing parochial about them; they were men of broad horizons and a continental outlook able to accommodate themselves to almost any conditions anywhere. Were life to become too restrictive in the settlements along the St. Lawrence or were a wife to nag too constantly, some of them at least could hire out as *voyageurs* for the west or as crew on a voyage to Labrador, France, or the West Indies. Even those who never made such a trip could feel that the opportunity was there, and this must have given them a sense of freedom. They could not help but hear the tales of those who had voyaged far afield, of the strange peoples with stranger customs in these distant lands. They, too, shared the experience, vicariously.

Royal officials in the eighteenth century, upon first arriving in the colony, were quick to remark that the Canadians had become a distinct

Habitant's house, Île d'Orléans, *ca.* 1730.

people with values and manners markedly at variance with those of the
same class in the mother country. Usually they were quite taken aback by
the attitudes and way of life of the Canadians. Only after they had been in
the colony for a few years did they come to appreciate the positive side of
what had at first seemed a society and people sadly in need of discipline
and reform. It was the free and easy, seemingly dissolute, ways of the
Canadians, their independent attitude, their insistence on being led not
driven, that irked the officials, both civil and military. Other observers were
struck by their profligacy, their feast or famine attitude, their recklessness. A
Sulpician priest upon arrival in the colony in 1737 remarked that the bulk of
the people—military officers, merchants, artisans, and *habitants* alike—were
"as poor as artists and as vain as peacocks" and spent every sou they had on
ostentatious living. He was shaken to see country girls who tended cows
during the week, on Sundays bedecked in lace and hoop skirts, wearing
their hair in the very elaborate, high-piled style known then as *à la
Fontange*.[16]

Despite these shortcomings, all observers agreed that the Canadians
were tough and hardy, gloried in feats of endurance that made Europeans
blanch, could travel from one end of the continent to another while living
off the land, and had no equal in forest warfare. It was also noted that these
same men, when in their homes, were uncommonly courteous, with a
natural air of gentility more usual among the nobility than the lower
classes.[17] In this respect they compared very favorably with their counterparts, the peasants of France and the settlers in the English colonies. Peter
Kalm was particularly struck by this and in his journal he noted that:

> The inhabitant of Canada, even the ordinary man, surpasses in politeness
> by far those people who live in these English provinces. . . . On entering one
> of the peasant's houses, no matter where, and on beginning to talk with
> the men or women, one is quite amazed at the good breeding and courteous
> answers which are received, no matter what the question is. . . . Frenchmen
> who were born in Paris said themselves that one never finds in France
> among country people the courtesy and good breeding which one observes
> everywhere in this land. I heard many native Frenchmen assert this.[18]

It would, of course, be very easy to ascribe these peculiarities to the
frontier environment of New France. There can be no doubt that the
frontier had a good deal to do with this, but the changes that took place in
Canadian society were very complex. It is therefore necessary to examine
conditions in the colony closely to discover the various elements that
differed from those of France and then decide which ones were occasioned
by the frontier.

Perhaps the basic factor was the abundance of free, fertile land, and the
peculiar terms of land tenure under the seigneurial regime. This meant that
the Canadian *habitants* were assured of as much land as they could
cultivate, and they paid for it only very modest seigneurial dues, if they
paid any at all, amounting to less than 10 percent of their annual income

from the land.[19] Apart from this obligation, and the tithe for the church, fixed by royal decree at one twenty-sixth of the wheat grown, the *habitants* paid no other taxes. Labor service for the seigneurs, in the form of *corvées*, was very rarely imposed and was, in fact, a violation of the *Coutume de Paris*. In the few seigneuries where it was imposed it consisted of one day's labor in March or an exemption payment of two *livres*. Parish and royal *corvées* for work on the seigneurial common land, roads, bridges, or fortifications were a form of taxation but they usually amounted to not more than three or four days of labor a year, and the seigneur was supposed to do his share, under the supervision of the militia captain.

Unlike the peasant in France who spent his life sweating, scrimping, cheating, and saving to put aside enough money to buy a small piece of land or to purchase exemption from manorial obligations, and who had to keep his little hoard well hidden, wearing rags, living in a hovel, giving every appearance of near starvation to prevent the tax collectors from seizing his savings, the Canadian could spend what he had earned without a care. He could buy land for his sons so as to have them near him and spare them the necessity of clearing virgin forest on a new seigneury, or he could spend his earnings on consumer goods and entertainment. Whereas the economics of the situation would tend to make the French peasant mean and grasping, the Canadian could afford to be openhanded, with little care for the morrow.

In 1699 the intendant Jean Bochart de Champigny commented that for the most part the *habitants* lived well, enjoying the right to hunt and fish, privileges that were stringently denied their European counterparts. In that age wood and leather were vital commodities; the Canadians had ample supplies of both. Canadians who moved to France complained bitterly of the shortage and high cost of firewood, and declared that they suffered far more from the damp winter cold there than they ever had in Canada. In the eighteenth century the intendant Gilles Hocquart remarked that no one starved in Canada. Of few lands in Europe could this have been said. The normal consumption of meat was half a pound per person a day, and of white wheat bread, two French pounds a day. Moreover, the climate allowed the Canadians to keep plentiful supplies of meat, fish, and game frozen hard for use throughout the winter; but a mid-winter thaw that lasted too long could be calamitous. At the town markets fish were sold frozen and cut with a saw. Eels, taken at Quebec by the thousand, were a staple food; smoked or salted, they were described by Frontenac as the *"habitants'* manna." They were also a major export item to France, being considered far better than the European variety. Ice houses were common, making possible iced drinks and desserts all summer, not just for the wealthy as in France, but for the majority of the population. The colored ices served by the French in hot weather were a source of wonderment to visiting Indians when entertained by the governor, and their effect on the decayed teeth of certain elderly chiefs was electric.

The vitamin content of the Canadian diet, being much richer in protein, was considerably higher than that of the peasants and urban working class in France, who had to exist on coarse bread and vegetable stews with meat only on very rare occasions.[20] In Europe the bulk of the population went to bed hungry most nights. Such was rarely the case in Canada. Mme. Marie-Isabelle Bégon, widow of the governor of Trois-Rivières, who in 1749 moved from Montreal to the family estate near Rochefort querulously asked, "Where are those good partridges we left for the servants? I would gladly eat them now."[21] It is not surprising that the fine physical stature of the Canadians occasioned frequent comment from persons recently come from France. In fact, the Canadians were better fed then than a sizable percentage of North Americans are today.

If the Canadians had been willing to work hard, they could all have been very prosperous. Some of the royal officials, charged with improving the colonial economy, declared that the men showed a marked distaste for hard work and that the unbridled vanity of their womenfolk kept them poor. In 1699 Champigny noted: "The men are all strong and vigorous but have no liking for work of any duration; the women love display and are excessively lazy."[22] Denonville, thirteen years earlier, had also remarked that the indolence of the men and the desire of the women to live like gentle ladies kept the people poor and the colony's economy backward. Such comments have to be considered in context.

The Canadian *habitant* could provide for his basic needs without too much effort, and he preferred to devote his extra time, not to produce an agricultural surplus to please the intendant or to add to his own store of worldly goods, but to the relaxed enjoyment of his leisure hours. He would grow enough flax or hemp to supply his own needs, but frequently declined to raise a surplus for export. Rather than raise more cattle, he raised horses; by the early eighteenth century all put the poorer families had a carriage and sleigh for social occasions, and every youth had his own horse, used not for the plow but for racing, or to pay calls on the neighborhood girls. During the War of the Spanish Succession the governor and intendant became concerned over this, claiming that in winter the men no longer used snowshoes because they always traveled by horse and sleigh. It was difficult, they stated, to find enough men who could use snowshoes when they were needed for war parties against New England. The question might well be asked; how many peasants in Europe owned horses and carriages, let alone used them for mere social purposes. The average horse cost forty *livres* (roughly $80.00 in today's money) and a good one a hundred *livres* or more,[23] thus the Canadian *habitants* were relatively affluent, and this could not help but have influenced their social attitudes.

Given these conditions it is hardly surprising that the Canadians were by no means as submissive or even respectful, on occasion, toward their social superiors as was thought fitting. As early as 1675 the members of the Sovereign Council were incensed by derogatory graffiti on walls in Quebec, and several years later the intendant had to threaten stern action against those who composed, distributed, or sang songs that he regarded as libelous and defamatory of certain prominent persons in the colony. This last, however, might be regarded as merely the continuance of an old French tradition that had flourished in the days of the *Mazarinades*. Thus, rather than the frontier environment, economic affluence and the French temperament were the more significant factors here.

Much is made of the prevalence of lawlessness on the Anglo-American frontier. To a limited degree this was also true of New France, and it is significant that it was at Montreal, the fur trade and military base, the main point of contact between European and Indian cultures, more than at Quebec, that respect for law and order was sometimes lacking. In 1711 the governor and intendant had to establish a police force in Montreal, consisting of one lieutenant and three archers, to make the citizens keep the peace and to control drunken Indians. An educated soldier in the colonial troops, newly arrived in Canada, remarked that the citizens of Montreal called those of Quebec "sheep," and that the character of the latter was gentler and less proud. The Quebecers reciprocated by calling the men of Montreal "wolves," a label that the soldier thought apt since the Montrealers spent much of their time in the forest among the Indians. In 1754 an officer recommended that Quebec men be employed to transport supplies to the Ohio forts because they were much "gentler" and almost as vigorous as those from the Montreal area.

Despite the frequent tavern brawls and duels, the incidence of crimes of violence was not great. But what is much more significant is that, given the nature of the populace, accustomed to the relatively unrestrained, wild, free life that the fur trade afforded, very rarely was there any overt resistance to authority. On the few occasions when the people protested openly and vigorously something done, or not done, the authorities were able to subdue them quickly without recourse to punitive measures. Most of these manifestations—some five in all—were occasioned by high prices charged for certain commodities, leading the people to believe that the merchants were profiteering and that the authorities were delinquent in not taking steps to stop them. The heaviest penalty inflicted on the leaders of these "seditious gatherings" appears to have been less than two months in jail.[24] The conclusion to be drawn from all this is that the Canadian people had little to complain about, but when they did complain too vigorously, order was maintained without the overt use of force.

The attitude of the Canadians toward the religious authorities makes it plain that their opinions had to be taken into account. When it was decided, immediately after the inauguration of royal government in 1663, to impose tithes on the people for the support of a secular clergy, the bishop stipulated that it be at the rate of one thirteenth of the produce of the land, payable in wheat. The people protested vigorously, claiming this to be more than they could afford. The bishop reduced his demand to one twentieth, but the *habitants* and seigneurs would agree to pay only one twenty-sixth of their wheat, not of all their produce, with a five year exemption for newly settled concessions. With this the clergy had to be satisfied. That it was not enough is made plain by the fact that the crown had to provide the clergy with an annual subsidy to make up the difference between what the tithe produced and what the *curés* needed. By the 1730s however, as more land came into production, many of the parish priests were relatively well off.

Further evidence that the Canadians were anything but subservient to clerical authority is provided by the frequent *ordonnances* of the intendant ordering the *habitants* of this or that parish to behave with more respect toward the cloth; to cease their practice of walking out of church as soon as the *curé* began his sermon; of standing in the lobby arguing, even brawling, during the service; of slipping out to a nearby tavern; of bringing their dogs into church and expostulating with the beadle who tried to chase them out. Frequently the bishop thundered from the pulpit against the women who attended mass wearing elaborate coiffures and low-cut gowns. But all to no avail; décolletage remained that of the Paris salons. When Bishop St. Vallier somehow learned that the female members of his flock wore nothing but petticoats under their gowns he was horrified. In a curiously phrased pastoral letter he demanded that they immediately cease to imperil their immortal souls in this manner.[25] What the response was is not known. And a practice that might be advanced in support of the thesis that the frontier bred initiative was the Canadian custom of *mariage à la gaumine*, a form of "do it yourself" marriage ceremony which both the clergy and the civil authorities frowned on severely.[26]

At the upper end of the social scale, the most significant feature of this Canadian society was the aristocratic and military ethos that dominated it. This was not unique to Canada; it was part of the French old régime heritage. In the seventeenth century the aim of the rising, powerful bourgeois class was to gain entry into the ranks of the nobility, or at least to emulate the way of life of the aristocracy. Molière made this plain in *Le Bourgeois Gentilhomme*. Despite the fact that the Canadian economy was basically commercial and dependent largely on the fur trade, bourgeois commercial values did not dominate society; indeed, they were scorned. The ambitious Canadian merchant wished to be something more than prosperous. That was merely one rung on the ladder. The ultimate goal was entry into the ranks of the *noblesse* and receipt of the coveted Order of St. Louis for distinguished service. More than wealth, men wished to bequeath to their sons a higher social status and a name distinguished for military valor, some great achievement, or the holding of high office. The proverb, *"Bon renom vaux mieux que ceinture dorée,"* summed up the Canadian philosophy at all levels of society.[27]

Wealth was, of course, desired, and ethics frequently went by the board in its pursuit. Men who might well have been ennobled for valiant service were denied if they lacked the means to live in a fitting manner. Wealth was

Seigneurial manor house, *ca.* 1730.

sought, not for itself, but to enable men to live in the style of the class they sought to enter. Father Charlevoix, the Jesuit historian, writing in the 1740s commented on one aspect of this proclivity: "There is a great fondness for keeping up one's position, and nearly no one amuses himself by thrift. Good cheer is supplied, if its provision leaves means enough to be well clothed; if not, one cuts down on the table in order to be well dressed." He then went on to compare the Canadians with the English colonists to the south: "The English colonists amasses means and makes no superfluous expense; the French enjoys what he has and often parades what he has not. The former works for his heirs; the latter leaves his in the need in which he is himself to get along as best he can."[28]

In Canada it was in some ways much easier than in France for ambitious men to adopt the values and attitudes of the nobility and even to become ennobled. Despite the fact that society was very much status ordered, it was relatively easy for a talented, ambitious man or women to move up the social scale. Four factors help account for this: the availability of free land, the economic opportunities presented by the fur trade, the Royal edict of 1685 which permitted members of the nobility resident in Canada to engage directly in commerce and industry, something that, with a few notable exceptions such as the manufacture of glass and paper, was not permitted in France, and the presence of a large corps of regular troops in the colony in which Canadians could obtain commissions as officers.

It is rather ironic that when the king issued the edict of 1685 allowing nobles in Canada to engage in trade, he intended merely to stimulate the colonial economy.[29] It quickly came, however, to function in a way not anticipated by Louis XIV, for if those who were of noble status could engage in trade, there was nothing to prevent merchants and entrepreneurs who were not noble from aspiring to become so, provided they fulfilled the other requirements. Thus a Canadian of humble origin could make his fortune in the fur trade, acquire a seigneury, have his sons, if not himself, commissioned in the Troupes de la Marine, and hope that one day he, or his sons, would be ennobled for valiant service. Enough Canadians accomplished this feat to encourage a much larger number to govern their lives accordingly. It was the old story, few are chosen but many hear the call.

To be a seigneur, the first rung up the social ladder, was a distinct mark of social superiority, made manifest in a variety of ways; hence there was never any lack of applicants;[30] but it necessitated accepting rather onerous responsibilities and in the seventeenth century most seigneurs had a hard time making ends meet. Yet so eager were the Canadians to attach the coveted particle *de* to their names that by 1760 there were nearly 250 seigneuries in the colony. Even more significant, it is estimated that there were some 200 *arrière fiefs,* or sub-seigneuries, that is, small seigneuries granted by a seigneur within his own seigneury to a friend or relative whom he wished to see get on in the world. Another significant point is that many seigneurs, the majority of whom lived in the towns and not on their lands, did not bother to collect the stipulated dues, *the cens et rentes,* from their *censitaires.* Clearly, many seigneurs were not interested in the economic aspect of land holding. The only other motive would appear to be the social prestige attached to the title. In other words, Joseph Blondeau was undoubtedly a good name, but Joseph Blondeau de Grandarpents, or even de Petitarpents, was much better.

There were some who sought to gain entry into the *noblesse* through the back door, by simply assuming a title and claiming its privileges. In 1684 a royal edict was enacted levying a fine of 500 *livres* on any Canadian who falsely claimed noble status. A few years later the intendant Champigny stated that there were many such in the colony, but in time of war he thought it unwise to initiate an enquiry lest it cool their ardor for military campaigns. He also declared that several officers had requested to be ennobled, and although some of them merited it, he could not support their requests because they lacked the means to live as members of the *noblesse* should.[31] Although gaining entry into the ranks of the nobility was by no means easy, it was remarked in the mid-eighteenth century that there was a greater number of nobles in New France than in all the other French colonies combined. It was not the actual number of nobles that was important; rather it was the scale of values that they imparted to the whole of society, the tone that was set, and the influence it had on the way of life of the Canadian people.

Inextricably mingled with, and greatly strengthening, this aristocratic ethos was the military tradition of New France. In Europe wars were fought by professional armies, and civilians were not directly involved unless they happened to get in the way while a battle was being fought. This was more true of France and Britain than of other countries, since they both had sense enough to wage their wars on other nations' territory. In Canada when war came, all the settled areas were a battlefield and everyone was obliged to be a combatant. The administration of the colony was organized along military lines. The entire male population was formed into militia companies, given military training, and employed in campaigns. In 1665 the Carignan Salières regiment arrived in the colony to quell the Iroquois; it comprised over a thousand officers and men, and many of them stayed on as settlers. This greatly enhanced the influence of the military, for at that time the total population was less then 3000. Twenty years later the Troupes de la Marine were permanently stationed in the colony, some 1300 men and 400 officers by the end of the century among a total population of 15,000.

In the campaigns against the Iroquois and the English colonies it was quickly discovered that Canadians made better officers in forest warfare than did regulars from France. Consequently this career was opened to the seigneurs and their sons. They seized on it eagerly. Youths in their teens were enrolled as cadets and served on campaigns with their fathers or elder brothers to gain experience, then were sent out in command of scouting and small raiding parties to capture prisoners for intelligence purposes. The minister, however, thought they were being enrolled at far too early an age, while still mere children, and suspected the practice was merely a means for their families to draw military pay and allowances. Mme. de Vaudreuil, wife of the governor general, declared, "It would be advantageous for the well-being of the colony to accept youths of good families as cadets in the troops at fifteen or sixteen; that would form their characters early, render them capable of serving well and becoming good officers." The minister and Louis XIV were not convinced; they ordered that cadets had to be seventeen before they could be enrolled.[32] The dominant values of Canadian society were clearly those of the soldier and the noble, the military virtues those held in highest regard.

The social circles of Montreal and Quebec, comprising the senior officials, the army officers, and seigneurs, were undoubtedly very urbane, reflecting the polish and social graces of the French *noblesse*. Certainly Peter Kalm found this society much more civilized than that which he encountered in the English colonies where few people thought of anything but making money and not spending it.[33] Some of the senior officials who came from France in the eighteenth century, men like the intendant Claude Thomas Dupuy and the Comte de la Galissonière, took a keen interest in natural science, as had earlier the doctor and surgeon Michel Sarrazin who was a corresponding member of the Académie Royale des Sciences, but few Canadians showed much interest in intellectual pursuits.

The parish schools provided a basic education for those who wished it, and the Jesuit college at Quebec offered facilities as good as those in the larger French provincial cities. The letters and dispatches of Canadian-born officers and merchant traders in the mid-eighteenth century demonstrate that, with the rare exception of an officer such as Claude-Pierre Pécaudy de Contrecoeur who although a competent commandant had obviously had little schooling, they were all well-educated men. They expressed themselves succinctly and quite often felicitously; their syntax was good, the subjunctive employed where required; the literary style as well as the contents of their letters make them a pleasure to read. In fact, these men appear to have been as well educated as their counterparts in the French and British armies.

Yet the colony did not develop a literary tradition; the published journals depicting life in the colony were written by men from France and were intended for a metropolitan audience. But then, Canadians would see little merit in describing what was familiar to all their compatriots. Several Canadians had large private libraries, but there was no public library. Nor was there a printing press in the colony, hence no newspaper, not because of any sinister repression of thought by the clergy, but because there was no great need therefore no demand for one. In these realms of activity Canada lagged far behind the English colonies. In short, New France was the Sparta, not the Athens of North America.

◁ **6** ▷

The Fur Trade Frontier,
1663-1700

*I*n 1663, when Canada became a royal province, the territory claimed by France extended a few miles past the junction of the Ottawa and St. Lawrence rivers. Beyond that point, on the shores of the Great Lakes, were only a handful of itinerant fur traders and Jesuit missionaries; the Indian nations still held undisputed title to the interior of North America. By the end of the century the French had explored, laid claim to, and in varying degree were in possession of the Great Lakes basin, the river routes west to Lake Winnipeg, and the Mississippi Valley to the Gulf of Mexico. Scattered throughout this vast wilderness area were fur trade and missionary posts, some with military garrisons. The Indian nations of the west were by this time bound to the French in a commercial and military alliance.

Treaties and alliances, then as now, were not made for something but against something; that is, they were directed against hostile powers. Without this hostility, latent or manifest, there would be no need for alliances. So it was in seventeenth-century North America. The earliest French commercial and military alliances with the Indian nations were intended to counter the competition of unlicensed traders at Tadoussac; subsequently they were negotiated to maintain French dominance in the fur trade against Dutch and English competition. At the end of the century they became the means to contain the English along the Atlantic seaboard and on the shores of Hudson Bay. This change from economic to political ends was to have drastic consequences.

Jean-Baptiste Colbert, who took over the direction of colonial affairs in 1663, strongly opposed French westward expansion. When the intendant Jean Talon, after being in the colony only a few weeks, proposed the establishment of a vast French empire stretching from north of the St. Lawrence, southwest to Florida or even Mexico, Colbert refused to entertain any such wild notions. He advised Talon that even had the king not been faced with urgent problems in Europe, it would be very poor policy to depopulate France in order to populate Canada. There was, he pointed out, a limit to the number of settlers the colony could absorb in a given time; to send more would only result in their starving to death, or at least bringing great hardship on both themselves and the colonists already established. "The true way to strengthen that colony," he wrote, "is to cause justice to reign, to establish a good civil administration, to take care of the settlers, to give them peace, tranquillity and abundance, and train them to defend themselves against all manner of foes, for these things are the basis and foundation of every establishment." In this way the colony would grow by degrees and in time could become very considerable. In conclusion, he declared that it was manifestly impossible to implement such grandiose colonizing schemes as Talon proposed unless one had surplus people to populate the new states, and France did not.[1]

It cannot be said that Colbert's plans for the diversification of the Canadian economy were a complete failure, but they did not enjoy the degree of success he had hoped for and took longer than he had anticipated to show appreciable results. Had it not been that the economic activities were overshadowed by the fur trade, their extent might well appear in a better light. Colbert had no desire to see the amount of fur shipped to France diminish, just the reverse in fact. All he wanted was to ensure that this trade did not hinder his long-range plans for Canada's economic development. It was with some misgivings that he allowed the Canadians to engage in the fur trade at all. "It is to be feared," he wrote, "that by means of this trade, the *habitants* will remain idle a good part of the year, whereas if they were not allowed to engage in it they would be obliged to apply themselves to cultivating their land."[2]

It is therefore rather ironic that it was Colbert and Louis XIV who inadvertently opened the floodgates to a vastly extended fur trade, and with it French expansion into the interior, which drained off the colony's limited supplies of both capital and labor so badly needed to develop the resources of the central colony. The regular troops they sent to Canada, in bringing the Iroquois to terms, allowed the fur trade to expand to limits previously

undreamed of. In 1665, while negotiations with the Iroquois were under-
way, 400 Ottawa arrived at Trois-Rivières with 150,000 *livres* worth of furs.
The following year, 100,000 *livres* worth reached La Rochelle, and in 1667,
550,000 *livres* worth were shipped to France.[3] This sudden flood of fur,
mainly beaver, forced a reduction in price from 9 *livres* the pound to 6 for
greasy beaver, and dry beaver had to be reduced to 3 livres the pound.[4]
Despite this 50 percent reduction, the profits to be made were still great, far
greater than could be made in any other way. Moreover, since it was now
possible for the western Indians to bring their furs to Montreal in safety, it
was by the same token possible for the Canadians to voyage to the Indian
villages to obtain the pick of the furs, and at cheaper prices. In their
attempts to forestall one another and to get beyond the Indian middlemen,
they pushed farther and farther west. Colbert issued stern edicts forbidding
the Canadians to leave the settled areas in the central colony to trade for
furs, but to no avail. The rivers led west and nothing could stop the men
from slipping away in their frail canoes.

Another factor that greatly stimulated this westward drive for furs was
the fixing of beaver prices by ministerial decree. Between 1665 and 1674,
when Colbert was finally obliged to admit the failure of his Compagnie de
l'Occident, close its books, and have its title to New France revert to the
crown, various devices were used to assure stability and facilitate the
marketing of the commodity. In 1675 Jean Oudiette, a tax farmer, was
granted the monopoly on the marketing in France of all beaver pelts and
moose hides for a ten-year lease. The Canadians had to sell these pelts, but
only these pelts, to the agents of this Company of the Farm, at prices
stipulated by the Ministry of Marine. In return, the company had to pay the
crown 350,000 *livres* a year for the lease. When Oudiette's bail expired, it
was taken over by a succession of companies, and the price of the lease in
1687 rose to 500,000 *livres*.[5] During these years the crown realized a profit
on its Canadian colony, and so did the lease holders, but the principal
beneficiaries were the Canadian fur traders. Under this system they were
not at the mercy of the vagaries of the market; the law of supply and
demand was held in abeyance; and at the established prices profits were
guaranteed, regardless of how much beaver was brought to the bureau of
the company. Nothing could have been better contrived to bring about
expansion in the fur trade, or of the numbers engaged in it, and nothing that
Colbert could do from his littered desk on the far side of the ocean could
stem the surge westward. It was too alluring, and much too profitable, to be
denied.

Colbert had warned the intendant Talon, "it would be better to restrict
oneself to an amount of land that the colony will be able to sustain on its
own, rather than to embrace too vast an area whereby one would perhaps
one day be obliged to abandon a part with some reduction of the prestige of
His Majesty and of the State."[6] But the Canadians, and Talon, lacked his

foresight. Talon began sending out parties, ostensibly to explore the lands west and north of the central colony, to seek mineral deposits, to discover a route to the western ocean, and to claim all the lands they traversed for France. His main purpose, however, was to bypass the Ottawa middlemen and enter into trade relations directly with the more distant Algonquian nations who supplied the Ottawa.[7]

In 1668 Jean Peré was sent to seek the copper mines of Lake Superior. The following year Adrien Jolliet was sent to join him. They returned to Quebec by way of Lake Erie, the Niagara portage, Lake Ontario, and the upper St. Lawrence, opening up an alternate route to the Ottawa River—Lake Huron route to the west. That same year two Sulpician priests, François Dollier de Casson, onetime captain in Turenne's cavalry, and Renée de Bréhaut de Galinée, with seven Canadians, voyaged to Lake Erie by way of Lake Ontario and claimed possession for France of the lands around these two lakes. Two years later Talon sent Jean-Baptiste de St. Lusson to explore the northwestern lands as far as possible. He went little farther than the Jesuit mission at Sault Ste. Marie, where he claimed the lands of the Ottawa nation for the French crown. The whole of the Great Lakes basin was to be regarded as French territory. Still another party was sent north to claim the lands from the St. Lawrence to Hudson Bay. They made a great haul of beaver.

Talon hastened to inform Colbert that these parties cost the crown nothing. The furs they garnered en route covered the expenses. Others in the colony, seeing the canoes of Talon's exploration parties returning heavily laden with prime furs, were not slow to follow suit. By 1670 French traders, men such as Nicolas Perrot and Louis Jolliet, had established trading posts on Green Bay and were trading on the Wisconsin River. Reports again began to filter back to Quebec of a great river, "Messisipi," flowing to the western or the southern ocean.

Colbert admitted only two reasons that could justify French expansion into the west: one was to forestall other nations that might seek westward expansion in order to interfere with the fur trade, but he could see little danger of this in the immediate future; the other was the discovery of a western route to a southern sea where an ice-free, year-round port serving Canada could be established. In May 1674 he informed the governor at Quebec that such a discovery would be of tremendous value since "the worst thing about Canada is the entrance to the river which, being so far to the north, allows ships to enter only during four, five or six months of the year."[8] Jean Talon and the recently appointed governor general, Louis de Buade, Comte de Frontenac et de Palluau, had, however, anticipated him. In 1672 they had dispatched Louis Jolliet to locate the Mississippi and discover where it led.

After Talon's return to France, Frontenac continued his expansionist policy in a much more aggressive manner. He was quick to see that with the proper organization great profits could be made in the fur trade. That this ran completely counter to Colbert's aims for French colonial development meant nothing to him; this was merely another problem to be circumvented one way or another. Prior to Frontenac's arrival Talon had proposed the establishment of garrisoned forts on Lake Ontario to defend that region against possible Iroquois or English incursions, but Colbert had refused to give his assent. Frontenac therefore decided to build a trading post on the lake and inform Colbert afterward. In 1673 he forced the *habitants* of Montreal to provide labor and materials throughout the summer and constructed Fort Frontenac at the eastern end of Lake Ontario. The Iroquois, who regarded this territory north to the Ottawa River as their hunting grounds, were gravely disconcerted but for the moment they could not oppose this invasion of their lands. Not only were the Andastes and Mohegan pressing them hard but their source of essential European goods had just been disrupted by the Dutch seizure of New York.

The Montreal fur traders, led by their local governor François-Marie Perrot, were every bit as disturbed as the Iroquois by Frontenac's move. They feared that this trading post would drain off a great deal of the furs that would otherwise have gone to them at Montreal, and also that it would serve as a staging post for Frontenac's men to engross the trade of the Algonquian nations farther west. This was exactly what Frontenac had in mind. The colony was soon divided into two hostile factions, that of Frontenac and that of the Montreal merchants. Conflicts between the two broke out within the colony as the rivalry became more intense, until the administration was completely disrupted.[9] And in the background the Iroquois sullenly watched, willing to trade at the new post while it suited their convenience, and unable to take any hostile action because the French held the upper hand as long as their war with the Andastes and Mohegan lasted.

The following year the role that this post was intended to play was made very plain. In August 1674 Louis Jolliet returned to Quebec after his epic journey with Father Jacques Marquette down the Mississippi almost to the mouth of the Arkansas, far enough to determine that the great river emptied into the Gulf of Mexico rather than the Pacific or Atlantic. As Frontenac was quick to point out, here was a direct route for canoes and sailing vessels from Quebec to the Gulf of Mexico; and Jolliet proposed the building of a canal at the Chicago portage which would enable sailing vessels to transport goods back and forth between Lake Erie and the Gulf. Colbert, although he could see the possibilities as well as the next man, did not intend this discovery to wreck his plans for colonial development. When Jolliet requested permission to establish a settlement in these new lands, the minister refused on the grounds that the population in the St. Lawrence Valley would have to be augmented considerably before there could be any thought of creating new colonies in the far interior.[10]

But Frontenac held very different views on the French purpose in

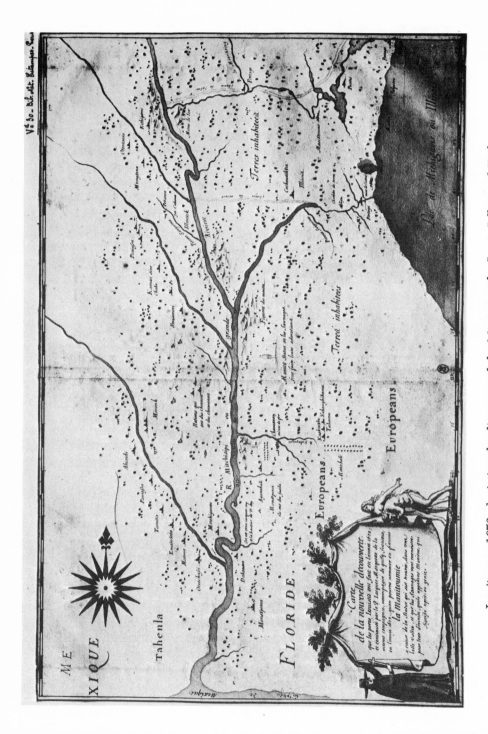

Jesuit map, 1673, depicting the discovery of the Mississippi by Louis Jolliet and Father Jacques Marquette, S.J. (Public Archives of Canada)

North America. Although he did not inform the minister that he thought his antiexpansionist policy was misguided, his actions make it plain that he favored the greatest possible increase in the fur trade. As he saw it, the agricultural colony in the St. Lawrence Valley existed merely as a base to serve the needs of this staple trade.[11] He never took into account what the consequences of this expansion would be; he was concerned only with the short-term benefits of increased fur trade profits. With the assistance of friends and relatives who possessed considerable influence at the Court, he was able to obtain privileges for members of his entourage that were denied to others. One of his coterie, the man for whom he had obtained title to a seigneury at Fort Frontenac, René-Robert Cavelier, Sieur de La Salle, was able, with Frontenac's backing, to obtain the right to establish fur trade posts in the Mississippi Valley and to engage in trade with the Indians along that river and its tributaries. The privilege was granted La Salle to enable him to explore the Mississippi to its mouth in the hope that it would provide a route to Mexico, but this exploration had to be accomplished within five years and entirely at his expense.[12]

Colbert and Louis XIV had clearly been led to believe that this was a means to have these lands explored and claimed for France at no expense to the crown. La Salle and Frontenac, however, used the permission to explore as a means to monopolize the fur trade of central North America. Within a few years they had established a chain of posts at the foot of Lake Michigan and on the Illinois and Mississippi rivers: in 1676 a staging post at Niagara, in 1679 a trading post on the St. Joseph River, in 1680 Fort Crèvecoeur on the Illinois, then Fort St. Louis and Fort Prud-homme on the Mississippi below the Ohio. Not until 1682 did La Salle proceed down the Mississippi beyond the point that Jolliet and Marquette had reached, and on to the Gulf. Once these posts were established, La Salle, with Frontenac's conni-vance, sought to prevent all but their own men from trading in the vast area south of the Great Lakes. Anyone caught doing so without La Salle's written permission had his goods seized. At the same time La Salle's men traveled north to trade with the Ottawa and Assiniboin, despite the fact that his commission specifically forbade him to trade with the nations that normally took their furs to Montreal, and La Salle himself was investigating the feasibility of shipping the furs to France by way of the Gulf of Mexico. This last would have enabled him to sever connections with New France and given him complete control of an independent commercial empire of the west.[13]

Needless to say, the merchant fur traders of New France and the *coureurs de bois* watched this development with mounting alarm. Any vague hope of their paying heed to the royal edicts forbidding trade with the Indians outside the confines of the colony quickly disappeared, and more and more canoes began voyaging westward. They made Michilimack-inac, at the junction of Lakes Michigan and Huron, their main base. When their men arrived from Montreal, they obtained new canoes and fresh food supplies, then pushed on farther into the interior to trade with the Sioux along the upper Mississippi, with the Assiniboin beyond Lake Superior, and north with the tribes above Lake Nipigon. In these areas they built their small cabins near the Indian villages, until the entire vast area from Lake Winnipeg south to the Ohio and north to Hudson Bay was dotted with trading posts. At some of them scores of traders gathered, at others only two or three men. In this fashion the form of the French Empire in North America took shape, in opposition to the policy of the crown.

It was a curious, indeed a unique, form of empire. The French did not really occupy the area they now claimed; in fact, much of it they did not yet claim. They were no more interested in occupying land than were New England seamen who voyaged to Africa for cargoes of slaves or tropical produce. Eventually they had to claim these lands and maintain military garrisons to protect their interests, in just the same way as, in the nineteenth century, European powers seized territory by military force in Africa and the Far East to protect the interests of their traders and missionaries. In North America in the late seventeenth century the French merely voyaged through the lands to trade with the Indians, obtain a cargo of furs, then transport it back to Montreal. The Indians were the important factor. It was they who provided the desired commodity in a semimanufactured state; thus their interests, their traditional way of life, their seminomadic hunting economy, had to be preserved. Yet the Indian's way of life was radically altered. Tribes ever more remote became enmeshed in this European economic empire and became dependent on European goods. They achieved a somewhat higher standard of living, but ultimately paid a very heavy price for it.

The consequences of this development for the French were also far-reaching. The number of Canadians traveling to the west each year increased immeasurably. An entirely new social group unique to Canada, had emerged. In 1672 Jean-Baptiste Patoulet, Talon's deputy, estimated their number at three to four hundred. According to the intendant Jacques Duchesneau, by 1680 there were at least 800 *coureurs de bois* off in the wilderness, and, he added, "I have been unable to ascertain the exact number because everyone associated with them covers up for them."[14] The great distances they traveled made it impossible to leave Montreal on a trading venture in the spring and return before freeze-up. Few men had the capital required to finance such voyages, thus the trade gradually came to be controlled by the wealthier men in the colony, split into the two rival and hostile factions.

The life of the *coureurs de bois*, or *voyageurs* as they later came to be known, was no calling for weaklings or the fainthearted. Squatting on a narrow thwart, legs cramped by bales of goods or furs, these men paddled hour after hour from dawn to dusk, pausing occasionally for a pipe while the professional raconteur spun a tale from his inexhaustible supply, singing folk songs to the dip of the paddle, forty-five to forty-eight strokes to the minute. For over a thousand miles the paddles thrust the canoes through the water. At rapids they were either roped upstream, the men wading up to the waist in the swift icy river, or the canoes and their cargoes were carried on a tump line, sometimes for miles around the turbulent waters. Going downstream the temptation was strong to run the rapids, and at every portage crosses marked where men had paid for this with their lives. Time could not be spared to hunt, the only food was two meals a day of corn meal mush flavored with salt pork, dried fish, or jerked venison, washed down with water, and a nip of brandy to aid the digestion. The casualty rate was high, and rheumatism too frequently made men old before their time, but the Canadians gloried in this life. Wherever a canoe could go these men went, seeking Indians with furs, bringing them within the orbit and control of this trading empire. But they changed the face of the land hardly at all. Their canoes left no marks on the rivers and lakes as they passed. A few trees were cut at a campsite or along a portage, or a larger clearing was made and a log house built where a post was established, but when abandoned in favor of a better and usually more distant site, only a few years were needed to erase all signs of its existence. Yet a few hundred such men held the west in fee for France.

Despite the constant demands of Colbert that the exodus of Canadians for the west be stopped, it continued apace. He ordered Frontenac to establish public markets so that when the western Indians came down to Montreal with their furs all the Canadians would have the opportunity to trade with them and be less likely to succumb to the temptation to desert the colony. For a few years these fairs were held at Montreal, on the common by the river's edge. Nearby was a large open space where the Indians camped, frequently numbering in the hundreds. The Canadians set up stalls to display the goods they had to offer in trade. They came from all over the colony to take part, or to see the sights. Bronzed, near-nude warriors, their womenfolk and children, and their savage dogs sprawled around their cooking fires on the common or wandered through the narrow streets of Montreal, streets lined with steep-roofed gray stone houses, rubbing shoulders with pigtailed homespun-clad *habitants,* merchants in knee breeches and long coats, officers and senior officials in lace, hair powdered and hand on sword, nuns and priests in gray, brown, or black, and ladies with elaborately dressed hair in gray, brown, or blue cloaks reaching the ground. The citizens of the town had to maintain a close watch on the cattle in the nearby pastures and keep their dogs tied up; the Indians were all too likely to barbecue either, preferably the latter.

But when the governor appeared, all was decorum. Seated in an arm chair, his interpreter, the officers of his guards, the senior officials, and members of the clergy beside him, he looked out over the serried ranks of silent impassive, obsidian-eyed faces, and listened to the long-drawn-out metaphors of the Indian orators. These declared eternal friendship for the French, complained about the high cost of trade goods, requested aid to repel their traditional foes, the Sioux or the Iroquois, and asked Onontio[15] to convey their greetings to the king across the ocean. To close their remarks they presented the governor with a few packs of choice pelts "to open his ears" to their pleas. The governor replied through an interpreter, heaping compliments on the Indians, exhorting them to heed the words of the Jesuits in their villages, to remain at peace, one tribe with another, and, above all, to have nothing to do with the English. After informing them how dearly both he and the king had their interests at heart, he distributed his presents from the royal warehouse: plumed hats, lace-bedecked coats, fancy hilted swords, dresses and trinkets for the women, and toys for the children. Then came the great feast, followed by enough brandy to make for conviviality, but not enough to allow the Indians to go berserk.

Despite such precautions, however, the streets of Montreal sometimes resembled Dante's inferno. Too often the Indians saved the brandy issued them, then drew lots, the winners getting it all. Lacking the inhibitions that control the subconscious of Europeans, to some extent at least, once drunk they ran amok. Incest, mayhem, and murder occurred without restraint. All that the people of Montreal could do when the uproar transpired was bar their doors and shutters, stay indoors, and wait for the hideous clamor in the streets to subside, then haul away the mutilated bodies, some dead, some merely unconscious but with ears and noses bitten off, knife and tomahawk wounds draining blood onto the cobblestones and wooden sidewalks.[16]

Economically if not socially, it was perhaps unfortunate that these annual trading fairs did not last many years, but it was almost inevitable that they could not endure. With the Canadians willing and eager to transport goods to the west, there was no need for the Ottawa to make the long journey to Montreal. They undoubtedly obtained goods cheaper there than from the *coureurs de bois*, but the time taken in the voyage could be employed in trapping, hunting, or lazing about. Moreover, a visit to Montreal sometimes was followed by an epidemic of smallpox, measles, cholera, or influenza. Then, in 1680, the Iroquois renewed their long-thwarted attempt to gain control of the western fur trade, and that marked the end of the Montreal fur fairs as an established institution. Montreal now became the outpost for voyages to the west. From this time on the trade itself centered at the western posts.

In 1681, Colbert was forced to admit defeat. His attempts to challenge geography and curb the acquisitive instincts of the French in Canada had, for a variety of reasons, been a complete failure. There were now so many *coureurs de bois* in the west it was admitted that it would be impossible to punish them all, even had it been possible to apprehend them.[17] A royal edict was sent to the Sovereign Council at Quebec granting amnesty to all *coureurs de bois*, provided that they returned to the colony without delay, and a licensing system for trading in the west was inaugurated. The governor general was now empowered to grant up to twenty-five trading permits a year, each of which allowed the recipient to send a canoe load of trade goods with three men to trade in the Indian villages. No one was to receive a permit two years in a row, and they all had to be viséed by the intendant.[18] Colbert's hope was that all the *coureurs de bois* would avail themselves of the amnesty, return to useful employment in the colony, and await their turn for a permit. In this too he was to be disappointed.

The minister was not the only party perturbed by the trend of events in North America. To him, expansion into the west represented a dispersal of French strength which placed everything in jeopardy. To others it looked different. The Iroquois, the governors of New York, and a few years later the Spanish, all viewed the presence of French traders in the west, particularly south of the Great Lakes, with alarm. In 1676 the Andastes ended their ancient war with the western Iroquois, made their peace, moved from their lands in the Susquehanna valley to the Seneca villages, and became part of this nation, thus greatly enhancing its strength. At about the same time the Mohegan to the east made their peace with the Mohawk. As long as the Iroquois had had these two nations to cope with, the French had held the balance of power. Now that balance was destroyed. The Iroquois had their hands free to renew their bid for control of the western fur trade. Their friendly attitude toward the French turned to hostility, and the Jesuit missionaries in their villages reported that an attack on Fort Frontenac and the French allies could come at any time.[19] But first, the western Iroquois turned their attention westward to the Ohio Valley, to lands which they claimed had been their hunting grounds and which the Illinois and Miami nations had occupied while the Iroquois were defending themselves against the Andastes. They were determined to regain this territory.

It was just at this juncture of events, while the Iroquois were organizing a full-scale campaign to deal with the Illinois as they had earlier dealt with the Huron, that La Salle and his men established their posts in the Illinois country. His commercial alliance inevitably meant that the Illinois and Miami were under French suzerainty and had to be given military aid if attacked. The western expansionist aims of the French and the Iroquois were in opposition. The newly established French bases in the Illinois country were a thousand miles from the central colony, and the communication route to them was flanked by Iroquois-dominated territory throughout most of its length. This was the sort of situation that Colbert had envisaged, and warned against, seemingly in vain.

Despite the reports from the missionaries in the west, the governor of

New France took no steps to counter the threat. Instead, he denied its existence.[20] In September 1680 the clash came. Six to seven hundred Iroquois warriors invaded the Illinois country. Henri Tonti, La Salle's commandant, was wounded, but he and his men managed to escape before the Iroquois launched their main assault. An Illinois village was destroyed and several hundred, mostly women and children, were taken prisoners. Frontenac refused to abandon his pusillanimous policy, and this merely encouraged the Iroquois to continue their aggression against all the French allies and to pillage French canoes on the river routes and even Fort Frontenac.

In the midst of these events Frontenac was dismissed from office; not, ironically, for his failure to counter the Iroquois threat, for he had successfully disguised its seriousness in his reports to the minister, who was loath to consider the expense of a war in the interior of North America and hence readily accepted the governor's accounts at face value. When Frontenac departed, the colony was without defenses. There were no forts in the scattered settlements; Montreal did not even have a palisade; the Iroquois could have devastated the colony at any time. His successor, LeFebvre de La Barre, upon arriving at Quebec in 1682 found himself faced with a totally unexpected and quite desperate situation. He conferred with the colonial leaders and then reported to the minister: "I have found this colony on the verge of being forced into war by the Iroquois and in a condition to succumb."[21]

The members of La Barre's assembly of notables maintained that it was the English who were inciting the Iroquois to break the French hold on the western fur trade, that the Five Nations would attack the French allies one at a time, destroy them piecemeal, drive the French out of the west, then launch their full strength against New France. They advised that the only safe policy the French could pursue was to give the western allies every support, obtain a few hundred regular troops from France to guard the settlements, and muster all the militia to invade the cantons of the western Iroquois and destroy them.

There is little or no evidence that the English colonies were responsible for the Iroquois aggression. Governor Thomas Dongan of New York was eager to contest the French hold on the west, but the merchants of Albany who dominated the English colonial fur trade showed little enthusiasm for such imperialist ventures.[22] Were the Iroquois to have gained control of the western fur trade, the Albany traders would have been very pleased, but as it was they obtained plentiful supplies of furs from two sources, the Iroquois and the Canadian smugglers. They paid higher prices for beaver than did the French Company of the Farm, and some of their English trade goods, particularly woolens, were much superior to anything the French had to offer. Consequently, there had long been a steady flow of contraband furs south to Albany from Fort Frontenac and Montreal. As long as this continued, the Albany merchants were content to let well enough alone. In any event, the Iroquois needed no incitement from the English to pursue their aggressive policy.

La Barre found the French position was threatened also from the north. For over a decade the English had had their trading posts in Hudson Bay, and the French had been hard put to it to prevent the tribes north of the Great Lakes from taking the bulk of their furs to the "Adventurers of England, trading into Hudson's Bay." The majority of the northern Indians had been retained in the French commercial alliance only because of the presence of so many *coureurs de bois* in their midst, the refusal of the English traders to adapt themselves to Indian ways or to treat them as anything approaching equals, and the long, difficult river voyage to the Bay. Yet the Hudson's Bay Company was able to sell on the European market large quantities of prime northern beaver, and this reduced the amount that the French Company of the Farm could dispose of.

Previously, Colbert had been loath to challenge the English presence in the Bay owing to the good relations between the two crowns, but in 1679–1680 he had sanctioned the formation of a Quebec-based Compagnie de la Baie du Nord. This led to armed clashes between the rival companies, but the French government did not provide adequate aid and the minister's decision that all furs taken at the Bay posts had to be brought to Quebec to have the tax deducted rather than taken directly to France proved a grave hindrance. The Canadian company under these conditions was able to annoy the Hudson's Bay Company, but not drive it out. This meant that the English had gained virtual control of the far northern entrance to the continent.[23]

What made these grave problems facing the French in North America much more difficult to grapple with, let alone resolve, was the removal of Colbert from the direction of Canadian affairs. In 1681 his son Jean-Baptiste, the Marquis de Seignelay, had been given this responsibility, and in 1683 Colbert died. Unfortunately, Seignelay was not the man his father had been.[24] The feeble reaction of the Ministry of Marine to the frantic pleas of La Barre and the newly appointed intendant, Jacques de Meulles, made this all too plain. In 1683 Seignelay neglected to deal with the Canadian dispatches before the annual convoy sailed for Quebec. A senior *commis* in the ministry took it on himself to send off very equivocal instructions to the effect that war with the Iroquois would be bad for the colony; therefore La Barre should reduce them to obedience without war, but if he should have to launch a campaign against them, he was to bring it to a swift and successful conclusion. To aid him, 150 Troupes de la Marine hastily recruited in the grogshops of Rochefort were sent, along with supplies of arms, the bulk of which were found to be worthless. Meanwhile, the aggressiveness of the Iroquois increased in direct proportion to the failure of the French to respond. La Barre dispatched some of his few available officers and men to garrison the threatened western posts, sent urgent pleas to the minister for more troops and munitions, and made preparations to march his available forces to attack the western Iroquois.

The dispatching of regular army officers as commandants at the western posts was in itself an important development, the significance of which was overlooked in this time of crisis. From 1683 on, military garrisons manned these posts, and inevitably, despite stringent orders from the minister, they became deeply involved in the fur trade. Officers and men became very eager for the appointments. A few years as commandant at one of the posts sufficed to make a small fortune.[25] They did, however, serve as an agency of control. Orders could be sent from Versailles to a military trading post in the heart of the continent, four thousand miles away, and when these orders did not run counter to the private interests of the commandants, or were too imperative to be ignored, they were obeyed. The writ of the king of France now extended much more firmly over half the continent, and its effectiveness was quickly put to the test.

In the spring of 1684 the Seneca launched an assault on Fort St. Louis in the Illinois country. The commandant, the Chevalier Henri de Baugy, with a garrison of twenty-four French and twenty-two Indian allies managed to withstand the Iroquois siege, but when La Barre received word of the assault in May, he had to anticipate the worst. Everyone in the colony urged him to attack the Iroquois in their villages before they overran all the western posts and drove the French out of the west. Here was the weakness of the French position. Their hold on the interior was extremely tenuous. The widely scattered fortified trading posts, manned by a few men, were very vulnerable and dependent on the maintenance of communications along the river routes to Montreal. The French hold on this vast area was dependent on their ability to retain their Indian allies in a commercial alliance. Were these tribes to lose confidence in French ability to maintain the posts and the supply routes to them, there was a grave likelihood that they would come to terms with the Iroquois. These tribes always had the alternative of trading their furs with the Albany merchants via the Iroquois would-be middlemen or at the Hudson's Bay Company posts. The Iroquois were very conscious of this and always sought to divide the French allies, making attractive overtures to one tribe while concentrating their attacks on another. The caliber of the French officers at the western posts now became vital. They had to be skilled diplomats, commercial agents, guerrilla leaders, and, most of all, men of exceptionally strong character able to hold the respect and allegiance of the western allies who considered themselves under no obligation to consult any interests but their own.

These were the circumstances that led La Barre in July 1684 to take a motley force of Troupes de la Marine, Canadian militia, and allied Indians, over eleven hundred men in all, to Fort Frontenac preparatory to an invasion of the Iroquois cantons. La Barre, however, lacked resolution. The deeper he went into enemy-controlled country, the more difficult his task appeared. His courage ebbed, as did the effectiveness of his men. An epidemic of the tertian ague, Spanish influenza, swept through the ranks. When the Iroquois offered to negotiate a treaty of peace, he immediately accepted. With the bulk of his men hardly able to stand, completely at the mercy of the Iroquois warriors, he had no alternative but to accept the Iroquois terms, which were couched in scornful, humiliating phrases. The Iroquois allowed the French to return to Montreal in safety, but they declared their determination to destroy the Illinois. A great nation allied to the French, under French suzerainty, had been abandoned. The significance of this was not lost on the other allies. Nor was it lost on Louis XIV when he received a copy of the treaty. For the first time he, and Seignelay, examined closely the situation in Canada. They found it deplorable; the king's pride and prestige could not tolerate it. La Barre was made the scapegoat and recalled in disgrace.

His successor was Jacques-Réné de Brisay, Marquis de Denonville, brigadier and colonel of the Queen's Dragoons, generally regarded as one of the better officers in the king's armies. He proved to be one of the better governors general of Canada. He was given a free hand to deal with the Iroquois problem as he best saw fit, and provided with over 1600 Troupes de la Marine, along with adequate supplies. When he landed at Quebec on August 1, 1685, he took stock of the situation and quickly became convinced that Canada was threatened by a giant pincers movement. To the north, the Hudson's Bay Company threatened French control of the northwest. Were the English company to succeed in its aims, the French would find themselves sitting impotent in a few isolated log-palisaded posts in the midst of the northern wilderness. To the south, the Iroquois, urged on by the governor of New York, threatened French control of the western Great Lakes basin and the lands south to the Mississippi. Denonville immediately set to work to counter both these threats. He dealt with the northern menace in 1686 by sending 105 men, regulars and Canadian militia, through the forest to James Bay. They seized three English posts at the "bottom of the Bay" and 50,000 prime beaver pelts. Despite the recently negotiated Treaty of Neutrality between the two crowns and the infuriated protests of Whitehall, the French maintained their position until the end of the ensuing war.

Denonville declared that the threat from the south could best be dealt with by purchasing the province of New York from its proprietor, James II. The possibility of this transaction being effected was, however, too remote to allow him to neglect other measures. All the reports he received from the Jesuit missionaries and the post commanders convinced him that the French position in North America could not be made secure until the Iroquois had

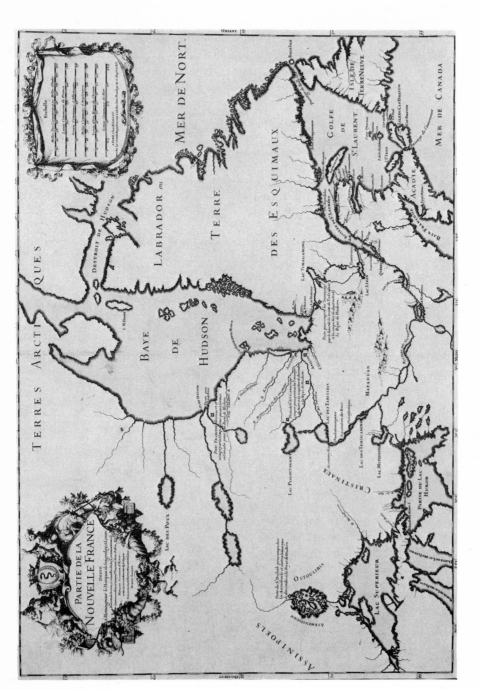

Hubert Jaillot's map, 1685, depicting the struggle for control of Hudson Bay. (Public Archives of Canada)

been crushed. He therefore began making very careful preparations for a full-scale campaign against the Seneca, the most numerous and the farthest removed of the Five Nations.

While he was engaged in these preparations, his fears and suspicions of the role played by the English authorities and traders of New York were confirmed. In 1686 Thomas Dongan sent a trading expedition to the Ottawa of Michilimackinac, offering them goods at very low prices. This further undermined the French position in the west, already gravely weakened by Frontenac's craven policy and the failure of La Barre's campaign. Dongan intended sending another expedition the following year, and Denonville had to counter it. This he did with such success that two parties of Albany traders going by different routes were captured and spent some weeks in jail at Quebec before being sent home to spread the good word. The Canadian renegades who had guided them were summarily executed. The Albany merchants made no further attempts to invade French-claimed territory north of the Great Lakes.

The Seneca campaign, launched in June 1687, did not enjoy an equal measure of success. Denonville reached the villages with his motley force of some 1500 men, regular troops, Canadian militia, *coureurs de bois,* and allied Indians. To have brought a force of this size so far into the enemy country was no mean feat, but after a brief skirmish with a few casualties on both sides, the Seneca fled. Their villages and food supplies were destroyed, but the enemy lived to fight another day.

It was clear that a much larger force than the colony could provide was needed to subdue the Iroquois. The alternatives were a long drawn-out war of attrition, which inevitably meant heavy casualties and destruction in the French settlements, or a negotiated peace settlement. The abandonment of the west was not even contemplated. The growing threat of war in Europe as the League of Augsburg mustered its forces against France precluded any hope that additional troops would be sent to Canada. To make matters worse, an epidemic of smallpox and measles decimated the colony. Of a total population of just over 11,000 including the troops, over a thousand died.[26] With the sanction of Louis XIV, Denonville entered into negotiations for peace with the Iroquois and was able to bring them to accept his terms. They agreed that their ambassadors would return in the spring of the following year, 1689, to ratify the treaty. Denonville availed himself of the respite to send a large party of *voyageurs* to Michilimackinac to bring back the furs stored there. His Seneca campaign had prevented them being brought down during the preceding two years.

The Canadians were now really in a bad way. The heavy death toll from disease had been a cruel blow; Iroquois war parties had already inflicted some casualties; and the interruption in the flow of furs from the west had reduced the people to penury. Conditions were no better during the spring and early summer of 1689. The people had to tighten their belts still further, and wait. Wait for the ships from France with badly needed supplies; wait for the fur brigade to return; wait for the Iroquois plenipotentiaries to come to ratify the peace treaty. Week succeeded week, as the summer passed. Neither the ships nor the Iroquois came. Elsewhere great forces were in movement. In Europe there was war; in England the "Glorious Revolution" had ousted James II and seated William of Orange on the throne. Word of the Revolution and impending war with France reached officials at Boston in March. The Iroquois were immediately informed.

Then, at dawn on August 5, the Iroquois came. Fifteen hundred of them fell on the settlement at Lachine, near Montreal. The settlers were startled awake by shrill war cries. Many of them were hacked down in their homes, others as they sought to flee. More were taken alive. Fifty-six of the seventy-seven habitations in the area were put to the torch. Surprise had been complete. Before nightfall the Iroquois horde retired across Lake St. Louis. The survivors, who had taken refuge in the garrisoned forts, were able to see the faint glow of their fires on the opposite shore. The Iroquois were celebrating their first victory of this war, which was to last to the end of the century, by burning a few of their prisoners slowly to death.

But not all the news was bad. The *voyageurs* sent to Michilimackinac the preceding year by Denonville returned safely with 800,000 *livres* worth of furs, and in October the ships finally arrived from France. With the convoy came the Comte de Frontenac as governor general, appointed to replace Denonville, who had previously asked for his recall. Frontenac immediately tried to enter into peace negotiations with the Iroquois and, predictably, failed. The Five Nations, now sure of English support, were confident that they could destroy New France. Unfortunately, when the western allies heard of Frontenac's return and of his peace overtures, they lost all confidence in the French and began their own separate negotiations with the Iroquois.

Meanwhile, the Iroquois attacks on the settlements continued. The Canadians wanted nothing more than to hit back, but the Iroquois war parties were too elusive. There was, however, Albany, whose people were presumed to have urged the Five Nations on. Were this Iroquois supply base to be destroyed, their ability to wage war would be greatly reduced. This was how the Canadians saw it; and they had good grounds for their view. They were confident that they could raze Albany to the ground. So were the colonial authorities in New York.[27]

Frontenac took full advantage of the Canadians' aggressive spirit, but instead of sending a single strong force to attack Albany, he made the serious blunder of forming three raiding parties, which attacked small frontier settlements not only in New York but also in New England, whose people had not harmed New France and could well have been left alone. During the winter the hamlets of Schenectady, and Salmon Falls on the Atlantic seaboard, were easily overwhelmed. In May, Fort Loyal and the

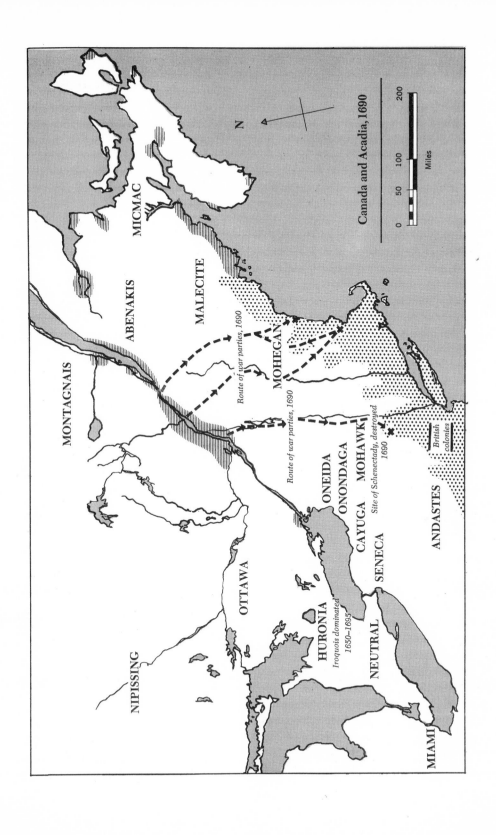

Canada and Acadia, 1690

MICMAC

ABENAKIS

MALECITE

MONTAGNAIS

MOHEGAN

Route of war parties, 1690

Route of war parties, 1690

ONEIDA

ONONDAGA

MOHAWK

Site of Schenectady, destroyed 1690

British colonies

CAYUGA

SENECA

ANDASTES

OTTAWA

NIPISSING

HURONIA
Iroquois dominated 1650–1695

NEUTRAL

MIAMI

N

0   50   100   200
Miles

surrounding settlements were razed. Over a hundred English settlers were killed and many more taken prisoner; farms and livestock were destroyed. Terror was sown all along the frontier.

It took a great deal to make the jealously independent English colonies unite in a common effort, but Frontenac's border raids accomplished it. The colonies combined their forces for a massive assault by land and sea to destroy New France. Encouraged by the easy success of a profitable pillaging expedition against Port Royal in Acadia the previous summer, an armada was assembled to attack Quebec by sea. At the same time an army was to march overland from Albany against Montreal. The land expedition collapsed for want of proper organization and martial spirit before it even reached Lake Champlain. The Boston fleet did succeed in reaching Quebec. The commander, Sir William Phips, sent Frontenac a bombastic demand for the surrender of the town. Frontenac rejected it with equal bombast, making his famous rejoinder: "I have no reply to make to your general other than from the mouths of my cannon and muskets." The New Englanders then landed, some thirteen hundred strong, on the tidal flats near the city. But when they saw several hundred regular troops lined up, with artillery, waiting for their assault, they thought better of it. After a few days of futile maneuvering, they re-embarked and sailed away.[28]

The failure of these expeditions made it plain that despite their vastly superior numbers, the English colonies could not conquer Canada and that Canada was unable to destroy the Iroquois. From this point on, the war became a series of savage raids by small war parties, what the French called *la petite guerre*. During the early years the Iroquois decidedly had the better of it, but the Canadians eventually mastered the technique of guerrilla warfare. Neither side had any great superiority in weapons; it was purely a question of skill and endurance. The training the Canadians had received in the western fur trade was the vital factor in their survival. In this type of warfare the Troupes de la Marine proved to be of little use, and the bulk of the fighting fell to the militia, led, however, by regular officers, many of them Canadians. The regular soldiers were, for the most part, used to garrison forts in the exposed seigneuries and as a labor force, helping the *habitants* on the land.

After the first disastrous Iroquois raids the French learned that it was no use looking for Iroquois war parties after an attack; they had to lie in wait for them along the routes they were likely to use. This proved more successful, and the Iroquois suffered heavy losses in sudden ambushes at a portage or river narrows. The French then began carrying the war to the enemy's country. In one swift raid several Mohawk villages were destroyed. Smaller parties of Canadians and allied Indians harried the Iroquois in their hunting and fishing grounds. Because of the ease with which the Iroquois learned of French military plans, which too often were discussed in Montreal's numerous taverns, the officers commanding these small parties were sent

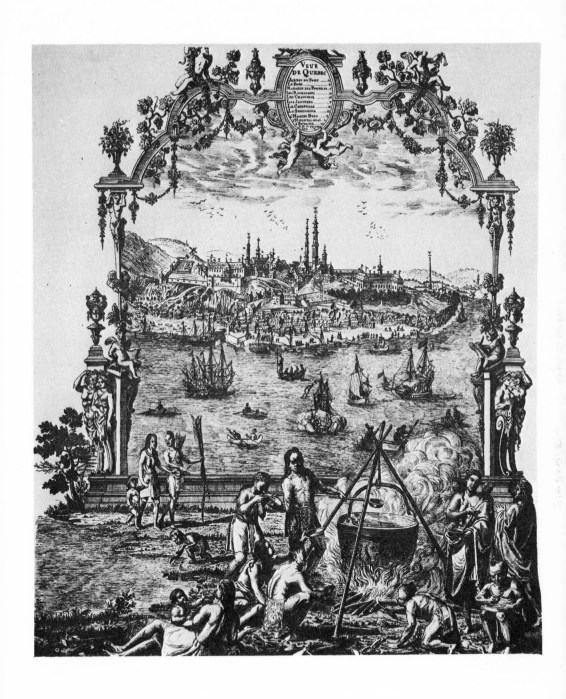

View of Quebec, 1699, from the cartouche on a map by J.-B.-L. Franquelin. (Public Archives of Canada)

off without being told their objective. Instead, the officer in command was given sealed orders, to be opened some ten miles out of Montreal. With these changes in methods, the Iroquois losses began to mount. The number of warriors who failed to return from a raid or a hunting trip increased. When, on Frontenac's orders, Iroquois captives were burned slowly to death in the French settlements in the same manner that the Five Nations dealt with their prisoners, the Iroquois ceased to press their attacks as recklessly as before. Not only did the Iroquois have to use far more caution in approaching the French settlements, but they had to be on guard near their own villages. To add to their difficulties, they received very little support from their Anglo-American allies. The New York border settlements were suffering drastically from French raids, and many settlers fled to the less exposed provinces. The Iroquois, too engaged in the war to hunt, were bringing little fur to Albany; nor was it receiving supplies of contraband from Montreal as formerly. When Governor Benjamin Fletcher of New York appealed to the other colonies for aid, he received only regrets, and the Iroquois received the same reply from the Albany authorities when they complained that they were fighting alone.

The French, on the other hand, were suffering no shortage of furs because of the war. Just the reverse in fact. Frontenac sent parties of some hundred and forty men to the western posts each year, ostensibly to convoy supplies to the garrisons and the Indian allies to aid them in prosecuting the war against the Iroquois. The intendant soon discovered that these military detachments were nothing more than trading ventures; the canoes were loaded not with military supplies but with trade goods, brandy being a major item. New posts were opened in the Sioux and Assiniboin countries; how many, and where, will probably never be known since Frontenac was careful to write as little as possible about these ventures in his dispatches to the minister. Suffice it to say that the war served as a marvelous means for a tremendous expansion of the western fur trade empire. There were now more French traders in the west than ever before.

The capital for this expansion came from three sources: the king's stores in the guise of military supplies for the Indian allies; the Canadian merchants; and the *marchands forrains*, merchants of La Rochelle who came every summer with trade goods, hired *coureurs de bois* at Montreal to transport the goods to the west to trade, and returned to France in the autumn with the furs brought back by other *coureurs de bois* sent out the previous year. What proportion of the fur trade was in the hands of these nonresident capitalists is not known, but it appears to have been considerable. The amount of beaver coming into the offices of the Company of the Farm as a result of this expansion is a good indication of its extent. At a time when the demand in Europe was shrinking, as a result of a change in hat styles decreeing a narrower brim and the use of blended felts by hat makers—beaver fur mixed with rabbit or Peruvian llama wool—the amount shipped from Quebec rose to four times annually what the French market could absorb. Over 140,000 *livres* weight of beaver a year was flooding in, and the Company of the Farm, by 1695, had an unsaleable surplus of 3,500,000 *livres* worth in its warehouses.[29] The Canadian beaver trade was on the verge of bankruptcy.

The political consequences of this unbridled fur trade expansion were even more menacing. The Ottawa, who had previously provided the bulk of the furs, found themselves being eliminated from their middleman role. The French traders, military and civilian alike, were voyaging far beyond Michilimackinac to trade directly with the Assiniboin, the Ottawa's main suppliers, and with the Sioux. As long as the Ottawa could remember, the Sioux had been their enemies. French firearms had enabled them to hold their own against the ancient foe, but now the French were supplying the Sioux with muskets.

It was at this juncture of events that the Iroquois, who badly needed a respite from recent French attacks to recuperate their strength, made separate overtures for peace to both the French and the Ottawa in a cunning attempt to play the one off against the other. When Frontenac, despite the warnings of his subordinates, agreed to a truce while negotiations were under way, the Iroquois informed the Ottawa that the French were abandoning them. The Ottawa, already disgruntled by French policies, were quick to accept Iroquois proposals for peace and an alliance. The entire French position in the west now teetered in the balance. Nothing could have made it more obvious how tenuous this empire really was. Were the Ottawa to have defected and allied themselves with the Iroquois, the French would have been swept out of the west and the Five Nations would have been able to concentrate their entire strength against the central colony.

This did not happen, but it came dangerously close. Frontenac's subordinates were able to bring enough pressure to bear to force him to undertake a full-scale invasion of the Iroquois cantons. In 1696 the villages of the Onondaga and Oneida were destroyed. They suffered only one casualty, but the loss of their food supplies was a hard blow. Disease and the steady toll of the *petite guerre* had reduced their strength to less than half what it had been when hostilities began.[30] The Ottawa, who had refused to assist the French in the campaign, could not resist the temptation to harry their old foes brought low. The Five Nations appealed to the English for aid, received none, and were then forced to ask the French for terms, this time in earnest. Their attempt to wrest control of the western fur trade from the French had failed.

Ironically, just as the French hold on the west was finally made secure, Louis XIV ordered that it be abandoned. He, and the minister of marine, had suddenly awakened to the fact that the glut of beaver had reached menacing proportions. The lease on the Canadian beaver monopoly expired in 1697, and there was a distinct danger that it would be impossible to find anyone to take it over. This would have meant a loss in revenue to the crown of half a million *livres* a year. With France extremely hard pressed by the cost of the war in Europe and the disastrous winter of 1694, which had reduced the masses to starvation, this loss of revenue was too serious to contemplate. The minister, a kinsman of Frontenac's, had refused to accept the intendant's complaints that the governor's sending of military detachments to the west was largely responsible for the oversupply of fur. Now he was forced to face reality. Procrastination was replaced by drastic measures.

When Frontenac returned from the Onondaga campaign, he received dispatches from the minister that spread consternation throughout the colony. All the posts in the west were to be destroyed and their garrisons recalled to the central colony, with the sole exception of Fort St. Louis des Illinois, which was to be retained only for military purposes and no trade in beaver was to be allowed at it. No more permits were to be issued for trade in the west; instead the western Indians were to bring their furs to Montreal to trade there. The Canadians were not to go beyond the settled areas along the St. Lawrence. This was a return to Colbert's old policy, but the circumstances were no longer what they had been in his day. For one thing, the war with the Iroquois and the English was not yet over. For another, the western allies had become accustomed during the past quarter century to having their needs supplied in their villages, and several of these tribes were not canoe men. To have withdrawn from the west in this fashion would have required them to reorganize their way of life drastically. It would also have left a power vacuum in the west, and there was no telling what forces would fill it.

The royal edicts sparked a vigorous trans-Atlantic debate. Even the intendant Champigny, who had vigorously opposed Frontenac's use of military resources for trading purposes and whose warnings of the consequences the minister had refused to heed, declared that the new policy would be disastrous. Very quickly lines were drawn in the colony. The Jesuits strongly supported the restrictive measures, for they would be allowed to retain their missions and they were utterly convinced that the presence of French soldiers and traders among the Indians undermined all their efforts to Christianize them. Others, led by Frontenac and his associates, men to whom he had given commissions in the Troupes de la Marine and appointed commandants of the western posts, men like Tonti, LaForest, and Cadillac, who were interested only in private profit, bitterly opposed the edicts, claiming that they meant the destruction of New France. In between were men such as Champigny and Denis Riverin, the latter one of the colony's leading entrepreneurs, who advocated a middle way.

Champigny proposed retaining the twenty-five annual *congés*, trading licenses, and three posts, Fort Frontenac, Michilimackinac, and St. Joseph

Wampum belt. Oral tradition has it that this belt depicts a clause in the great treaty that ended the French and Iroquois wars in 1701. (McCord Museum, McGill University)

des Miamis at the foot of Lake Michigan, along with adopting much tighter restrictions on the trade to prevent the old abuses. Denis Riverin, with remarkable prescience, proposed that the French retain their posts north of the Great Lakes and abandon those south of them. He pointed out that the bulk of the poor-grade beaver that had flooded the market came from the more southerly lands; hence this region was of no real value to France. Moreover, he stated, the Alleghenies were not an insuperable barrier to the Anglo-Americans. If France retained the region south of the Great Lakes, when the English began to penetrate the west, the French would be obliged to expend blood and treasure to keep them out of these lands that were really only an economic liability. The country north of the Great Lakes, on the other hand, produced better-quality furs, and he maintained that the French could easily hold this territory against English encroachment.[31] Riverin had no way of knowing it, but he was then advocating the very division of the continent that was to emerge, under different auspices, after the American Revolution.

The minister, after perusing the spate of memoirs that flooded in protesting the new edicts, adopted a middle course, which did nothing to solve the basic problem; in fact, it only made it worse. He allowed the posts at Michilimackinac, St. Joseph des Miamis, St. Louis des Illinois, and also Fort Frontenac to be retained; no more trading licenses were to be issued; and the price of beaver was reduced. This meant that control of the entire western trade fell into the hands of the men whom Frontenac appointed to command at these posts. Some, if not most, of the other posts were clandestinely maintained, and the *coureurs de bois*, seeing Frontenac's men carrying on the trade as before, refused to obey the royal edict and return to the colony, except to slip in and out with their cargoes of furs and merchandise.

After Frontenac's death in 1698 his successor, Hector de Callières, made a more determined attempt to stop the contraband trade, but with small success. By this time there were some two hundred *coureurs de bois* who knew no other way of life. Had it been possible to force them to return to the central colony, they could never have readjusted to that ordered society. They were prepared to defy the king's officers, even to turn renegade and trade out of Albany or Philadelphia, rather than abandon the west. One French officer, sent to Michilimackinac in 1702 to enforce the new regulation, reported back to the governor that the *coureurs de bois* there had merely laughed in his face. "It is very fine and Honourable for me, Monsieur" he wrote Callières, "to be charged with your orders but it is also very vexatious to have only ink and paper as means to enforce them."[32]

Callières did have much more success in another sphere. In 1697 hostilities in Europe had ceased, ended more by the exhaustion of the combatants than by anything else, and by the need to resolve the knotty problem of the succession to the throne of Spain. Peace with the Iroquois

Pierre Le Moyne d'Iberville, founder of Louisiana. (Public Archives of Canada)

was more difficult to arrange but in 1701 a firm treaty was finally ratified. By one of its clauses the Five Nations bound themselves to remain neutral in any future conflict between France and England. This was a great gain for the French, a terrible blow to New York. No longer could that province rely on the Iroquois to act as a shield for their northern frontier. At the same time the Iroquois remained sufficiently strong to bar the way to the western Indians who otherwise would have flocked to Albany, as an alternative to Montreal, to trade their furs. This allowed the French to retain their tenuous hold on the west, and with it the problem of reconciling the conflict between the economics of the fur trade and the politics of Indian alliances.

Then, suddenly, the whole context was radically altered. Decisions were made in Europe that drastically affected the future course of events in North America. Almost overnight factors that had been regarded as intolerable liabilities became either of no account or were transformed into assets. The issue of the Spanish succession had, by 1700, resolved itself to three possible solutions: either a grandson of Louis XIV was to gain the throne and with it control of the Spanish empire, or it was to go to a member of the House of Habsburg, or the empire was to be divided between them. The Spanish people rejected the last; either of the other two could hardly be effected without war, since both solutions meant upsetting the European balance of power. Louis XIV took steps to meet any eventuality. One measure was to strengthen the French position in North America in order to be ready either to defend or to assault the Spanish colonies, depending on who received the Spanish Empire. The great Canadian naval captain Pierre Le Moyne d'Iberville was ordered to establish a French colony at the mouth of the Mississippi. Military posts were to be established from the Gulf of Mexico to the Great Lakes to bar the English from the west, prevent them from expanding southwestward to threaten Mexico, and hem them in east of the Alleghenies. This was imperialism with a vengeance. A handful of French officers, fur traders, and priests were to hold the allegiance of the western nations and seek to retain possession of most of North America—this at a time when traders from the English colonies were beginning to move into the trans-Allegheny west.

Once the first settlements in Louisiana were founded, any hope there might have been of forcing the *coureurs de bois* to return to New France was lost. They began taking their furs down the Mississippi, as La Salle had once planned to do, and obtaining fresh supplies of trade goods from Iberville's men. The Montreal merchants protested vigorously, declaring that Louisiana would be the ruin of Canada, but the minister was no longer concerned about such matters. The economic problem of the fur trade was all but lost to sight, dwarfed by the vastly greater political and military problems posed by the new policy for North America. When one of his staff suggested that the *coureurs de bois,* being tough, ruthless, and capable of anything, should be encouraged to trade in the Mississippi Valley and, in alliance with the Indian nations of the south, bar the way of the Anglo-Americans to the Spanish mines of New Mexico, he merely minuted the *memoire* with one word *"Essayer."*[33] In this laconic fashion a sweeping new policy was inaugurated. The *coureurs de bois,* up to this point regarded as outlaws and renegades, a social group to be eliminated by one means or another, were suddenly transformed into useful agents of crown policy. Grave economic and social problems had been submerged by political expediency in a manner that must have made Colbert spin in his grave.

The Imperial Frontier, 1700-1750

*A*t the beginning of the new century and on the eve of a new war, the War of the Spanish Succession, Canada's future looked bright. The French in North America had weathered a long, bitterly fought war without loss of territory. During these years of fighting they had extended their authority over a vast expanse of the continent and were in a much stronger position than ever before. The Iroquois had been subdued, and the Anglo-Americans were regarded with something akin to contempt. An officer in the Troupes de la Marine, after a tour of the northern English colonies, reported:

> It is true that this country has twice the population of New France, but the people there are astonishingly cowardly, completely undisciplined, and without any experience in war. The smallest Indian party has always made them flee; moreover, they have no regular troops. It is not at all like that in Canada. There are twenty-eight companies of infantry, the Canadians are brave, much inured to war, and untiring in travel; two thousand of them will at all times and in all places thrash the people of New England.[1]

The degree of truth contained in this statement is not really important; what is significant is the light it casts on the self-confidence of the Canadians at this particular time. During the ensuing half century they were to suffer reverses, endure harsh privation, see a large part of Acadia lost to France, their bases on Hudson Bay were to be sacrificed like pawns at the European conference table, but they were still to emerge strong, the economy of the central colony more diversified and prosperous, their hold on the interior of the continent firmer than before. All this came about only as a result of strenuous efforts on the part of the Canadian people, the resilience of their institutions, and the adroit policies pursued by the senior officials at Quebec. Ironically, certain policy decisions made by the Minister of Marine were among their greatest handicaps during this period. It took a great deal of skill on the part of the Governor to cope with the serious problems these decisions brought in their train.

When hostilities between the French and the English resumed in 1702, some in Canada were all for launching full-scale attacks on New York and New England, confident that these provinces could easily be conquered. More prudent councils, however, prevailed. The intendant Champigny, who had been recalled to France to serve as intendant at Le Havre and whose counsel was sought by the minister, advised that nothing could be worse for Canada than to launch such attacks. He maintained that the Anglo-Americans wanted only to be left in peace and that were the French to attack them it would merely stir up a hornet's nest, and might well bring the Iroquois into the fray. He strongly advised that a treaty of neutrality, similar to that with the Iroquois, be concluded with the English colonies, but that it not be negotiated through the agency of the Five Nations; instead, the Jesuit missionaries should subtly indicate to the Iroquois that if the English wished to suspend hostilities, the French might be willing to follow suit. In this way, the onus could be made to appear to rest on the English, and the French would not appear to be the supplicants.[2]

The governor at Quebec, Philippe de Rigaud, Marquis de Vaudreuil, was of the same opinion. Some years later, in 1711, he had occasion to state his views very succinctly to the minister on the Iroquois problem, and there is no doubt that he had held this opinion all along: "It is in our interest, My Lord, to avoid war with this nation for as long as possible. The five Iroquois villages are more to be feared than the English colonies. . . . Twenty-four years experience has convinced me that war with them is bad for this colony. I know only too well how much it has cost us and how difficult it was for the people to recover from it."[3] He therefore gave the Iroquois to understand that he would not be the first to strike, but were they, or the Anglo-Americans of New York, to reopen hostilities, he would throw his entire forces against them both.[4] He was, however, fully aware that the English colonies could muster a far larger force than the 3350 active men he could raise in the colony. He had to rely on defense works and skillful tactics to offset the enemy's superiority in numbers.[5]

The French had managed to bring the Iroquois to terms, but only after

Philippe de Rigaud, Marquis de Vaudreuil, governor general of New
France, 1703–1725. (Public Archives of Canada)

ten years of grinding guerrilla warfare, and neither side wanted any more of that. Yet it had long been a cardinal principle of French policy that the Iroquois must be kept in a state of hostility with the northwestern Algonkin tribes upon whom the French depended for their supplies of furs. The Iroquois were essential to prevent these tribes from taking their furs to Albany rather than to the French at Montreal or at the western posts. Previously, the inducements for the French allies to trade with the English had not been great; the better prices for furs offered by the Albany merchants had been offset by the refusal of the Iroquois to allow them to trade directly with the western nations, since this would have prevented the Iroquois from making the middleman's profit. For this reason the Five Nations refused to allow the authorities at Albany to establish a fort on Lake Ontario.

After 1700, however, it became increasingly difficult for both the Iroquois and the French to maintain their positions. As a result of the huge surplus of beaver in French warehouses, the price paid by the new company was reduced to 1 *livre* 10 *sols* the pound. Previously prices had varied, according to quality, from 5 *livres* 10 *sols* to 3 *livres* 10 *sols*. Now much more emphasis was placed on furs other than beaver, and these *menues pelleteries*—fox, martin, bear, weasel, otter—which were sold on a free market, made up over 50 percent of the total trade. In fact, the French paid higher prices for these furs than did the English. They even encouraged some of their allies to sell their beaver to the Albany merchants, and the smuggling of beaver by the Canadians to Albany rose by leaps and bounds.[6]

Yet beaver was still the mainstay of the trade and with the Montreal price so low the western nations were more inclined to look to Albany than ever before, but as long as the Iroquois barred the way, requiring that the trade pass through their hands, the French hold on the western fur trade was secure. The Iroquois, however, had suffered such heavy losses in the past war that they had to secure their western flank against future attacks by the Algonkin nations. When the Huron, in 1703, entered into negotiations with the Iroquois for the right to pass through the lands of the Five Nations to trade at Albany, the Iroquois decided to allow it, the alternative being the likelihood of renewed hostilities, which the Iroquois could not afford. In the ten years that followed, the Ottawa, Huron, and Miami began to trade directly at Albany. For the French, this was a disaster. The Iroquois barrier that they had relied on since the days of Champlain had finally been breached.[7] As yet it was only breached one way; the western tribes were going to Albany but the Albany traders were not venturing into the west. Ample supplies of fur were being smuggled to them from Montreal, and the Iroquois were not yet prepared to allow the Anglo-Americans to establish trading posts on, or to pass through, their lands. Whereas before, Iroquois strength had been the main threat to New France, Iroquois weakness now proved to be an equal, if not greater, menace.

The French had to bend their every effort to prevent this bad situation from becoming worse, and ministerial policy did much to make the task more difficult. The crux of the problem was that for political and military reasons the French wished to maintain their hold in the west, but for economic reasons—the glut of beaver—they wanted to reduce the number of men in the west to a bare minimum. The minister was painfully aware that the more soldiers and traders there were in the west, the more beaver would come to Montreal each year. Yet it was difficult to hold the western nations in the French alliance without maintaining garrisoned posts in their villages. Thus, when Lamothe Cadillac proposed to the minister of marine the creation of a large French settlement at Detroit with all the allied nations in the Great Lakes basin removed from their existing villages and settled about it, the minister was persuaded that such a French-Indian settlement would serve both to cow the Iroquois and forestall any Anglo-American plans for westward expansion. Despite strong opposition from the governor and the intendant at Quebec, in 1701 Cadillac was allowed to proceed. Michilimackinac was abandoned and the tribes were persuaded to move to the new base.[8]

Not only was the entire concept of Detroit ill-advised, but it would have been difficult to find a worse commander for the new post than Cadillac. He was completely without scruples or honor, incompetent, and a coward to boot. By 1708 there were only 63 settlers at Detroit, of whom 29 were married soldiers of the 100-man garrison, and only some 200 acres of land were under cultivation, with 3 cows, 6 or 7 bulls and calves, and 1 horse. What really prospered was Cadillac's trade in brandy at seven times the Montreal price. When the minister sent a trusted official from France, François Clairambault d'Aigremont, to investigate the plethora of charges and complaints against Cadillac, he confirmed them all. In his lengthy report he declared: "I was able to observe that M. de la Mothe . . . was generally hated by all the French and Indians. . . . I can assure you My Lord, that this aversion was not without cause, he is not hated for nothing. The tyranny that he maintains over them both is sufficient to warrant it."[9]

Yet Cadillac did get the settlement established. It was not long, however, before the warnings of Governor Vaudreuil were borne out. The relocation of the French allies brought them into closer proximity to the Iroquois, made it much easier for these old enemies to come to an understanding, and for the Huron, Ottawa, and Miami to take their furs to Albany. As the commercial ties between the western nations and Albany became closer, the Iroquois began to adopt a less neutral attitude toward the French. In 1709 and again in 1711, when expeditions were organized in the English colonies for full-scale attacks on New France, several hundred Iroquois warriors were prepared to accompany them. Fortunately for New France both expeditions came to nothing, but it was clear to the governor, the intendant, and the *commissaire* d'Aigremont that Detroit was a source of considerable danger to Canada. They recommended strongly that the settlement be abandoned, the Michilimackinac be restored with a commandant and garrison, and that the twenty-five annual licenses be reinstituted. Making Michilimackinac the main western base, they argued, would remove the allies from too close proximity to the Iroquois, and the garrison and license holders would be able to exert enough influence and pressure on the western tribes to hold them in the French alliance. The minister, however, could not admit that Detroit had been a mistake; nor would he entertain any measure that might increase the amount of beaver traded.

When Charon de la Barre of Montreal submitted a memoir recommending the establishment of a fort at Niagara as a barrier to Anglo-American penetration of the north and west, the officials at Quebec opposed the suggestion. They were of the opinion that it would prove to be even more dangerous than Detroit, drawing the French allies into still closer proximity to the Iroquois. They maintained that the Iroquois would never allow the Anglo-Americans to establish a post there; hence there was no need to forestall them. On this issue the minister agreed with the Quebec officials.[10]

The crux of the matter was that the French could only keep their hold on the west by maintaining a controlling influence over their Indian allies. To do this they had to prevent them from having commercial dealings with Albany and the Iroquois. As long as the price paid by the French for beaver was so far out of line with Albany prices, this was extremely difficult. The French were, therefore, reduced to all manner of expedients to maintain their position, and some of them were quite illegal. Smuggling played a major role in the involved game of western power politics. How much beaver was traded at Albany by the Canadians is not known—it may well have been more than the amount shipped to France.[11] Whatever the amount, the trade had two beneficial results for Canada; it prevented the surplus in beaver on the French market from becoming that much larger, and it was one means whereby the Canadians were able to obtain the English woolen cloth, duffel, and stroud that the Indians preferred to the poorer quality French cloth. This removed one inducement for the French allies to go to Albany to trade.

Vaudreuil allowed a small force of Canadian traders, some fifteen in all, to be maintained at Michilimackinac. With his connivance these men were kept supplied with trade goods.[12] Elsewhere in the west renegade *coureurs de bois,* estimated to number 200, maintained the French presence, along with the missionaries. The lavish use of presents to the Indians was another means of holding them in the French alliance; 20,000 *livres* a year on the colonial budget was employed by Vaudreuil for this. To woo the chiefs thirty silver and ten enamel medals were especially manufactured, and Vaudreuil declared that the awarding of these medals as a mark of distinction would have a desirable effect.[13] Eventually, the medals were produced in Montreal, proving to be a very useful bread-and-butter trade

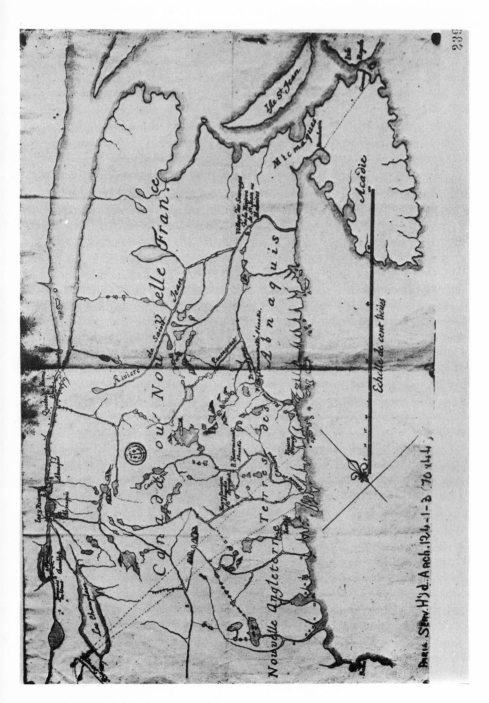

Map of Acadia and Canada, 1713, by Father Joseph Aubry, S.J. (Public Archives of Canada)

for the local silversmiths. But the most important factor enabling the French to hold the west was undoubtedly the nonaggressive policy pursued by the English of New York during most of the war.

On Canada's eastern frontier the situation was entirely different. Throughout its history, Acadia had been the neglected stepchild. During King William's War the French had maintained their hold on this area only with the help of their Indian allies, the Abenakis, Canibas, Etchimin, and Malecite, and by well-timed and executed assaults on the New England strong points, such as that which resulted in the capture of Fort Penobscot in 1696. Yet in 1701 the French population in the province was only 1134.[14] That the French had retained their grip on the area for the past century was more a measure of New England's military ineptitude than of French strength.

When hostilities were renewed in Europe French policy in Acadia was the reverse of that in New France. Whereas Vaudreuil declared that the French must not attack New York for fear of arousing the Iroquois, it was felt that the New England colonies could be attacked without danger of the Five Nations coming to their support. Whenever the Acadian Indians hearkened to the efforts of the New England authorities to make peace, Vaudreuil had to disrupt the negotiations by inducing the wavering allies to join with the Canadians in attacks on the Anglo-American settlements. In 1703 the settlements from Wells to Falmouth were ravaged by 500 Indians and a few Canadians led by Leneuf de Beaubassin. Over 160 settlers were killed or taken prisoner. In February 1704 Hertel de Rouville, with 50 Canadians and 250 Abenakis and Caughnawaga Iroquois, after a 300-mile journey on snowshoes, fell on Deerfield, Massachusetts, and destroyed it, killing some fifty settlers and carrying off over a hundred.

Smaller parties harried the New England frontier continually without the Anglo-American settlers being able to defend it successfully, let alone respond in kind. They had no body of men capable of traveling through hundreds of miles of trackless wilderness at any time of the year, let alone in mid-winter, to attack New France. In 1709 Vaudreuil reported that two thirds of the fields north of Boston were untended, and that his war parties were now returning without prisoners after spending up to three weeks amid these settlements because the Anglo-Americans remained cooped up in their forts, afraid to venture out.[15]

The New Englanders did have one way to strike back—by sea. In reprisal for the Deerfield raid a maritime expedition destroyed the inoffensive Acadian settlements at Grand Pré in the Bay of Fundy; but a sea-borne assault on Port Royal was ignominiously routed by a small French force under the command of a veteran officer, Daniel d'Auger de Subercase. In 1709 a much more ambitious undertaking was planned, the conquest of both Acadia and New France. A land army under Colonel Francis Nicholson, a tough Yorkshireman, was to muster at Albany to attack Montreal, while a

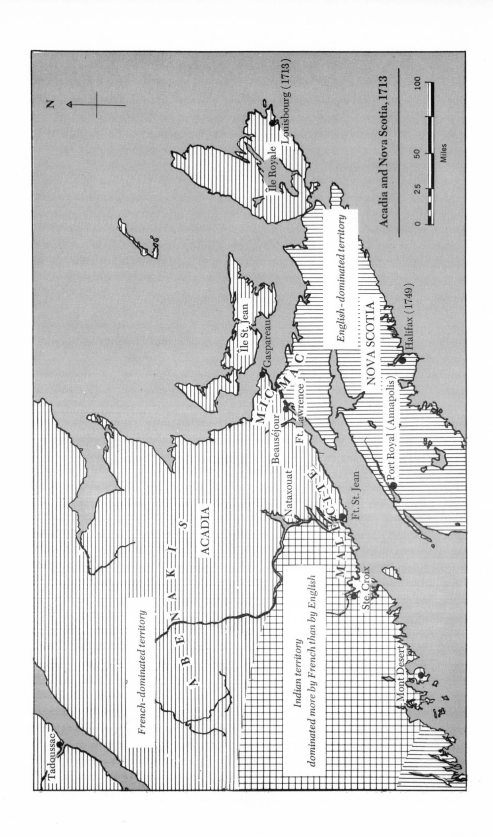

N

Tadoussac

French-dominated territory

A B E N A K I S

ACADIA

Indian territory
dominated more by French than by English

Île St. Jean

Gaspareau

M I C   M A C

Beauséjour

Ft. Lawrence

Nataxouat

M A L I C I T E

Ste. Croix

Ft. St. Jean

Mont Desert

Île Royale

Louisbourg (1713)

English-dominated territory

NOVA SCOTIA

Halifax (1749)

Port Royal (Annapolis)

Acadia and Nova Scotia, 1713

0   25   50   100
Miles

maritime expedition sailed from Boston to assault Quebec. It was the same strategy that had been tried, without success, in 1690. Then, the maritime expedition had at least reached Quebec. This time both expeditions came to grief, largely owing to poor organization. The following year a combined force of British regulars and colonial militia, over 1900 men, sailed to Port Royal. After withstanding a siege and bombardment for a week, Subercase surrendered the fort and was granted the honors of war—as well he should since his garrison numbered 258 officers and men.[16] Although the British occupied only Port Royal and the surrounding area, they were able to maintain their hold on it until the end of the war.

In Hudson Bay, as in the west, political aims and economic reality were in conflict. In 1697, while the diplomats were hammering out a peace treaty, the French government sent Iberville to capture the English-held forts in the Bay, not because they would be an economic asset to France, but because it was feared they would be to England. After a crushing naval victory over the English ships in the icy waters at the mouth of the Hayes River, Iberville captured York Fort on September 13, one week before the Treaty of Ryswick was signed. The Hudson's Bay Company still held the posts at the Bottom of the Bay, and despite the fact that the peace treaty called for the French to regain them and the English to hold York Fort, the exact opposite prevailed. Both sides retained what they held. Throughout the next war the French held on to York Fort, which they renamed Fort Bourbon, but it had to be supplied directly from France, and Canada was unable to mount an expedition against the English posts in James Bay.

In 1712 the fighting in Europe came to an end, and the following year the Treaty of Utrecht ushered in three decades of peace between France and England. This phenomenally long period without war between the rival powers did not arise because the treaty had removed all causes for war, rather because the internal situation in both countries made peace essential. Both were almost exhausted, but had great recuperative powers; and both had unstable governments. In Britain the Hanoverian succession required time to be consolidated, and the Jacobite uprising of 1715, although quickly repressed, was a source of worry lest another and stronger attempt be made. In France the health of the infant Louis XV gave cause to fear a contested succession in the event of his early demise. By the time these problems had been resolved, power was in the hands of ministers—Robert Walpole and Cardinal Fleury—who firmly believed that peace, not war, was in the best interests of their respective countries.

In North America the terms of the Treaty of Utrecht appeared at first glance to be an initial step in the loss by France of all its possessions on the continent. France ceded to England Hudson's Bay, Newfoundland, and Acadia "with the ancient boundaries." In addition France had to recognize British suzerainty over the Iroquois, and commerce with the far Indians was to be open to traders of both nations. Had the British interpretation of these sweeping clauses been implemented, French power in North America would have been rendered virtually negligible. This the French were able to prevent. They did relinquish Fort Bourbon on Hudson Bay, but that merely relieved them of an economic liability. As long as the English made no attempt to move inland, the Hudson's Bay Company posts did not constitute a serious threat to Canada. In Newfoundland, the French retained fishing rights on the northern coast, and this was all that really mattered to them. They were still able to harvest the maritime wealth of the Grand Banks, maintaining a large fishing fleet as a training school for sailors, and it was this last that both powers regarded as of vital importance.

In Acadia the British chose to interpret the "ancient boundaries" as extending north through present-day New Brunswick and Quebec to the St. Lawrence, including also Cape Breton and the peninsula of Nova Scotia. The French, however, were able to retain possession of Cape Breton and the mainland as far south as the Kennebec River. This territory was occupied by the Abenakis who, with French moral and material support, were able to resist the attempts of the Anglo-Americans to seize their ancestral hunting grounds. During the ensuing years, although there was to be savage intermittent fighting along the frontier, the area was preserved as a buffer zone to protect Canada.

In the west French interests were more gravely threatened. Clause fifteen of the Treaty of Utrecht granted the English the right to trade with the Indian nations in the interior. This would have allowed the Anglo-American traders to flood into the west with their cheap merchandise, and cheaper rum, eliminating the French entirely. But the Canadians had no intention of allowing this to happen, and they were in a position to prevent it. By 1712 the minister of marine was forced to conclude that the Detroit settlement had been a big mistake. He could not openly admit this, or that his choice of Lamothe Cadillac to establish and command the settlement had been disastrous; he therefore gave orders that Detroit be allowed to wither on the vine. Cadillac, in typical bureaucratic fashion, was kicked upstairs and made governor of Louisiana. This removed two liabilities. Michilimackinac was ordered restored and garrisoned, the license system was reintroduced, and several new trading posts were established in the west to hold the tribes firm in their allegiance.[17]

That the French were determined, regardless of the Treaty of Utrecht, to take strong measures to bar the west to the Anglo-Americans was made clear in 1720. Rumors had reached Vaudreuil that the Albany merchants were preparing to erect a trading post at Niagara. Although Vaudreuil had, in 1706, rejected Charon de la Barre's proposal that the French build a fort there, this threatened English move had to be blocked. An English post at Niagara would have enabled the Albany merchants to tap the trade of all the nations in the Great Lakes basin, making the French position in the west, if not untenable, at least extremely difficult.

The swift and decisive manner in which Vaudreuil countered this threat makes very plain the effectiveness of the French military form of government and the caliber of his subordinate officers. Niagara was Seneca territory, and the French had acknowledged British suzerainty over the Five Nations in the Treaty of Utrecht. Vaudreuil was able to get around that. Chabert de Joncaire, one of his officers in the Troupes de la Marine, had been taken prisoner in the 1690s by the Seneca and had so impressed them by his brave demeanor in the face of a slow, horrible death that they had spared his life and made him an adopted member of their nation. Joncaire was now sent to their village and at a council meeting asked permission from the chiefs to build a house on their land. This being granted, he quickly collected a party of soldiers from Fort Frontenac and constructed a trading post on the east side of the Niagara River, well below the falls.[18] The French were solidly entrenched at this vital passage before the New York men had done more than talk about making such a move.

Governor William Burnet of New York protested vigorously to Vaudreuil, to no avail. He tried to persuade the Iroquois to drive the French off their lands, but although the Five Nations were deeply concerned, they feared that if they attacked the French they would get no armed support from New York. In this they were undoubtedly right, for the *entente presque cordiale* between Britain and France precluded open hostilities in the colonies. The Iroquois, however, were not prepared to see the French gain the upper hand in the area. To retain some semblance of independence, they had to keep the British and French in balance. For this reason, in 1724 they gave their permission to Governor Burnet to built a fortified trading post at Oswego. The Iroquois had been obliged to give way under pressure from first the French then the English. Their sovereignty over their own lands was diminished still further. The balance of power was preserved, but only by a reduction of their own power.

When the Marquis de Beauharnois, Vaudreuil's successor, learned of this development, he was incensed. The French had struggled long and hard to keep the English away from the shores of Lake Ontario. Now they were there. The danger was great that the French allies, lured by cheaper goods and unlimited supplies of liquor, would take their furs to this post. Governor Beauharnois sent an ultimatum to the commandant of Oswego, demanding that he raze the fort on the strange grounds that it was contrary to the terms of the Treaty of Utrecht. Needless to say, that officer rejected the ultimatum. Beauharnois then wrote Burnet, protesting the establishment of the fort, declaring that the shores of Lake Ontario were French territory, citing the French posts—Niagara, Frontenac, La Famine, Fort des Sables, and others—as proof of possession, and stating, menacingly, that Fort Oswego's existence threatened the peace between the two crowns. Burnet rejected the demand, politely, firmly, and at length. Beauharnois began mustering an army to attack the fort, but wiser counsel prevailed and he referred the

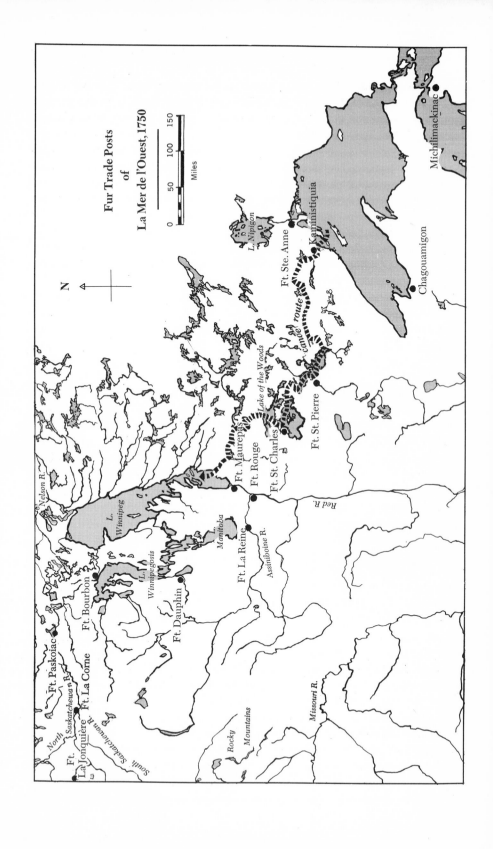

Fur Trade Posts
of
La Mer de l'Ouest, 1750

Miles

0   50   100   150

N

Michilimackinac

Chagouamigon

Kaministiquia

Ft. Ste. Anne

L. Nipigon

canoe route

Lake of the Woods

Ft. St. Pierre

Ft. Maurepas

Ft. Rouge

Ft. St. Charles

Red R.

L. Winnipeg

Manitoba

Assiniboine R.

Ft. La Reine

Nelson R.

L. Winnipegosis

Ft. Bourbon

Ft. Dauphin

Ft. Paskoiac

Ft. La Corne

North Saskatchewan R.

Ft. La Jonquière

South Saskatchewan R.

Missouri R.

Rocky Mountains

matter to the minister. The following year the answer came that no overt military action must be taken against Oswego.[19] It had been a near thing.

All that the French could do was to keep the price of their trade goods at Niagara as low as possible. For this reason the fur trade at this post and at Fort Frontenac was not farmed out to the highest bidder. These forts were maintained as the king's posts. By adroit diplomacy and the lavish use of presents the French were able to hold their position. Yet they had had a nasty shock. The wooden, stockaded post at Niagara was replaced by a massive stone fort, and the construction was begun on a chain of forts down Lake Champlain, guarding an area which they were determined to hold for its timber and reputed mineral wealth as well as for military reasons. Chambly and St. Jean on the Richelieu had been built earlier. Now Fort Frédéric at Crown Point was built at the southern narrows of the lake, in the hope that it would effectively bar this main invasion route in any future war. During the ensuing fifteen years the lands on both sides of the northern part of Lake Champlain were conceded as seigneuries, but only around the fort was any attempt made at settlement.

Meanwhile, in the west the French position improved greatly when the fur trade was suddenly revitalized. In 1714 it was discovered that the huge surplus that had glutted the market had been ruined by vermin, and beaver was now in short supply.[20] The market responded swiftly. The following year the price of greasy beaver rose to 60 *sols* and by 1746 the price was up to 80 *sols* for greasy beaver and 75 *sols* for dry beaver. To meet competition of the English traders with their better quality duffel and strouds, and to curb the Albany smuggling trade, supplies were imported from England. Efforts were made to have the Languedoc woolen mills produce cloth of comparable quality.[21] Vaudreuil and the intendant Michel Bégon declared that with commandants and garrisons once again at the western posts the renegade *coureurs de bois* could be kept in line and disputes between Indian nations adjudicated. They also maintained that as long as the Indians could obtain trade goods close at hand they would not trouble to make the long voyage to Albany or the Hudson's Bay Company posts. This became French policy after 1713: to maintain garrisoned posts throughout the west wherever there was the possibility of the Anglo-American traders breaking through, and with the handful of men at the posts to retain the Indian nations in the French alliance.

Every spring some hundred canoes, each manned by from five to ten men, left Montreal for the western posts, transporting trade goods and supplies for the garrisons, up the Ottawa River to Michilimackinac, west from Lake Michigan to the Sioux country, over the height of land from Lake Superior to the Mer de l'Ouest—the vast region centered about Lake Winnipeg—and beyond it along the Saskatchewan River to the foothills of the Rocky Mountains.[22] Some of them went no farther than Michilimack-inac, Green Bay, or Kaministiquia, then returned with cargoes of pelts for the merchants of Montreal. Some stayed on to trade with the Indians, and still others were almost permanent residents in the west, going out from the main posts in three-man canoes to trade with the far distant nations.

There was nothing casual about the procedure that had to be followed before the men embarked for the west. The merchant had to obtain a permit from the governor general permitting him to send one or more canoes to a specified post and to trade only within the limits of that particular post; the number of men, their names, and places of residence in the colony were specified; the men were all required to have muskets and were limited to four jugs of brandy each, which they were not allowed on any pretext to use in trade with the Indians. It was strictly forbidden on pain of a 300 *livres* fine to make any changes in the crew list, for *voyageurs* to give false names, or to list as place of residence parishes other than those where they usually resided. By means of these regulations the authorities kept a careful check on all who left the colony for the west and knew approximately where the men were at all times. The individual *voyageurs* signed contracts, duly notarized, with the merchant who hired them. These contracts stipulated the destination, duration of the voyage, wages, and the position in the canoe—stern, bow, or center. If the men were permitted to take some goods to trade on their own account, the amount was stipulated.[23] In the weeks before the brigades left Montreal the notaries were kept busy drawing up and filing the contracts; the local authorities were equally busy registering the permits, checking the crew lists, and making sure that the men had their muskets and no more than the stipulated amount of brandy. Needless to say, evasion of the latter restriction did not tax the ingenuity of the *voyageurs* unduly.

The minister wanted the western posts to be maintained at little or no cost to the crown. To this end the fur trade at most of them was leased to the officers appointed to command. Detroit, Niagara, and Fort Frontenac were maintained as the king's posts to ensure that trade goods there would be competitive with Oswego prices, and at Michilimackinac the trade was open to all licensed traders. The commandants of the leased posts had to pay the costs of maintaining the garrison, and also a padre, a surgeon, and a blacksmith. At first the cost of these leases was kept low, about six to seven thousand *livres* a year, to ensure low prices to the Indians for goods and maintain good relations with them.

Some commandants could not resist the lure of profit and charged all that the traffic would bear, making their fortunes in a few years. Since there was seemingly no way of preventing this, the minister decided that the crown might as well be the gainer, and the posts were auctioned off to the highest bidders. This drove the price of trade goods higher than ever, and French relations with the Indians suffered in consequence. To curb these abuses the Comte de La Galissonière, who served as governor general in 1748–1749, decided to lease out only such posts as Temiskaming, Nipigon,

Kaministiquia, Chagouamigon and those in the Mer de l'Quest area where the Indians were far removed from any contact with the Anglo-American traders. At the other posts the trade was carried out by permit holders, traders licensed to trade at a specified post and nowhere else. Galissonière hoped by these means to keep the price of goods low and the Indians satisfied.[24]

Under his successor, the Marquis de la Jonquière, and the intendant François Bigot private profit was the main consideration. The governor general appointed the post commanders, but reserved the trade at two of the most profitable posts for himself. This resulted in all manner of intrigues, as the leading Canadian families contended for the governor's favor. Those who were disappointed, or did not receive the particular post they had hoped for, were at daggers drawn with the more successful contenders.[25] On at least one occasion the commanders at different posts quarreled over the limits of their territories. In the 1750s Joseph Marin, commandant at La Baye, and the Chevalier de La Vérendrye, who commanded at Chagouamigon, disputed the territory at the headwaters of the Mississippi. Marin claimed that La Vérendrye had confiscated his men's goods and had forbidden the Indians to trade at his posts in the disputed area.

Large amounts of capital were required to provide the trade goods needed at the posts, and to transport both goods and furs to and from Montreal. The officers who obtained posts formed companies, consisting mainly of relatives, to raise the capital and handle the trade. Business alliances were cemented by marriage alliances; the family of one post commander married into the family of another, the better to protect their trading interests. The lion's share of the western fur trade was controlled by a coterie of interrelated, wealthy families forming a military and commercial colonial aristocracy with the governor general and the intendant at its head.

In the mid-eighteenth century the profits to be made at certain of the posts were reputed to be enormous. It was claimed that La Baye, which comprised the territory from Green Bay to the Mississippi, north to the Lake Superior watershed, south to a point below the Wisconsin River, and which contained at least four sub-posts—Forts La Jonquière, Beauharnois, Vaudreuil, and Duquesne (the last not to be confused with the fort of the same name on the Ohio)—gave an annual clear profit of 150,000 *livres*; and that the commander, Joseph Marin de la Malgue, lieutenant in the Troupes de la Marine, received two-thirds of it, the rest going to the governor and intendant.[26] The private correspondence of the post commanders would, however, lead one to think that their profits were not nearly as great as they were sometimes made out to be.

In return for these emoluments the post commanders were required to police the west, to strive to keep the peace among tribes that were constantly warring with each other and make sure that they remained in the French allegiance and had no dealings with the English; to maintain order among the *voyageurs* and oblige them to abide by the regulations governing their activities. In addition they had to search constantly for workable mineral deposits, and those who commanded the more westerly posts were enjoined to search for the western ocean. Most of them appear to have had little time to spare for this last. Keeping peace among the nations was a full-time job, and too often Canadians were killed in the intermittent tribal skirmishes. When this occurred, little could be done; those responsible could not be brought to account, as the Indians in the west did not submit to the law of the French. Sudden death at the hands of the Indians had to be accepted as an occupational hazard.

The journal of Joseph Marin, commandant at La Baye in 1753–1754, tells of an Illinois attack on the Saki in which three Indians and a French blacksmith were killed. Marin traveled from village to village cajoling and threatening the Sakis, Fox, and Sioux tribes, and with the aid of brandy and presents he persuaded them to abandon their plans for reprisals, pointing out that the Illinois had merely sought revenge for much greater losses suffered earlier at their hands. Marin informed the governor general: "I can assure you that since last autumn, when I arrived at the Wisconsin, it has cost me at least 10,000 *livres* to restrain that large war party as well as several others and make them agree to remain at peace."[27] On occasion more subtle ways were used to influence the Indians. When a party of Sakis decided to go to Quebec to see Governor Duquesne, Marin arranged to have them call on his brother-in-law in Montreal and be entertained one evening with a magic-lantern show.

Sometimes, despite the best efforts of the post commanders, war could not be avoided. Such was the case in the Fox wars in the early years of the century. More, however, was at issue here than tribal blood feuds. Just as the Huron, Ottawa, and Illinois had earlier sought to retain a middleman's position and prevent the French from trading directly with the western nations, so too had the Fox of the Wisconsin River area sought to prevent the French from traversing their lands to trade directly with the Sioux. This powerful tribe barred the way to French westward expansion at the time when the fur trade was reviving, and launched stinging attacks on the tribes commercially allied with the French. Since it was the posts in the Illinois country that were suffering the most from this warfare and the attendant disruption of trade, and since these posts in 1717 had been placed under the authority of the governor of Louisiana, the governor general at Quebec, Rigaud de Vaudreuil, was accused of being less than anxious to take firm measures against the Fox. It appeared to the minister of marine that Vaudreuil and the Canadian fur traders regarded the Fox almost as allies in a struggle with Louisiana for control of the western trade.[28]

With beaver becoming scarce in the Great Lakes area and the regent, the Duc d'Orléans, much interested in the discovery of a route to the western ocean, it became imperative that the Fox barrier be breached.

Vaudreuil's successor, the Marquis de Beauharnois, launched a full-scale campaign against them. Four hundred Canadians and 1200 allied Indians destroyed their abandoned villages. Further campaigns were launched in 1730, 1731, and 1734, before they were crushed. The lesson was not lost on the other western nations. The French had finally demonstrated their ability to muster large forces in the west to destroy any nation that opposed them. There was nothing the Indian nations respected so much as strength; fear of the long arm of the governor at Quebec, more than anything else, kept them in the French allegiance. And the French could maintain their hold on the west by means of their far-flung network of fur trade posts only because of their alliance with these western nations.

While the Fox were still a threat, and the Sioux nation was both too powerful and too suspicious of the French to allow easy trade or travel west of the upper Mississippi, Pierre Gaultier de Varennes, sieur de La Vérendrye, his sons, and nephew began their active search for the western sea. From 1728 until 1744 the Vérendryes traveled far over the western plains, reaching, it is believed, the foothills of the Rockies, the Big Horn Mountains. To finance their explorations, they were granted the usual form of fur trade lease on the area around Lake Winnipeg, known as the Mer de l'Ouest, and the minister was never able to disabuse himself of the notion that, like La Salle a half century earlier, the Vérendryes were using exploration merely as a means to exploit the fur trade of the far west. Yet there can be no doubt that they explored a vast area and discovered the most practical routes—and best trading regions—for extending French control of the interior. It was they, for example, who discovered that the Saskatchewan River system was a much better route to the west than the Missouri. By using the northern route the dangerous Sioux country was bypassed; moreover, the furs of the north were of better quality and posts in this area blocked the flow of furs to Hudson Bay. Canoe travel was much easier on the Saskatchewan than on the Missouri, and along the entire northern route, until the Blackfeet were reached, the Cree tongue was understood and sufficed for trade with all the tribes.

During these years the trade in Indian slaves at the western posts became a sizable item, up to sixty a year being shipped to Montreal. Most of them appear to have been Panis, or Pawnee, a numerous tribe inhabiting lands on the Missouri, but many were Sioux, captured by the Ottawa and Cree tribes of the north. Indeed it was said of La Vérendrye that while he commanded the posts of the Mer de l'Ouest, he shipped more slaves to Montreal than bales of fur. This cost him dearly; one of his sons was killed by the Sioux in reprisal. In the 1730s Governor General Beauharnois strictly forbade the purchase of Assiniboin slaves, obviously for political reasons, but in 1748 his successor, the Comte de La Galissonière, wrote Le Gardeur de St. Pierre, commandant at Michilimackinac, to complain that no slaves had been sent down to Montreal from Michilimackinac that year and that they were badly needed. The only way he could persuade the Mission Indians to give up the Anglo-American captives taken in raids on the English colonies was to exchange them for Indian slaves. St. Pierre was therefore instructed to purchase six or eight next spring for the king's account, if they were not too expensive. The governor noted, "that will serve to satisfy the most stubborn of our *domiciliés.*"[29]

In 1743 the long era of peace came to an end. The commercial element in England had become more than uneasy over the economic resurgence of France. French overseas commerce had grown by leaps and bounds; in the West Indies, India, the Levant, French manufactures were pushing English goods, even woolen cloth, off the market. France signed a commercial treaty with Turkey in 1740, and it strengthened its alliances with Spain and Sweden. Once again France was the leading power in Europe.[30] Spain too began taking a firmer stand against England. English ships, long accustomed to disregard Spanish trade regulations, were now seized by the *guarda costas*. The loss of this rich contraband trade brought shrill protests from British merchants and shipowners. During one skirmish with the Spanish a certain Captain Jenkins had an ear severed, but he preserved it in pickle and it was subsequently to enjoy considerable prominence.

Although Robert Walpole, George I's prime minister, was opposed to war with Spain or France for fear of uniting these powers against Britain, his control over Parliament was slipping. His political foes, led by the Duke of Newcastle, allied themselves with the merchants of the seaport towns to bring on hostilities with Spain. This faction was convinced that peace was ruinous, that France in particular was the beneficiary of peace, and that only war with both Spain and France could prevent the latter country becoming predominant in Europe and also in America. What the commercial element and Walpole's political foes wanted was a preventive or spoiling war with France.[31] By the end of June 1739 their maneuvers had succeeded in bringing on hostilities with Spain, and a declaration of war followed in October. Only the death of the emperor Charles VI, which upset the balance of power in Europe and necessitated involved diplomatic realignments, prevented hostilities from breaking out between France and England a few months later. This only delayed the conflict. By spring 1743 the Royal Navy was attacking French ships on the high seas; a year later, after the death of the ever cautious Cardinal Fleury, France declared war on Great Britain.

In America the War of the Austrian Succession, or King George's War, followed much the same pattern as had the War of the Spanish Succession. New York was not at all anxious to take an active part. Its ships still traded with the French West Indies, and the contraband trade continued with Montreal. The Iroquois showed no desire to engage in offensive military operations against Canada. Pennsylvania wanted no part of any war, except commercial profits. Only New England saw something to be gained by taking the field; namely, Louisbourg. This fortress on the desolate, fog-bound, eastern shore of Cape Breton served as a haven for the French navy and privateers, who were causing havoc among the New England fishing and trading fleets. It had also become a thriving entrepôt for trade between Canada and the West Indies. Its capture would eliminate the menace and allow New England ships more scope in the contraband trade with the French West Indies.

In 1745 Governor William Shirley of Massachusetts succeeded in orga-nizing an expedition of colonial militia to attack Louisbourg. Commodore Peter Warren of the Royal Navy was persuaded to bring his three ships from Antigua, and by the end of April they had invested the walled town. The commandant, Louis Du Chambon, was gravely concerned lest his men, who had mutinied the previous year, deliver the place to the foe. When the enemy appeared, however, they responded well enough upon being prom-ised a pardon. After a heavy bombardment lasting nearly seven weeks the town was in ruins, and with no hope of relief from France, on June 27 the garrison capitulated. The terms of surrender were promptly dishonored by the undisciplined New England forces bent on pillage. Subsequent French attempts to retake the fortress ended disastrously and New England held it until the end of the war.

The loss of Louisbourg caused consternation in Canada. The fortifica-tions at Quebec and Fort Frederic on Lake Champlain were hastily strengthened; beacon fires were made ready down the St. Lawrence; and the old Canadian policy of frontier raids began once again. In November 1745 a force of 400 Canadians and 200 Abenakis struck deep into New York territory, destroying Saratoga; some 30 settlers were killed and about 100 taken prisoner. Smaller parties ravaged other settlements from the environs of Albany to the outskirts of Boston. Attempts by the authorities in the English colonies to induce the Iroquois to attack New France were una-vailing. These nations once again declined to risk attacks by the French and their western allies merely to protect the Anglo-Americans. Only the Mo-hawk launched a few raids on the outlying French settlements along the Richelieu, killing some people and burning outlying farms. The English colonies had to fend for themselves, and in this type of warfare their militia was no match for the Canadians.

In the west, however, the French faced a more serious threat. Traders from Pennsylvania had flooded over the Alleghenies, and the low prices of their goods were very tempting to the Indians south of the Ohio. This occurred at a time when, owing to profiteering on the part of the merchants in France who supplied the colony and the avarice of the leaseholders of the western posts, trade goods at the French posts were in very short supply and were selling at exorbitant prices. In 1747, after the capture of Louis-bourg had completely disrupted trade between France and its American

Rolland Michel Barrin

Chev Marquis de La Galissoniere

Chevalier de l'Ordre Royal et militaire de St Louis

Capitaine des vaisseaux du Roy, Commandant General

pour sa Majesté dans toutte la nouvelle france, Terres

et pais de la Loüisianne.

Il Est Ordonné au S. Groschene Rimbault

Cadet dans les troupes, d'aller a la guerre avec le

parti de sauvages commandé par le S. Gaultier de Varenne.

Il luy est recommandé de traitter humainement les

prisonniers qu'il pourra faire, et d'engager les sauvages

a faire la même chose; a Montreal le 24. May 1748.

La Galissoniere

Par Monseigneur

colonies, the price of goods in the west was higher than ever, and some post commanders had no goods at all. Not only were supplies from France cut off but the Mohawk had effectively stopped the normal flow of contraband goods from Albany to Montreal. Given these circumstances, all the western and northern tribes were more than usually willing to entertain suggestions from the Anglo-American traders, brought surreptitiously to their villages by emissaries of the western Iroquois.

The conspiracy to drive the French out of the west spread from village to village. But the tribal chiefs were unable to control their young braves, or one tribe to trust another very far. With communications dependent on word of mouth passed along the canoe routes, coordination was extremely difficult. At Detroit, on May 20, 1747, a band of Huron captured and tortured to death five *voyageurs,* and stole their canoe load of furs. Later they killed all the cattle in the settlement. Three other *voyageurs* were killed en route from Detroit to Michilimackinac. Two eight-man canoes were attacked near Lake Michigan, en route to the Mer de l'Ouest; only one escaped. At Grosse Île a Canadian was stabbed by the Saulteur, who intended to attack the fort. When the garrison made ready to defend themselves, the Indians thought better of it, but here too they killed the cattle.

From all the posts in the Great Lakes basin came reports that a general uprising was being planned. The commandants abandoned their outlying posts, concentrating their men within the main forts, and tried to reason with the chiefs, employing all the usual threats and blandishments. The situation was eased in September when a reinforcement of 150 men reached Detroit from Montreal, and the *voyageurs* from the Mer de l'Ouest arrived at Michilimackinac with the furs from the posts on the northern plains. The following year several ships reached Quebec from France, bringing news

---

Commission for a war party against the English colonies, 1748. (Archives du Séminaire de Québec)

> Rolland Michel Barrin, Chevalier Marquis de La Galissonière, Knight of the Royal and Military Order of St. Louis, Captain of the King's ships, Commander General for His Majesty in all New France, lands and territories of Louisiana.

> The Sieur Groschène Raimbault, cadet in the troops, is ordered to go to war with the Indian party commanded by the Sieur Gaultier de Varenne. He is charged to treat humanely the prisoners that he takes and to urge the Indians to do the same.

> At Montreal, 24 May 1748

> [signed] La Galissonière

that hostilities had ceased in Europe. With this, the price of goods was reduced by more than half.[32] The commandants in the western posts were now able to regain control of the situation. The threatened insurrection had shown all too clearly that the French hold on the west was completely dependent on their maintaining control over the Indian nations, who had no desire to be subservient—whether to France, England, or another Indian nation. They would remain in the French allegiance not a day longer than it served their interests to do so.

In Europe meanwhile France and Britain sacrificed the interests of their allies and in July 1748 came to terms. In October, at Aix-la-Chapelle the peace treaty was signed. For France, colonial commerce and the Grand Banks fishing had become such large items on its economic balance sheet that Louis XV, urged on by the Comte de Maurepas, the minister of marine, was willing to cede the Maréchal de Saxe's conquests in the Netherlands, as well as Madras, in return for Louisbourg. This fortified naval base was regarded as vital to protect the French fisheries, to guard the entrance to the St. Lawrence, and as the entrepôt in the Canada–West Indies trade. Moreover, Maurepas was determined to rebuild the French navy to the point where it could protect French overseas trade against the English. The fishing grounds off Cape Breton were regarded as vital to train a large number of seamen who could serve in a reconstituted navy in time of war. The French populace and the people of New England failed to appreciate these factors. The one regarded the abandonment of the Netherlands conquests as wanton stupidity; the other considered the return of Louisbourg to the French as a sacrifice of their great efforts and interests.

During the course of the war French overseas commerce had suffered drastically at the hands of the Royal Navy. Between 1710 and 1741 the value of trade with the French colonies had increased from 25 million *livres* a year to 140 million *livres*. In 1741 the total of France's overseas trade was estimated to be worth 300 million *livres*.[33] In the final year of the war this trade had been seriously disrupted, while England's imports from the West Indies alone rose from £7,500,000 to £11,500,000 a year.[34] The French colonies were far too important an item on the national balance sheet to be treated lightly. A strong navy had become a necessity for France, yet there was little hope that it could establish a navy equal to, let alone greater than, that of Britain. Even a combined French and Spanish fleet would be no match for the British. Means had to be found to disperse Britain's naval strength and prevent it from blockading French ports, as it had done in the final year of the war.

In Canada the Comte de la Galissonière, sent to serve as governor general in 1748, took careful stock of the imperial situation. Soldier, scientist, man of letters, polished product of the Enlightenment, and, unlike some of his predecessors, with no private interests to push in the colony, he sat in the Château St. Louis at Quebec, studied maps, and questioned everyone. Very quickly he grasped the essence of the North American situation, and, what is more, saw clearly its relevance to the greater strategic problem implicit in the continuing Anglo-French imperial rivalry. In short succinct dispatches to the minister of marine he stated what had to be done, the reforms that had to be made in the administration of the west, the fortifications that had to be strengthened or built where none existed, the need to increase the colony's permanent military establishment, and the need to destroy Oswego.

But of all his recommendations, those contained in his dispatch No. 10, dated September 1748, were the most significant. He declared categorically that the Illinois country was of very little economic value to France, that for a long time posts and settlements there would merely be a source of expense to the crown and that the French settlers in the region would certainly not become very prosperous. Yet, he declared, the crown must maintain them, regardless of the expense, to protect the investment already made, but, more significantly, because they served as a barrier to English expansion, enabling the French to dominate the Indian nations of the lower Mississippi and retain their trade and allegiance. If, he noted, there had been four to five hundred French in the area during the past war, the posts in the southwest would not have been threatened by the Indian nations; instead the very tribes that had insulted the French could have been led in war parties to attack the heart of the English colonies. He then made the most significant point of all: "we should never delude ourselves that our colonies on the continent . . . could ever rival the neighbouring English colonies in wealth, nor even be commercially very lucrative, for with the exception of the fur trade the extent of which is limited and the profits continually declining, these colonies can furnish only goods similar to those of Europe at higher prices and of poorer quality."

This was merely the negative side of the colonial picture. He then turned to its other aspects. Although France could not hope to reap large or easy profits from Canada and Louisiana, these colonies were extremely fertile and could sustain a large population with little or no outside help. For a long time to come their only real value would lie in the caliber of the men they nourished, and in a short while they would produce men in such numbers that far from having to fear the English colonies or the Indian nations, they could lay down the law to both. Moreover—and here was the crux of his argument—the English set such great store by their American colonies that they would be forced to divert a sizable part of their navy and army merely to protect them, thereby reducing the forces that they could employ aggressively in other theaters. But were the Anglo-Americans ever to seize the Illinois country—and they had easy access to it—Canada's trade with the interior would be destroyed, Louisiana would quickly be lost, and the Spanish colonies, even Mexico, would then be in grave danger.[35]

Here it was, a restatement of Louis XIV's policy decision of 1700; the encirclement of the English colonies to bar them from the west, for reasons of imperial strategy. Basically, it was a dog-in-the-manger policy, but according to the prevailing eighteenth-century concepts it was perfectly correct. Colonies existed to further the aims of the mother country, not the other way around. If hindsight be eliminated, and given the facts of the situation as they were known to La Galissonière, his policy had much to recommend it. The Canadian population, which was now over 55,000, was doubling every generation, and given the fact that the Canadians had more than held their own in the past everywhere except in Acadia, where they had suffered defeats more in consequence of bad luck and bad management than as a result of Anglo-American military effectiveness, there were good grounds for believing that the French could both deny the west to Britain and cause the British to dissipate their maritime strength in the North American theater.

La Galissonière had no way of knowing that the ground rules in this North American conflict were about to be changed. A powerful element in England was still determined to destroy French overseas trade, and to its clamor was now added that of land speculators, including some of the leading men in Virginia, North Carolina, and Pennsylvania, and also of influential men in London. A few months after La Galissonière wrote his dispatch of September 1, 1748, the Ohio Company was formed. With capital provided by some of the leading Virginia plantation owners—Lees, Fairfaxes, Washingtons—and by prominent London merchants, this company acquired title from the crown to half a million acres in the Ohio Valley. Before the anticipated vast profits could be realized by selling sections to land-hungry settlers, the region had to be surveyed and the Indians bought or driven out. The directors of the company were determined that nothing, least of all the French, should stand in their way, and with the backing of the English mercantile war hawks they had good reason to be sanguine. The French now had to contend with a force far more formidable than Anglo-American fur traders. The military fur trade frontier was about to clash, head on, with the Anglo-American land settlement frontier.

◁ **8** ▷

The Military Frontier, 1748-1760

*B*y 1748 Anglo-American fur traders, some from Virginia but mainly from Pennsylvania, controlled the fur trade of the Ohio Valley. For a quarter of a century they had been trading with the Indians west of the Alleghenies and had established a chain of outposts along three main routes leading to the main trading posts of Venango and Logstown on the Ohio and in the Miami village of Pickawillany well north of the river. Their posts and close commercial relations with the Indian nations, the Delaware, Miami, Shawnee, and Iroquois, gave the British a *de facto* degree of sovereignty over this vast region similar to that exercised by the French north of the Great Lakes. In 1749 the Comte de Raymond, commandant at Fort des Miamis, reported that there were 300 Anglo-American traders in the area, cheap English goods were pouring in, and the Indian nations were solidly in the English interest.[1]

Some of these fur traders, men like George Croghan, were also agents of land speculation companies that were springing up like mushrooms to exploit the lands west of the Alleghenies. The rapid increase in population in the English colonies, by mid-century estimated to be about a million and a quarter, and the scarcity of cheap land in the older settled areas caused land-hungry men to look westward to the virgin wilderness beyond the mountains. Here was rich land, waiting to be grasped. That it was the hunting grounds of the Indian nations meant nothing to them. Would-be settlers began moving through the gaps in the mountains, building their cabins, and clearing the forest.

In a somewhat more legal fashion men with the right connections in high places and some capital formed companies to obtain title to vast areas from the colonial and home governments. Negotiations were entered into with complacent Indian leaders to cede the lands, roads were begun, and the grants surveyed. Once all this was done sections could be sold, and every section settled raised the value of the adjoining lands. The company shareholders reserved choice tracts for themselves and could hope that within a few years they would end up as the rich, respected possessors of large estates, secure in the knowledge that they had helped to advance civilization and their nation's destiny. Before all this could come to pass the conflicting claims of rival companies had to be reconciled and the Indians appeased or eliminated, but the speculators were confident that these problems could be overcome or somehow circumvented. Events were to prove them right, even though it required a world war, a revolution, and the disruption of two great empires to accomplish their aims.

In the 1740s the Iroquois Confederacy claimed that the headwaters of the Ohio and adjacent lands belonged to them and that their sanction had to be obtained before anyone, Indian or European, made any arrangements affecting the territory. Unlike the English land speculators, the French felt obliged to recognize the Iroquois claim, but they were not prepared to see this strategic area fall to the English by default. They saw, more clearly than did the Ohio tribes, that English fur trade posts would eventually give way to farming settlements and towns supporting a sizable, stable, Anglo-American population. Chabert de Joncaire, officer in the Troupes de la Marine, warned the Iroquois of this, declaring that, unlike the English, the French had no designs on their country. "The English," he said, "are much less anxious to take away your peltries than to become masters of your lands . . . and your blindness is so great, that you do not perceive that the very hand that caresses you, will scourge you, like negroes and slaves, so soon as it will have got possession of those lands."[2] A few years later, in 1754, the French Mission Iroquois put the entire issue very succinctly:

> Brethren, are you ignorant of the difference between our Father and the English? Go see the forts our Father has erected, and you will see that the land beneath his walls is still hunting ground, having fixed himself in those places we frequent, only to supply our wants; whilst the English, on the contrary, no sooner get possession of a country than the game is forced to leave it; the trees fall down before them, the earth becomes bare, and we find among them hardly wherewithal to shelter us when the night falls.[3]

That this appraisal of the situation was a very sound one there can be no doubt. The Ohio Company, having gained title to these lands in the Ohio Valley, intended to settle them, and its schemes made no provision for Indian hunting grounds. Yet the Iroquois, Miami, Shawnee, Delaware, all the tribes of the Ohio region, declined to heed the warnings. Some of them may well have recognized the ultimate threat posed by the presence of Anglo-American posts on their territory, but they were dependent on them. Were the Anglo-American traders to have been driven out, they would have had to take their peltries either to the French in the Illinois country, at Fort Miamis, Detroit, or Niagara; or to the Anglo-Americans at Oswego; or to the Pennsylvania traders in the Susquehanna valley. If the French had had posts on the upper Ohio, their attitude might have been different; as it was, they saw only that life would be more difficult were the Anglo-American posts to be removed.

The governor general at Quebec, Galissonière, decided that a show of force was needed to bring the Indians to their senses. He dispatched an expeditionary force of Canadian militia, some Troupes de la Marine, and a small party of Mission Iroquois and Abenakis, some 230 men in all. To lead the expedition, he chose a Canadian, Pierre-Joseph Céloron de Blainville, a regular officer with years of experience as commandant in the west. With him went several other experienced Canadian officers, as well as Father Joseph-Pierre de Bonnécamps to serve as chaplain and secretary. Father Bonnécamps' duties included writing a description of the area traversed and preparing maps, because the French still had only a very imperfect knowledge of the region.[4] The main purpose of the expedition was to claim the Ohio Valley for France, persuade the Indian tribes to break with the English and ally themselves with the French, and drive the Anglo-American traders out.

Going to the Ohio by way of Niagara, Rivière aux Boeufs, and the Allegheny, Céloron buried lead plates at various points along the way and nailed to trees metal plaques bearing the arms of the French crown. The Anglo-American traders they encountered en route were ordered to leave the country at once and not to return. It proved much easier to overawe these few individual traders than the Indians, who remained singularly unimpressed by the French presence and made their hostility obvious when they were in sufficient numbers. It was so marked at the Miami village of Pickawillany that Céloron was obliged to leave hurriedly, proceeding to Fort des Miamis, where he found the buildings dilapidated and the twenty-two man garrison all ill with fever. The situation in the Ohio was worse than had been feared.

La Galissonière's successor, Pierre-Jacques de Taffanel, marquis de La Jonquière, decided to try to woo the Indian nations away from the Anglo-Americans by means of persuasion and presents rather than by force. Captain Philippe de Joncaire was dispatched to the Ohio with a small party. At Logstown he confronted George Croghan and Andrew Montour, who had come from Pennsylvania with ten other traders bringing some £700 worth of presents. Although Joncaire remained in the region, he was able to make little headway in his attempts to win over the Ohio tribes, as they had no desire whatsoever to be forced to choose sides. They wanted neither European power to dominate them, but if they had to choose, it would be the side able to muster the most strength. In 1752 this appeared to be the Anglo-Americans. That year nine Canadian traders were killed by Indians in disputes of one sort or another in the country south of Lake Erie. It was clear that the French could not hope to prevail upon the Indians to drive the English back over the Allegheny Mountains. They would have to do it themselves.

The minister of marine agreed with this view of the situation. In his instructions to Ange de Menneville, marquis de Duquesne, appointed governor general of New France in 1752 on the death of Jonquière, the minister reasserted that the Ohio and its tributaries were to be held by France. The English traders were to be driven out and French forts established to hold the area, with provision of ample trade goods to supply the needs of the local tribes. The Indian nations were to be free to go to the English colonies to trade if they wished, but no Anglo-American traders were to be allowed to trespass on French-claimed territory.[5] Before Duquesne could put these orders into effect, Charles-Michel Langlade, at the head of some 240 Saulteur and Ottawa from Michilimackinac, descended on Fort Pickawillany. After a brisk engagement they took some of the English traders prisoner, burned their cabins, killed, boiled, and ate the Miami chief La Demoiselle, who had been a staunch supporter of the Anglo-Americans, then swiftly departed. From this point on English influence in the Ohio began to wane.

At Quebec Duquesne was making plans to hold the headwaters of the Ohio with forces sufficient to repel any attempts the English might make to occupy the area. In the spring of 1753 he sent 300 Troupes de la Marine, 1700 Canadian militia, and some 200 Indians to Lake Erie under the command of Captain Pierre-Paul de la Malgue, sieur de Marin, a tough veteran of the west born, as Duquesne put it, with a tomahawk in his hand. Although Duquesne was uncertain where the limits of French territory actually lay, he assumed them to be the crest of the mountain range thought to run south of the Ohio. Marin's orders were to construct a road from Lake Erie to the headwaters of the Ohio and to establish forts at strategic points in the area.[6] The expedition built and garrisoned Fort Presqu'île, began a wagon road to the head of the Rivière aux Boeufs, then hauled supplies over it to build a fort there and another to be named Fort Duquesne further on at the forks of the Ohio.

Marin drove himself and his men brutally hard. His own health ruined, he refused to return to Montreal to recuperate, preferring to die on campaign like a soldier. Several hundred of his men were not given the choice;

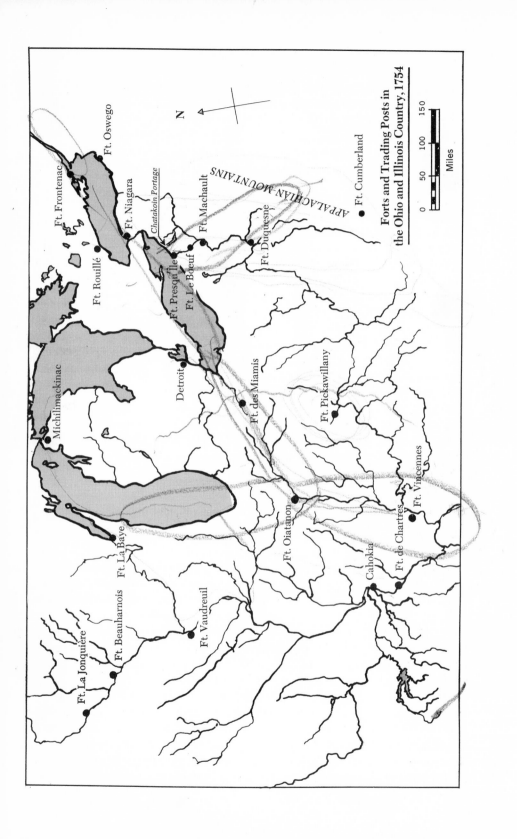

N

Forts and Trading Posts in the Ohio and Illinois Country, 1754

Miles

0   50   100   150

Ft. Oswego

Ft. Frontenac

Ft. Niagara

Chatakoin Portage

Ft. Machault

Ft. Duquesne

Ft. Cumberland

APPALACHIAN MOUNTAINS

Ft. Rouillé

Ft. Presqu'Ile

Ft. Le Boeuf

Detroit

Michilimackinac

Ft. des Miamis

Ft. Pickawillany

Ft. La Baye

Ft. Oiatanon

Ft. Vincennes

Ft. de Chartres

Cahokia

Ft. Beauharnois

Ft. La Jonquière

Ft. Vaudreuil

they were worked to death hauling supplies on their backs through swamps and forest, down the shallow river, unloading and hauling the goods over portages ten to fifteen miles long. Before the Allegheny was reached, fewer than 800 of the more than 2000 men who had left Montreal were fit to walk. Weakened by bad food, worn out by their exertions, over 400 perished. The plan to build Fort Duquesne had to be abandoned for the time being. Forts Presqu'île and Le Boeuf were garrisoned and the survivors made their way back to Montreal. When Governor Duquesne reviewed them on their return, he was shaken. Had they been forced to go on to the Ohio, he stated, the route would have been paved with their corpses, and the hostile Indians would likely have seized the opportunity to slaughter any who had not succumbed.

What made the dire consequences of this expedition all the more bitter for the Canadians was the belief that the intendant François Bigot and his coterie had made their fortunes out of the supplies purchased for it.[7] Nor was this all. At Fort Presqu'île, where the men of the garrison received only salt pork and sea biscuits for rations, 200 came down with scurvy, but the officers were well supplied with white bread, fresh meat, and brandy. Adequate supplies of corn and meat could not be obtained from the Indians. In order to counter the French threat, the English colonies had sent the Indians presents of vast amounts of goods, including the inevitable liquor. They had so much of the latter that they were incapable even of hunting for their own meat supplies, let alone providing meat for the French.[8]

Despite the heavy casualties, the newly established presence of the French south of Lake Erie shattered the hold of the English over the area. Their trade dwindled away and several of the Anglo-American traders who had granted very extensive credit to the Indians were ruined. All that the English colonies were able to do in response was dispatch an eight-man party in 1753, led by George Washington, with a letter from Lieutenant Governor Robert Dinwiddie of Virginia to complain of the invasion of British territory by the French and demand their immediate withdrawal. At the first French outpost, Fort Machault—Venango to the English colonials—they were dined and wined by the commandant Philippe de Joncaire. They then proceeded to Fort Le Boeuf, where Washington presented his missive to Jacques le Gardeur de Saint-Pierre. There was something symbolic about the confrontation of these two men. The one was striving to make his way in the world, and as yet giving no indication of certain qualities that later events were to make manifest; the other, an officer of over twenty years' service, most of them as commandant at the western posts among the Sioux and the Cree of the northwestern plains, still retained the manners and bearing of the *noblesse*.

Saint-Pierre's reply to Dinwiddie's rather hectoring missive was couched in restrained phrases; politely but firmly it rejected the governor's assertions that the French had committed acts of hostility against the English or done anything contrary to the treaties between the two crowns. It then stated: "As for your demand that I should withdraw, I do not believe myself obliged to submit; no matter what your instructions may be I am here by virtue of my General's orders, and I beg you not to doubt for one instant that it is my unshaken resolve to comply with them with all the exactitude and firmness that one would expect of the best officer."[9] With that the Virginia embassy had to straggle back in bitter weather to Williamsburg, taking a month to do it. The shareholders of the Ohio Company were not going to gain these lands and realize their hoped-for profits by such means.

Before Governor General Duquesne had received Dinwiddie's letter, he had already made plans to send heavy troop reinforcements to the Ohio and to establish Fort Duquesne before the English could return in force. In early February 1754, 800 troops and militia left Montreal, each man dragging a toboggan with two-months' food supplies. By February 25 they were at Niagara. A hundred men were left to strengthen the garrison there; and 200 remained at Fort Presqu'île, after the ten-mile portage had been improved sufficiently to transport cannon to Rivière aux Boeufs. From there 500 men swept down river by boat and pirogue to the Allegheny, and down the Allegheny to the junction of the Monongahela, where a small Virginia militia force commanded by Captain William Trent had been striving for the preceding few weeks to build a fort. When summoned to surrender, Captain Trent had no choice. He and his forty odd men marched back over the mountains; the French destroyed the unfinished fort and began the construction of Fort Duquesne nearby. This made it plain to the Indians that the French were able to transport much larger forces to the area more quickly than could the Anglo-Americans.

Prior to this the sieur de la Chauvignerie, commandant at the French outpost at Logstown, a few miles downriver, had reported that the Shawnee were hostile to the French, being fearful that the new forts were intended to encompass their destruction; that all the tribes of the region—Miami, Huron, Iroquois, Loup, and Shawnee—were preparing to attack the French and were being urged on by the English. To La Chauvignerie, with only thirty men and short of supplies, amid a horde of seemingly hostile Indians, the situation doubtless looked menacing. To Duquesne, at Quebec, things appeared in a better light. He was convinced that a show of force would bring the Ohio Indians to see where their best interest lay.[10] Claude-Pierre Pécaudy de Contrecoeur, who replaced Le Gardeur de Saint-Pierre as commandant in the Ohio country, informed the Indians bluntly that he would push the English back over the mountains. If the Indians supported the English, they would be crushed; it was up to them whether or not they wished to be destroyed.[11] With the Anglo-American force driven out and the French with their large force clearly in command of the river, the

Indians had little choice. Langlade's earlier swift assault on Pickawillany, followed by the establishment of Fort Duquesne, had shown that the French could strike from both flanks. From this point on, the Indians of the Ohio Valley inclined to the French. It had been close, but the military administrative framework of New France, the ability of the Canadian militia to travel great distances through the wilderness in all seasons, and the governor general's disregard for cost were all in striking contrast to the inadequacies that beset the Anglo-Americans.

The ineffectual attempts the English colonies now made to drive the French out of the Ohio Valley made their inability to cope with the situation even more obvious. George Washington, leading a motley collection of militia, once again crossed the Alleghenies. Contrecoeur, warned of their approach by the Indians, sent a small party of thirty-three men led by Ensign Joseph Coulon de Villiers de Jumonville to meet them and deliver a summons requiring them to retire or suffer the consequences. Should they reject the summons, Contrecoeur declared, force would be met with force and the English officer commanding would be held accountable for the outbreak of hostilities, as "it is our intention to maintain the union that exists between two friendly monarchs."[12] Jumonville appears not to have taken adequate precautions. His party was surrounded at daybreak by Washington with forty of his men and some Iroquois. Controversy has raged from that day to this on what then ensued. Suffice it to say that Jumonville and nine of his men were killed; one man was wounded, and twenty-one were taken prisoner, one escaped and informed the garrison at Fort Duquesne of what had happened.[13] This was the first clash of arms between duly commissioned troops of the rival powers, and it occurred in time of peace.

The reaction of the French was swift. After the incident Washington received reinforcements, of dubious quality, and foolishly decided to hold his ground at his base camp at Great Meadows. The men were set to work strengthening the crude log breastwork of what they aptly named Fort Necessity. Upon learning of the attack on Jumonville's party, Contrecoeur immediately sent a detachment of 500 men and a sizable body of Indians led by Jumonville's brother, Louis Coulon de Villiers, to intercept Washington's party, demand satisfaction for the murder of Jumonville, and drive the Anglo-Americans off French territory.[14] In this they were successful. After a short engagement in which the undisciplined Anglo-American militia, many of them drunk, had thirty killed and seventy wounded, Washington accepted de Villiers' hastily drafted terms. The preamble of the capitulation contained the controversial statement that the French intention was not to disturb the peace which existed between the two monarchs, but to "avenge the murder of one of our officers, the bearer of a summons, and of his escort, as well as to prevent any establishment being made on the lands of the King." Washington signed the capitulation and fled precipitately back over the mountains. He and his men were indeed fortunate that the French officers were able to restrain their Indian allies from massacring them.

In his haste to depart, Washington left behind his papers, including his diary, which Contrecoeur sent to Quebec. Its contents confirmed Duquesne and his officers in the low opinion they had formed of Washington in particular and the Anglo-Americans in general. "So many deserters, so much trouble in the provinces Washington traversed," exclaimed Duquesne when he read it, "so much discord among these troops of different provinces that claim to be independent! It is that which convinces me that we will always defeat such forces, as badly organized as they are unwarlike."[15] Duquesne was, however, disturbed by one of the terms of the capitulation of Fort Necessity. Clause six stated that the English agreed not to work on any establishment beyond the height of land for one year from that date, and Duquesne feared that this was tantamount to an admission that once the year was up the English had the same right as did the French to claim possession of the Ohio country.[16]

The French were now dominant in the Ohio Valley. The Indian nations had all swung to their support. In his brief stand at Fort Necessity, Washington had not had a single Indian ally with him. The French, however, were under no illusions that they could depend on the Ohio nations. Duquesne remarked, before the defeat of Washington's army, that although up to the present the conduct of the Indian allies was highly satisfactory, he would not have been at all surprised to see them remain in stubborn neutrality, to which they naturally inclined "since they feared both sides." He also felt it necessary to keep 500 men at the Ohio posts to check any moves the English might make and to win over the Indians by letting them see that the French were there to stay.

Contrecoeur was ordered not to take any aggressive action against the English, but to remain strictly on the defensive. Anglo-American traders captured by the Indians were to have their goods given to their captors and then to be incarcerated for three months before being sent back over the mountains, but on no account were they to be killed. The Ohio Indians were to be allowed complete freedom to go to the English colonies to trade, but no English traders were to be allowed on French territory. In early spring 1755, three English traders were captured near Fort Duquesne. They claimed they had come only to collect the trade goods they had been obliged to leave behind the previous year. Contrecoeur sent them back over the mountains with a French escort to ensure that the Indians did not harm them. The French were, in fact, being deliberately scrupulous to prove to themselves and everyone else that their conduct was above reproach.[17]

To gain the reluctant support of the Indians by impressing them with French military superiority was one thing, retaining their allegiance was another. To do this the French had to provide them with the goods that the Anglo-American traders had previously supplied, and at similar prices. This proved to be singularly difficult. With the exception of one or two Montreal merchant-traders, the Canadians showed a great reluctance to venture into the Ohio country. Their trade at the older established posts was well organized, and the recent military activity caused them to fear the loss of their goods and probably of men's lives among tribes so markedly hostile in the recent past. Duquesne offered all manner of inducements to persuade traders to send canoes to the Ohio. He promised that they would be given every assistance by all the post commanders; their goods would be transported over the portages by the garrisons free of charge; and if they ran short of trade goods, Contrecoeur was to supply what they needed from the king's stores at low prices. Duquesne still could get only some eleven or twelve canoe loads sent out, despite "the bridge of gold" he made available to save traders the costs of transport. Some of the traders who went did so only out of a sense of duty, and under considerable pressure. In exasperation Duquesne remarked that he could have made the entire colony march more easily than he could get "that breed" to move.

Duquesne also gave strict orders that the traders were to sell the staples of the trade, blankets and powder, at little above Montreal prices; the rest they could charge more for. Before the year was out he ordered that a price list for all goods be established at the posts to keep the Indians from being cheated and remove all grounds for complaints on their part. Contrecoeur was ordered to be more generous than he was reported to have been in giving presents to the Indians, and he was informed that he could regard as his perquisite any presents received from the Indians in return. Duquesne was, however, very displeased to learn that junior officers at the Ohio posts had engaged in trade with the Indians. He ordered this stopped at once. The officers concerned, who had been restricted to taking with them from Montreal only a portmanteau, were to be reported to him and disciplined. Duquesne declared that such actions lowered the dignity of the crown in the eyes of the Indians, and that under the existing circumstances it would be far better to give the goods to them.[18] This was why he was so anxious to have Montreal traders established in the Ohio country, taking merchandise right to the Indian villages. The reluctance shown by the Canadians, despite all Duquesne's pressure and subsidies, makes it very plain that this region was not seized by the French for the fur trade, quite the contrary. Had the Canadians had any say in the matter, they would probably have been quite content to let the English have it. As it was, the crown had to pay heavily to ensure that the Ohio Indians obtained enough goods from the French at prices sufficiently low to keep them satisfied.

Another major problem was keeping the forts themselves adequately supplied. Everything had to be transported from Montreal by canoe to Fort Frontenac, from there to Niagara by canoe or barque, portaged around the gorge, transshipped by barque to Fort Presqu'île, then carted to Fort Rivière aux Boeufs and reloaded on pirogues to navigate that shallow river to the Allegheny and on to Fort Duquesne. Maintaining an adequate supply of canoes, barques, horses, and pirogues was a difficult task. The horses in particular were a problem. They were quickly worn out, and fodder had to be transported from Detroit, or even Montreal.[19] Supplies dictated the number of men that could be maintained at the Ohio forts, and before the onset of winter the majority had to return to Montreal. In February they were marched back over the snow and ice so to be ready to meet the English threat once again. In addition 400 *voyageurs* were kept busy during the summer transporting supplies to the posts, and they consumed goodly quantities of food. Spoilage and breakage sometimes amounted to more than 50 percent of a shipment. Barrels of wine and brandy were particularly vulnerable. In one convoy alone forty-eight canoe loads of supplies were spoiled or stolen at the Niagara portage. Watching the seemingly endless wagon loads that left Montreal for the embarkation point at Lachine gave Duquesne nightmares.

Duquesne had to count on holding the Ohio country with a garrison strength of 500 men at the three forts: 300 at Fort Duquesne and 100 each at Forts Le Boeuf and Presqu'île. The largest number maintained at one time appears to have been less than 1400, and many of these were workmen employed on the construction of the fortifications or *voyageurs* transporting supplies.[20] The only way this many could be maintained was by reducing the bread ration from two to one and a half *livres* a day. This did not improve morale, and the desertion rate gave cause for concern. Considering the back-breaking work the men had to perform, up at three in the morning, hard at it until ten at night, on a diet of bread, stew, and salt pork, the officers frequently running short of wine, and with a heavy drain from sickness, it is amazing that the men gave such a good account of themselves.

Attempts were made to raise food at the posts: pigs, corn, peas, and greens. Duquesne declared that if the forts could not feed themselves, in the same way that the posts in the *pays d'en haut* did, the crown would soon have to abandon them. Nor were matters helped when some officers, more concerned with points of honor—one officer at Fort Duquesne was killed in a duel—than with tedious bourgeois honesty, availed themselves of every opportunity to fill their pockets at the king's expense. The moral climate of the colony had declined drastically with the arrival of Jonquière and Bigot. Their example had convinced too many of the Canadians that to rob the crown was no crime.[21]

In Europe, meanwhile, when the minister of marine received word of the initial clash of arms at Fort Necessity, he expressed doubt that the British government would support the colonial forces in their breach of the peace. He instructed Duquesne "to avoid giving them any just cause of complaint; to manage on occasions in which there may be acts of violence, in such a manner as not to appear the aggressor; and to confine yourself to the adoption of all possible measures to be in a position to repel force by force."[22] It was, of course, relatively easy for the French to adopt this attitude; their forces had not suffered a rather ignominious defeat, and they remained in possession of the Ohio country. The British could not allow this state of affairs to remain uncontested. Moreover, it was apparent that the English colonies, despite their vast preponderance in numbers, were unable to cope with the better organized and more warlike Canadians.[23] The British government therefore decided to send an experienced regular officer, Major General James Braddock, as commander in chief for North America, with two regiments of foot. Two more regiments of regulars were to be recruited in the colonies. With these forces attacks were to be launched on the French at four points: the Acadian frontier, Lake Champlain, to open the invasion route into Canada, Fort Niagara, and Fort Duquesne.

French agents in England were quick to report an increase in activity at the naval dockyards, and this was rightly interpreted to presage offensive action in America. Louis XV ordered 4000 regulars sent to strengthen the garrisons at Louisbourg and Quebec. This would have released the Canadian regulars and militia for service on the frontiers. To prevent this the Honourable Edward Boscawen, Admiral of the Blue, was ordered, although France and England were still at peace, to cruise off Newfoundland and destroy the lightly armed French convoy. The British intercepted only three of the French ships. After declaring, upon being challenged, that their countries were at peace, they got in the first shattering broadsides at close quarters. Two of the three French ships, heavily outgunned, had to strike their flags; the third was too fast for her pursuers and reached Louisbourg. The rest of the convoy also reached Louisbourg or the Gulf of St. Lawrence unscathed. Thus the French lost only ten of the seventy-eight companies of regulars sent out.

This attack on the high seas in time of peace—reminiscent of a similar attack in another ocean some two centuries later, but by no means as successful—had been a distinct failure, and the French were able to proclaim loudly in all the courts of Europe that Albion was more perfidious than had been imagined. Elsewhere the Royal Navy did better. Again without warning, more than 300 French merchant ships and 8000 sailors were seized on the high seas or in English ports.[24] At the very onset of hostilities the French found their maritime strength seriously reduced, and in the end it was this factor that made the difference in North America.

On land the British had no better success than Boscawen had had. General Braddock encountered great difficulty in organizing and supplying his expedition against Fort Duquesne. One element he lacked was Indian allies. He was delayed in his preparations long enough to avoid breaking the letter of the terms of the Fort Necessity capitulation, but the evidence indicates that neither the British nor the colonial authorities had intended to honor it.[25] That he was able to get his army, 2200 strong, over the mountains at all, encumbered as it was by wagon trains of supplies, women camp followers, a herd of cattle, and a siege train of heavy artillery, is a tribute to

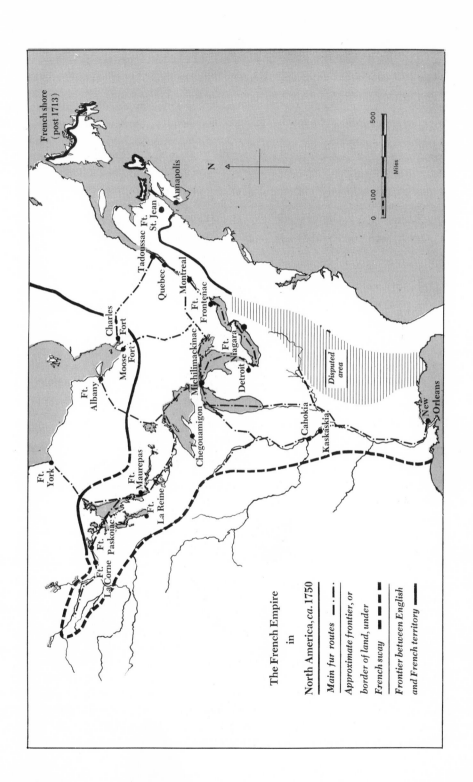

The French Empire
in
North America, ca. 1750

Main fur routes

Approximate frontier, or
border of land, under
French sway

Frontier between English
and French territory

N

Miles
0   100   500

French shore
(post 1713)

Annapolis

Ft.
St. Jean

Tadoussac

Quebec

Montreal

Ft.
Frontenac

Charles
Fort

Moose
Fort

Ft.
Albany

Ft.
Niagara

Michilimackinac

Detroit

Chegouamigon

Cahokia

Kaskaskia

Disputed
area

New
Orleans

Ft.
York

Ft.
Maurepas

Ft.
La Reine

Ft.
La Corne

Ft.
Paskoiac

Artist's concept of the fall of Braddock, by C. Schuessele. (Public Archives of Canada)

his organizing abilities. Duquesne had been convinced that it could not be done. At Fort Duquesne Contrecoeur had to rely on using his Canadians and Indians to harass the advancing foe, drive off their horses and cattle, and try to prevent them from reaching the fort by these guerrilla tactics. Yet he still forbade his scouting parties to cross the height of land, and he tried to prevent the Indians from attacking the English beyond it, but some of them refused to heed this order.[26]

Once Braddock's army had crossed the line into what the French claimed to be their territory, it came under attack, but with little effect. When the British were only twenty miles from Fort Duquesne, the situation looked desperate, but the French were determined to make a stand. The Indian allies, not liking the odds, at first declined to join in an attack on the advancing army. Captain Daniel de Beaujeu, chosen to lead this seemingly forlorn hope, shamed them by marching out with 108 colonial regulars and 146 Canadian militia, declaring that whether they accompanied him or not he intended to attack the enemy. This appeal to their personal honor demanded that they show equal courage. Some 600 Indians, from the north, from the mission settlements of Canada, from the Ohio, rushed to join him.

In the ensuing battle Braddock's army was shattered by the French and Indian force only half its size. British regulars and colonial militia proved no match for the Canadians and Indians in this type of warfare. Over two thirds of the British force were killed or wounded; the great train of baggage, supplies, and artillery, including 100 cattle and four to five hundred horses, was abandoned as the terrified survivors fled back over the mountains—this at a cost to the French and their allies of twenty-three killed and twenty wounded.

For days afterward the French gathered up the spoils of war, with the Indians taking the lion's share. To Contrecoeur's dismay, the Indians brought the captured horses and cattle to Fort Duquesne, where they promptly ate their way through the corn fields that had been counted on to feed the garrison during the coming winter. With the equipment abandoned by the British were Braddock's papers containing the British plans for the expeditions against not only Fort Duquesne, but also Forts Niagara, Beaubassin, and St. Frederic on Lake Champlain. This enabled the French to muster their forces in time to counter two of these threats.

Command of the expedition against Niagara had been entrusted to William Shirley, governor of Massachusetts. Although a military amateur he was given the rank of major general, and on the death of Braddock he succeeded briefly as commander in chief in North America. After the usual intercolonial bickering and chicanery he managed to muster 2400 hastily raised, untrained, colonial regulars and militiamen for the assault on Niagara. By the time he reached Oswego the French had moved sizable reinforcements to Lake Ontario, and his own troops were reduced to 1400 by sickness and desertion. In mid-September it was decided to defer the assault until the following year. The colonial forces were then concentrated for an attack on Fort St. Frederic at the narrows of Lake Champlain. Again the French forestalled them by swiftly moving to Lake George a strong force led by Jean-Armand, baron de Dieskau, commander of the regular troops recently arrived in the colony. A confused day's fighting ensued, reflecting little credit on the military abilities of either side. The French withdrew, leaving their wounded and very disgruntled general a prisoner in enemy hands. Neither side could claim a victory. The Anglo-Americans had been stopped in their drive to Lake Champlain; the French had failed to destroy the enemy or capture Fort William Henry at the foot of Lake George.

On the Acadian frontier the French were unable to avert defeat. For years the partisan leader Abbé Jean-Louis Le Loutre, missionary to the Micmac, had incited these warriors to give the British settlers in Nova Scotia no rest. He had also done everything in his not inconsiderable power to force the reluctant Acadians to quit British-held territory and relocate around the French forts at the head of the Bay of Fundy. His aim, and that of the officials at Quebec, was to use them in the struggle to regain the lost section of Acadia for France. These Acadians, simple peasant farmers and fishermen, wished only to be left alone, but preferably under the French flag. By the terms of the Treaty of Utrecht their land had been ceded to Britain and the British authorities had encouraged them to remain, but they had consistently refused to swear an unconditional oath of allegiance to the British crown because this would have required them to take up arms against the king's enemies, namely, the French. This they could not bring themselves to do.

When Fort Beauséjour on the Acadian border fell to a large force of English colonial militia on June 16, 1755, some 300 Acadians were found in it under arms. They had, however, taken the precaution of obtaining from the French commandant a declaration that he had forced them to serve under pain of death. The terms of the capitulation included a clause that they would be pardoned, and they surrendered with that understanding; but the British officer commanding in Nova Scotia, Colonel Charles Lawrence, had previously decided to expel all the Acadians from the province. He made this decision for military reasons. Despite the absence of an official declaration of war, hostilities had begun and he had no desire to fight the French with some ten thousand Acadians in his midst who might very well support an invading French army. This decision—but hardly the manner in which it was carried out—might be justified on the grounds of military expediency, but if so, the actions of Abbé Le Loutre and of the Acadians who resisted the British must also be condoned. Regardless of the way it was done and the moral and legal issues involved, the fact remains that the Anglo-American forces successfully removed the French and Acadian threat to the Nova Scotian frontier.

The French, however, were able to salvage something out of the disaster. The fate of the Acadians was given great publicity in Canada. Although some of the Acadians escaped to French-held territory, they had lost everything. The less fortunate were driven from their homes, which were put to the torch. They were then herded onto ships, with members of families separated, children from parents, some never to be reunited, and dumped in various ports in the English colonies, in England, and some in France. The Canadians were quick to grasp the point; were they to be conquered, this was the fate they too could expect. Nothing could have been better contrived to make them fight with unbridled ferocity.

With hostilities begun by the British, Pierre-François de Rigaud, marquis de Vaudreuil-Cavagnal, successor as governor general to Duquesne, felt no compunction whatsoever in striking back with every means available to him. He was a Canadian by birth and training, being the son of an earlier governor of the colony. His strategy was to employ the *troupes de terre* sent from France to secure the approaches to the central colony, and then to use the colonial regulars, the Troupes de la Marine, the Canadian militia, and the Indian allies to ravage the Anglo-American frontiers, and oblige the English colonials to use their vastly greater numbers to defend their frontier settlements. Initially, this strategy enjoyed success. Indian nations from the east, north, and west rushed to join in the assault. Along the whole length of the Alleghenies, from Carolina to New York and down the eastern slopes to within thirty miles of Philadelphia, the Anglo-American settlements went up in flames. Those who survived fled toward the seaboard and pleaded for protection. The situation eventually became so desperate word reached Quebec in October 1757 that the governor of Pennsylvania sought to treat with the Indians to grant them unopposed passage to attack Virginia, provided they spared the settlements of Pennsylvania en route.[27] Half a century earlier the Canadians had experienced the same sort of attacks in the Iroquois war and initially they had suffered heavy casualties, but they had mastered the art of guerrilla warfare and then beat back the Iroquois by using their own tactics of surprise, ambush, and swift assault where least expected. In that cruel war the Canadian military tradition was born.

The Anglo-American frontiersmen proved quite incapable of coping with the assaults on their settlements. They could only plead for help, which the colonial authorities were unable to provide. Herein lay the difference between the rival colonies. The Canadian frontier experience garnered in the western fur trade was the best training imaginable for this type of warfare. The Anglo-American frontiersman, more familiar with the axe and the plow, than with the musket and canoe paddle, eager to convert virgin forest into cleared farm land, rejecting all authority that sought to curb his private interests for the common good, was no match for the Canadians and their allies.[28] For the ensuing two years the Anglo-Americans suffered a series of crushing defeats. It was not Fort Niagara that was captured in 1756 by the Anglo-Americans, but Fort Oswego by the French and Canadians, and this caused the Iroquois to incline, ominously, to the French.[29]

The following year went even worse for the British. The French had built a massive fort at Ticonderoga. Although poorly sited, it served as a base for offensive operations. The English frontier settlements, and areas once well behind the frontier, were again ravaged with heavy loss of life. During the summer of 1757 a convoy reached Quebec with 3500 more regulars. In July, Louis-Joseph, marquis de Montcalm, who had succeeded Dieskau as commander of the French regulars, moved 5000 troops supported by a host of Indians to the foot of Lake George and laid siege to Fort William Henry. Although the British commander, General Daniel Webb, had 7000 troops at his disposal, he failed to concentrate them where they were needed and the fort surrendered after a few days of bombardment. Then occurred the infamous attack on the surrendered garrison by the French Indians, who saw no reason why they should abide by European rules of war in their own country. Perhaps not more than 200 of the more than 2000 men in the fort were killed or carried off, and once the massacre started Montcalm and his officers did all they could to end it; but it should never have happened. Montcalm, as commanding officer, has to be held responsible for not taking more effective measures to prevent it.

The borders of the English colonies had been driven far back, south of Lake George and over the Alleghenies; Lake Ontario was now a French lake, and the French and their allies were carrying the war to the enemy along the entire length of the frontier. In New France there was jubilation and the sweet, heady smell of victory; in the English colonies, nothing but defeat, cries of woe and rage; fear that the situation could only get worse, and pleas for peace before it did. Even before word was received in France of the victory at Lake George, a friend of the Comte de Broglie wrote to him from Versailles: "The news that we receive from America by way of Holland and England is so advantageous for us that we still don't dare believe it. If it were really true the English would have no recourse but to make peace quickly in order to conserve part of their colonies."[30] And in London Lord Chesterfield wrote: "This winter, I take for granted, must produce a peace, of some kind or another; a bad one for us, no doubt, and yet perhaps better than we shall get the year after."[31]

Everyone knows, of course, that the following year the tide turned, and eventually Canada was conquered. Given that fact, and the relative populations of the British and French colonies—roughly 1,500,000 and 70,000 respectively—it is all too easy to assume that this outcome to the war was inevitable. If that were so, one can only wonder why the Canadians and the French regulars put up such a desperate fight. The truth is, they expected at least to hold their own until peace in Europe forced the British in America to desist; and given the military situation as it was in 1757, they had good cause to be sanguine. They had beaten the Anglo-Americans in almost every engagement, and were convinced of their own military superiority. The Royal Navy had not yet succeeded in preventing supplies and reinforcements from reaching the colony from France, and the tremendous advantage in manpower enjoyed by the Anglo-Americans was more apparent than real. Lacking the large numbers of guerrilla fighters that the French had at their disposal, they had to remain on the defensive. A handful of Indians led by Canadian officers appearing near the settlements created panic and tied down large defensive forces; and fear of a slave insurrection in the southern colonies made the authorities there fearful of removing many of their men far from their own frontiers.

The French also enjoyed the advantage of both interior and exterior lines of communication. Externally, their river routes to the Ohio allowed them to keep their distant bases supplied and to ravage the English colonial frontier, then quickly retire. Within the central colony of New France they had the St. Lawrence and the Richelieu–Lake Champlain routes along which to move large forces swiftly. The enemy could only approach by ship up the St. Lawrence to Quebec; by small boat down Lake Champlain and the Richelieu, where the chain of French forts could delay them; and by way of Lake Ontario then down the St. Lawrence to attack Montreal, but this route was so hampered by rapids that a relatively small force could have inflicted heavy casualties by guerrilla tactics. Even were three armies to move along these three routes against New France, they would have been completely out of touch with one another and operating along difficult and lengthening supply lines. The chance of their all arriving on the doorstep of the colony at the same time was remote. Most important of all, the problem of communications and supply limited the number of men the British could employ in the campaigns; if the British had had even a far greater advantage in numbers, it is unlikely that they could have put larger forces in the field. If the conquest of New France was inevitable owing to the inferiority of numbers, the conquest of England's ally, Prussia, in this same war was also inevitable.

The gravest weakness of the French forces was their divided command. Montcalm, hot-tempered, supercilious, continually fuming over petty slights, real or imagined, commanded the French regulars and had tactical direction of the forces in the field. Vaudreuil, resentful, vain, unsure of himself, as governor general had overall command and dictated strategy. These two men, the one French and the other Canadian, and very conscious of it, quickly came to detest each other. Before long they were devoting more of their energies to feuding than to the direction of the war. This animosity spread to some of the subordinate French officers, who found campaigning in North America not to their taste, and Montcalm made no attempt to curb it; just the reverse in fact. Vaudreuil wanted to wage offensive war, employing Canadian and Indian war parties to ravage the English colonies, forcing them to keep their troops in defensive positions so that they would be unable to strike at Canada. Montcalm, his military experience gained on European battlefields, had little but contempt for this type of warfare and the men who waged it. He wanted to fight set-piece battles, where superior tactics, fire power, and discipline brought victory. In 1758, upon appealing to the Court, Montcalm won his battle with the governor general. Promoted to lieutenant general, he was given supreme authority over all the military forces, and Vaudreuil was ordered to defer to him in all military affairs. Unfortunately for the French cause, Montcalm was a confirmed defeatist. He regarded the colony as already lost.[32]

Lower down the military ladder there was ill-feeling between the officers of the colonial regulars, the Troupes de la Marine, and the officers of the French regular army, the regiments of the Troupes de Terre. The latter bitterly resented that many of the Canadian officers were appointed to command at the western posts, where they made fortunes in the fur trade, and that others were making even greater fortunes in the supply services with the connivance of the intendant François Bigot, while they themselves could not live on their meager incomes owing to inflation. They were particularly disgruntled at receiving their pay and allowances in wartime paper scrip issued by Bigot at a sizable discount. By contrast, in the lower echelons the French regular soldiers and the Canadians got along well together. During the winter months the bulk of the regulars were billeted on the Canadians, and this caused relatively little trouble. With Montcalm's permission many of the soldiers married Canadian girls and obtained grants of land; many more planned to do so. They were assured that when the war ended they could obtain their discharge and remain in the colony. Montcalm commented, significantly: "We cannot leave here too many soldiers from our battalions; were we to take them back they would be no good for service in Europe but they will prove good for America."[33]

In 1757 an epidemic, brought by the troop ships bringing reinforcements, was accompanied by a crop failure. This last was particularly disastrous at a time when the colony had an additional 9000 mouths to feed: troops, refugee Acadians, and western Indians who had come down to fight on the Lake Champlain front. The hospitals at Montreal and Quebec held 500 men, three or four dying every day. Between May and October, 250 of the Troupes de Terre alone succumbed, reducing their strength to 3730. As though that were not bad enough, the reinforcements who had introduced the disease into the colony were raw recruits of the worst quality, the dregs of the army. Nearly twenty were court-martialed and a prodigious number punished by their regimental officers, but the rot spread throughout the battalions, ruining discipline.[34] Nor was morale improved by a forced reduction of the food rations from two *livres* of bread per day to less than a quarter of a *livre*. The housewives of Montreal vigorously protested having to accept horse meat, and a nun at Quebec wrote in her order's journal: "Three scourges stalk our land: plague, famine, and war. Of the three famine is the most terrible."

Too much should not be made of this situation. The worst of the shortage occurred after the harvest, at a time when military operations were curbed by the onset of winter. Soldiers and civilians alike had to tighten their belts and subsist on unpalatable foods, but they survived. A great deal—perhaps too much—has been made of the corrupt practices of the intendant Bigot and his clique, who amassed huge fortunes from their monopoly on colonial supplies; while the mass of the population were reduced to a bare subsistence level, they entertained like oriental potentates. Balls and banquets with groaning tables, lavish dinner parties, gambling for fantastic stakes—these were the amusements in Bigot's circle during the winter months. In one night at cards he was reputed to have lost 200,000 *livres*, and this at a time when junior officers were running into debt just to live.[35] Yet the fact remains that French military operations do not appear to have been seriously hampered by these activities. Montcalm professed disgust at what was going on but he rarely declined an invitation; and the supplies he needed for campaigns, Bigot provided, albeit at greatly inflated cost to the crown. The intendant was undoubtedly a scoundrel; he was also a very efficient administrator. Indeed, the British generals, striving desperately to cope with supply problems made worse by petty corruption, short-sighted selfishness, and incompetence, would probably have been glad to have had a Bigot take charge for them. It was not until after the war that the aftermath of Bigot's system brought terrible hardship to the colony, when the huge sums of paper money he had issued were repudiated. The fall of New France cannot be blamed on him.

In Britain, meanwhile, William Pitt had acceded to power. While others contemplated treating for peace, he concentrated on winning the war. Realizing that the war in America could not be won, and might well be lost, if reliance continued to be placed on the colonists to carry the war to the enemy, he shipped several thousand British regulars to the colonies for campaigns against Louisbourg, Ticonderoga, and Fort Duquesne. New general officers were appointed, and Pitt assured the colonial legislatures that the British taxpayers would reimburse them for the cost of raising and maintaining the 25,000 men they were called on to provide for their own defense. This put a new complexion on things, and the colonial assemblies at last began to cooperate in the war effort.

To command the assault on Louisbourg, Pitt chose Colonel Jeffrey Amherst, whose chief characteristic proved to be plodding thoroughness. By May 28 the British fleet, with 8000 troops, was off Louisbourg. This great fortress, claimed by some to bar the St. Lawrence entrance to Canada, could in fact bar nothing beyond the range of its cannon. Intended as a base to maintain a fleet to guard French interests in North America, it was not Louisbourg itself but the fleet it could harbor that was the danger, but in 1758 there was no fleet; the Royal Navy had seen to that off Cartagena and La Rochelle. There was really no need for an assault on Louisbourg; it could have been left to wither on the vine. Amherst's siege lasted until July 26. One of his brigadiers, James Wolfe, caustically remarked: "If it had been attacked by anybody but the English, it would have fallen long ago."

Louisbourg had at least held out long enough to prevent the intended expedition against Quebec from being launched that year, and on the Lake Champlain frontier the British plans had again come unstuck. There, Major General James Abercromby was directed to march on the French forts with an army of 27,000 men, 20,000 of them provincials. Although only 9024 colonial levies were provided, and they were mostly raw recruits, Abercromby still had over 15,000 men, opposed to Montcalm's 3500. Without bothering to study the terrain, Abercromby launched his regular troops against the French entrenchments at Ticonderoga, where they were slaughtered by intense musketry fire. Assault after assault failed to reach the French lines. The intervening ground became carpeted with red-coated bodies. Eventually even these highly disciplined troops could take no more. Abercromby's demoralized army retired in confusion. The British regulars had suffered nearly 1600 casualties, the provincials 334. The French had 106 killed and 266 wounded.[36]

In the west things were different. In August, Lieutenant Colonel Bradstreet, with some 2600 provincial troops and 157 regulars, caught the French at Fort Frontenac completely by surprise. The garrison, numbering just over a hundred men, was able to resist only long enough to surrender with honor. Bradstreet made no attempt to occupy and hold the fort, and with good reason. Had he done so, a relief expedition from Montreal would have forced him to surrender in turn. As a fortress, Fort Frontenac was of little value, but the destruction of the supplies intended for the Ohio posts, and the boats in which to transship them, was a serious blow to the French position in the southwest.

This was made plain when General John Forbes and Colonel Henry Bouquet invaded the Ohio country with nearly 7000 men. They had made a close study of French methods of waging war in the interior, particularly of their practice of establishing a chain of bases and supply entrepôts along their lines of communication. Slowly, and painstakingly, they thrust their way forward over the mountains. Their main difficulty was obtaining wagons and teamsters from the colonials, who demanded military protection but refused to aid those affording it. An advance scouting party over 800 strong approaching Fort Duquesne was badly mauled by the garrison and attendant Indians, losing nearly 300 men. The French suffered only sixteen casualties. It appeared to be another Braddock defeat on a smaller scale, and the French remained convinced that they were still masters of the situation.

In October the French launched a spoiling attack on the advanced British post at Loyalhanna. It did not enjoy the same success as previous assaults, and the Ohio Indians suffered quite heavy losses. These tribes needed a respite and were now willing to listen to peace overtures from the Pennsylvania authorities. After lengthy negotiations they allowed themselves to be persuaded that the Anglo-Americans were sincere in their declarations that they did not covet the Indians' lands. At a conference held at Easton, Pennsylvania, in October 1758, delegates of the Ohio Iroquois and nine other nations made their peace with the English. The Pennsylvania authorities solemnly renounced all claim to lands beyond the mountains. The Indians mistakenly assumed that the pledge was binding on all the Anglo-Americans and would be honored.

This defection, combined with a shortage of supplies, forced the French to destroy Fort Duquesne in November and withdraw to Fort Machault. They thereby preserved the French presence on the Ohio. The British, however, made no attempt to follow up their success; instead they devoted their energies to consolidating their extended supply lines and to the construction of a stockade and winter quarters at Fort Pitt. This disturbed the Indians. It appeared that the French had been displaced only to be replaced by an even more menacing British presence on their lands. Lieutenant François de Ligneris at Fort Machault was able to win back the support of some of the wavering tribesmen. When fresh supplies and troop reinforcements reached him from Montreal, he made preparations to regain dominion over the Ohio.

The defeats in the west, first Fort Frontenac, then Duquesne, came as a severe shock to Montcalm and Vaudreuil. Montcalm had dismissed the reports of Forbes' advance as a British ruse to dupe him into moving part of his army from the Lake Champlain front to the west.[37] Despite his victory at Ticonderoga, he became more defeatist than ever. He had earlier advised that the forts in the Ohio Valley be abandoned on the grounds that they were too great a drain on the colony's supplies and manpower, and served no vital military purpose. He easily convinced himself that Canada was lost unless peace were made before the next year's campaigns began,[38] but the situation did not warrant such pessimism. The loss of Louisbourg and Fort Duquesne and the destruction of Fort Frontenac had not affected the ability of the central colony to defend itself. Communications with the western fur trade posts were still open and the furs were still coming down to Montreal. In fact, in 1758 at least 220 men, and probably many more, left Montreal for the western trading posts.[39] Obviously not everyone in the colony regarded the situation as hopeless. With their interior lines of communication and short supply lines, the Canadians were still in a fairly strong position. The events of the following year were to make this plain.

Pitt's plans for the campaign of 1759 called for New France to be attacked by three armies along the river lines: a sea-borne assault up the St. Lawrence to attack Quebec, an army to advance up Lake Champlain to attack the center of the colony by way of the Richelieu, and a force to proceed from Lake Ontario down the St. Lawrence to attack Montreal. The

French abandoned their forts at Ticonderoga and Crown Point, and then retired to Fort Île aux Noix at the outlet of Lake Champlain. Amherst, moving with the speed of a glacier, advanced only as far as Crown Point. The massive fort he then proceeded to construct there indicates clearly that he entertained little hope that Canada would be conquered. Similarly, the advance of the western army got no farther than Lake Ontario. The naval force, transporting an army under Major General James Wolfe, reached Quebec unopposed before the end of June. Montcalm and Vaudreuil sat back behind their lines at Quebec and allowed Wolfe's army not only to establish itself on the Île d'Orléans, but also to seize the point of land on the south shore of the St. Lawrence opposite Quebec. Once the British were securely established there, they mounted batteries of heavy cannon and during the ensuing weeks pounded the buildings and homes of Quebec to rubble. Worse still, under cover of this fire Admiral Sir Charles Saunders was able to get his ships up the river beyond Quebec. This meant that the army could land either above or below Quebec for an assault on the walled town.

Wolfe failed to take advantage of the mobility the fleet afforded him. Instead, he spent the summer striving without success to break the French lines below Quebec. In frustration, he turned his American Rangers loose to ravage the countryside. This calculated policy of terror would, he hoped, bring Montcalm's army out of its entrenched position to give battle. He was convinced that the superiority of his regiments made victory in such an engagement certain, but Montcalm refused to abandon his position. All he had to do was hold on, and beat back the enemy attacks. At summer's end the British would be forced to withdraw down river.

The Rangers, aided by detachments of regulars, set about their grim work with enthusiasm. Upward of 1400 well-built stone homes and manor houses went up in flames all along the river. In late August Jeremiah Pearson, soldier in the Massachusetts forces, wrote in his diary: "the Raingers and the lite Invitery embarked aboard the flatbotum Boats and went down the river about 30 miles and Lay in the Brig that night. Ye 23 we went on Shore for to set the houses on fire we had an ingagement with the french and kild and Sculped 16 of them and came all the way up by Land and got Sheep and geese and hens a nuf of them and set all the houses on fire as we came."[40] Every male Canadian over fifteen was a member of the militia and under orders to oppose the enemy by every means. Wolfe, however, took the European view that they were civilians and if caught in active opposition subject to punishment under military law. The Canadians had to suffer what the Anglo-American frontier settler had had to endure, but they fought back savagely in defense of their homes, despite heavy losses.

In the west the British had more success. By the end of June 1759, Brigadier-General John Prideaux had reoccupied Fort Oswego. Leaving a strong garrison he proceeded to attack Fort Niagara with 2000 regulars and, what was most ominous for the French, 1000 Iroquois. Captain Pierre Pouchot, commandant at Niagara, had only 486 French troops and Canadian militia, and a small force of allied Indians. He managed to persuade the Iroquois to sit on the side lines and let the Europeans fight it out. He also got word to Fort Machault of his plight, and the commandant, Lieutenant François de Ligneris, rushed to his aid with 600 French and a thousand western Indians. Their route was blocked by a British force of 500 regulars, 100 provincial troops, and 600 Iroquois. The French advanced on the British position, within sight of Fort Niagara, full of confidence. But the British troops had learned much since the days of Braddock. Under Colonel Henry Bouquet they had received intensive training in light infantry tactics in wooded country, and in marksmanship. This time the French came under withering and sustained fire that broke their attempts to flow around the British position. When they wavered, the British charged. The French turned and fled. At this the Iroquois, who had not taken part, joined in the pursuit. Their blood lust roused, the British had a hard time restraining them from butchering the French who had surrendered. This defeat of the relief force gave Pouchot no alternative but to surrender Fort Niagara. On July 24, after three weeks of bombardment he capitulated. With the loss of Niagara, the French hold on Lakes Ontario and Erie, and the Ohio country, was finally wrested away. Yet the French still held the regions north of the lakes, and French canoes still went out of Montreal to the western posts. The military frontier in the southwest had collapsed, but to the north the fur trade frontier remained.

At Quebec, Wolfe had been frustrated at every turn. With little time left before being forced to raise the siege, he finally accepted his brigadiers' proposal to effect a landing above the town. This, the brigadiers insisted, would force Montcalm to give battle since he had to keep his supply route from Montreal open; he maintained food supplies in Quebec sufficient only for a few days. Wolfe made one drastic change in the brigadiers' plan. Instead of forcing a landing a few miles above Quebec astride the Montreal road, he chose Anse au Foulon at the foot of a steep 175-foot cliff, less than two miles from the town walls. It was a last desperate gamble before being forced to admit defeat and return to England with the remnants of the army.

Montcalm, right up until the landing, was convinced that Wolfe would attack on the other side of the city or on the center. The British achieved complete surprise and on the morning of September 13, before Montcalm knew it, they had some 4500 men on the Plains of Abraham. Without waiting for Colonel Louis-Antoine de Bougainville to come up with the 3000 regulars stationed at Cap Rouge less than ten miles upstream, Montcalm gathered his forces from the opposite flank and rushed into battle with 4500 men, less than half the force he had available. His troops lacked the training and discipline possessed by the British regulars. He had mustered Canadians, untrained for European style fighting in line, even British deserters, into his regular regiments to bolster their diminishing numbers.[41] They fired too soon, broke ranks to reload, lost the shock effect of volleys fired at effective range. The British lines held their fire until the enemy was within sixty yards—some accounts say forty. Then came the crashing volleys by platoons, all down the line. The French lines were shattered. Those left standing broke and ran, the British in hot pursuit. The battle was won in a matter of minutes. Most of the 658 casualties suffered by the British were inflicted before, and after, the main engagement by Canadian skirmishers fighting the only way they knew, from cover. The French reckoned their casualties at 44 officers and about 600 men. Among the fatal casualties were both Montcalm and Wolfe. The fact that both generals were killed is evidence enough that the tactics employed were rather dubious.

The British had won the battle but the French still held Quebec, and Vaudreuil was able to get the bulk of the French forces around and past the British army—something he would not have been able to do had Wolfe landed where his brigadiers had suggested—to join up with Bougainville's forces. The Chevalier de Ramezay was left in Quebec with a token force and orders to hold until his food supplies were exhausted. By September 17 the Chevalier de Lévis, who had succeeded to command of the French forces, had rallied the army and was marching back to relieve the garrison. Before he arrived, de Ramezay had capitulated and the British occupied the shattered city.

The loss of Quebec was a harsh blow to the French. Yet the British held only the city and its outskirts; the French, the rest. After the British fleet had sailed, Lévis got ships away to France, to plead for reinforcements to be sent early the next year. Everything depended on which fleet would arrive first. In April, before the ice was out of the river, Lévis marched his forces to Quebec, and General James Murray, who had succeeded to command, obliged him by giving battle outside the town. This time the decision was reversed. The British forces were sent reeling back into Quebec from the battlefield at Ste. Foy. Lévis then invested the town, waiting for the hoped-for reinforcements to arrive. On May 9 the first ship came up the river—a British frigate with word that more were on their way. On May 16 Lévis had to abandon the siege and retire to Montreal.

Three armies now converged on the dwindling French forces. Murray's strengthened army moved up from Quebec; Brigadier William Haviland forced his way up the Richelieu; and Jeffrey Amherst finally put in an appearance with an army brought down the St. Lawrence from the reconstructed Oswego. Lévis still wanted to give battle, not because he had any hope of defeating the British and saving the colony, but because he could not bring himself to surrender without a fight. He was an ambitious man. New France might be finished, but his career was not. Many of the

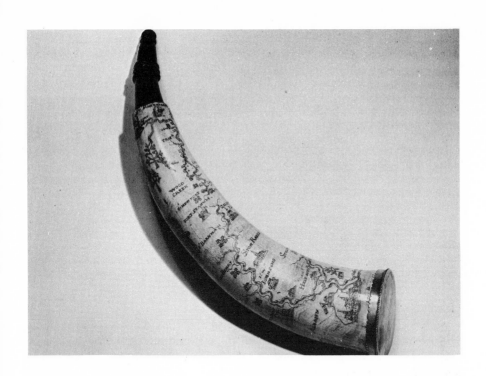

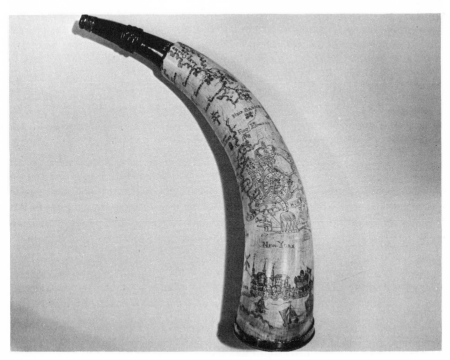

Powder horn of a British soldier in Amherst's army 1759. (McCord Museum, McGill University)

Canadians however, had different ideas. They were under no illusions that anything was to be gained by prolonging the agony. In mid-June word was received at Montreal that the few ships sent from France with meager troop reinforcements and supplies had been destroyed by the Royal Navy in Restigouche Bay. Some refugee Acadians brought the dispatches from the ships. These dispatches caused everyone, French regulars and Canadians alike, to despair. Payment on the vast sums of paper money issued by the intendant was suspended. This meant that eight months' back pay for the troops was worthless, and apparently not a *sou* in the future; as for the Canadians, many of them faced the loss of everything. It was clear to all that the French government regarded Canada as lost, had abandoned the colony and its people to the foe. In this assumption they were correct. In December 1759 the minister of foreign affairs, the duc de Choiseul, had consoled himself over the loss of the North American colonies by declaring that this would increase the strength of the English colonials and foster their urge for independence.[42]

The only thing that now mattered to the Canadians was protecting their families and their homes. Many of them began to desert, despite orders that any doing so would be shot and their homes burned. With the colony swiftly coming under enemy occupation they could hardly be blamed for refusing to throw away their lives in futile gestures. Large numbers of the regular troops also disappeared, most of them men who had married in the colony. The officers reported that the majority of their men were resolved not to return to France.[43] Yet some of the Canadians still preferred to fight, even though they had to march as far as twenty-five miles in a day, many of them without boots.

By September 7 Vaudreuil and Lévis had only some 2000 troops left. Amherst, at Montreal's outskirts, had 17,000. Very wisely Vaudreuil refused Lévis' demand that Amherst's terms be rejected because he had churlishly refused to grant the French the honors of war. In defiance, the night before the British occupied the city, Lévis burned all the regimental colors.

Before the month was out the French officials and the Troupes de Terre were embarked for France. That is, some of the Troupes de Terre left Canada. In addition to those who had decided earlier to become Canadian citizens under whatever flag, after the capitulation more than 500 more slipped away to be harbored by the *habitants*. Of the 3700 odd who had been on strength a few months before, fewer than 1600 landed at La Rochelle.[44] On the other hand some Canadians preferred to abandon everything and go to France rather than live under British rule. These were for the most part seigneurs and officers in the Troupes de la Marine, many of them holders of the Croix de St. Louis for distinguished military service. The clergy all remained, ordered to do so by their superiors.

In the British colonies there was unbounded jubilation at the final defeat of the old foe. Yet it is extremely doubtful, despite their overwhelming superiority of numbers, that the Anglo-Americans could have conquered Canada by their own unaided efforts. It was the British regulars, the Royal Navy, and the British taxpayer that finally defeated the French. Given better leadership on the French side, Quebec might well not have fallen in 1759, and that would have put quite a different complexion on things. But the fact remains that the battle was lost, and that before Quebec fell British troops had wrested control of the southwest from the French. The French garrisons in the remaining posts in the far west surrendered to British or colonial officers who were sent to take over. West to the Mississippi, north to the Arctic, and in the northwest as far as the most distant French post, all now came under British control. In Europe and elsewhere in the world the war still raged. North America had been only one theater in Britain's drive to dominate world trade. The other powers now began to entertain grave doubts about the safety of their interests were Britain's ambitions not somehow to be curbed. And in North America the Indian nations quickly came to realize, too late, that the French would have been the lesser of the two evils.

◁ **9** ▷

Epilogue: The Closing
of the Canadian
Fur Trade Frontier

*A*s soon as the fighting ended in North America, the fur trade frontier revived and within a few years was more flourishing than ever. All through the war the fur brigades had left for the west. In 1758 over two hundred *voyageurs* from the Montreal region alone went to the western posts— Michilimackinac, Detroit, Chagouamigon, the Mer de l'Ouest. Even in 1759, over one hundred men went out. The following year, with British armies investing Montreal from three directions, only thirty-three men were sent. In 1761 over two hundred *voyageurs* were hired; significantly, seven of the thirty-two merchants who hired canoe men bore English or Scots names, Alexander Henry, from Albany, among them; but they hired only some twenty *voyageurs*. Within a few years the preponderance of Canadian merchants in the trade was reversed and before the end of the century the names of only twelve Canadian bourgeois appear. These twelve sent out seventy-six men; the British merchants, 453.[1] During those intervening years the role of the Canadians in the fur trade, for a variety of reasons, was steadily reduced from that of the bourgeois, the entrepreneur, to that of wage earner, *voyageur* and *commis*. The fur trade was now a partnership:

186

British capital and direction joined with Canadian technical skill, the profits going to the former.[2]

In 1763 and 1764 the trade was disrupted by Pontiac's uprising. Once again the Anglo-American frontier was threatened as the Indians, disgruntled at the treatment they received from the new men at the old western posts, tried to regain control of their lands and their destinies, which, they realized too late, they were losing. The garrisons at the western posts were taken by surprise and several of them overwhelmed. War parties fell on the frontier settlements south of the Great Lakes, burning and destroying. Over 2000 settlers were slaughtered; the survivors fled to the east. Once again the Anglo-American frontiersmen and the colonial authorities proved incapable of dealing with the problem which they themselves had created. Pontiac's warriors had to be crushed by British regular troops.

During the ensuing half century the Montreal fur traders—Scots, English, American, and a handful of Canadian merchant traders—with Canadian *voyageurs* pushed the fur trade frontier ever farther into the northwest, into the Peace River country and over "the shining mountains." By 1778 Peter Pond, late of Connecticut, was trading on the Athabasca. On July 14, 1789, Alexander Mackenzie reached the Arctic Ocean at the mouth of the river that today bears his name. Four years later he crossed the Rocky Mountains. On a rock overlooking the Pacific he wrote in bold letters with trade vermillion: "Alexander Mackenzie, from Canada, by land, the twenty-second of July, one thousand seven hundred and ninety-three." The Canadian fur trade frontier had now reached its outermost limits.

Just as the new men in the fur trade employed old Canadian techniques, so the new political rulers of Canada after 1763 were forced to continue old Canadian policies. It seems ironic that after fighting a savage war to wrest the Ohio country from the French, the British were obliged to continue doing what the French had sought to do: to bar the region to Anglo-American settlement. The old conflict between the fur trade frontier and the settlement frontier continued there a while longer. The American Revolution however, in part caused by this problem, ultimately resolved it; and again it is ironic that the Americans finally won this area only with the aid of France. It is ironic too that the new masters of the Canadian fur trade had to take up the bitter struggle with Canada's old rivals, the merchants of Albany and the Hudson's Bay Company. The former were virtually eliminated during the American Revolution—many of them merely transferred their operations from New York to Montreal. Then in 1783 came the division of the continent north of the Spanish empire. In the west this division was made along the Great Lakes line first suggested by the Canadian, Denis Riverin, in 1696.[3]

In the northwest the struggle between the Hudson's Bay Company and the North West Company of Montreal was waged by the Montreal men as ruthlessly as the earlier military conflicts between Canada and the English

Beaver Club medal. The wintering partners of the Nor' Westers wore these gold medals as insignia of membership in the Beaver Club. Each medal bore the date 1785, the year the Club was founded in Montreal, and on the other side the year of the member's first voyage to the Indian country of the northwest. The medal of another member, Hypolitte Des Rivières, bears the dates 1785 and 1743. (McCord Museum, McGill University)

colonies. When in 1812 Lord Selkirk of the Hudson's Bay Company established a settlement at Red River athwart the North West Company's main supply line, it was savagely attacked in much the same way that Schenectady, Deerfield, and Haverhill had been dealt with in the Anglo-French wars. The fur trade frontier in the north was not yet ready to yield to settlement.

The new masters of the Canadian fur trade, tough Scots, Englishmen, and some few from the old northern colonies, were themselves in many subtle ways conquered by the way of life of the Canadians. The Nor' Westers had quickly adopted the techniques and many of the cultural traits of the old Canadian military and fur trade *noblesse*. Become bilingual and tri-cultural, they too spent money recklessly, built fine homes, married into the old seigneurial families, and entertained lavishly. The annual meetings of the wintering partners at Grand Portage, and at Beaver Hall in Montreal, are legendary for the liquor consumed as these men roared out the old *voyageur* songs and gloried in the hardihood the life of the *pays d'en haut* had demanded of them. Their moral values too acquired a flavor of the old frontier. While in the northwest these men took Indian wives, "savoured the wine of the country," and Montreal society accepted the custom by feigning ignorance. When one compares the attitudes and values of these fur trade bourgeois with those of the old Canadian *noblesse* and of the mercantile class of either Britain or the colonies to the south, it is apparent that they had abandoned those of the class whence they had come, adopted those of their new environment. The Canadian frontier had, in fact, assimilated them to a remarkable degree.

Eventually rising costs over the long haul to and from the northwest, declining prices for furs, the profligacy of the Nor' Westers and their resulting lack of financial reserves, drove them to the wall. In 1821 the surviving partners were glad to merge with the old foe, the Hudson's Bay Company. Montreal had finally been defeated; the fur brigades of *grands canots de maître* no longer departed from Lachine every spring. The furs and supplies moved through Hudson Bay by ship, then by York boat to the posts on the northern plains. The life of the *voyageur* was over; the western frontier was closed to the French Canadian. His world was no longer one of vast horizons, but the restricted world of the St. Lawrence Valley,[4] its economy dominated by grasping men who thought only of profit—speculators in the essentials of life, land, and wheat. There was no intendant, no *capitaine de milice*, to appeal to for social justice or redress of grievance. The consequences of this are still being felt today.

Inexorably the old fur trade frontier was submerged by westward-moving settlement. The axe and the plow finally defeated the canoe and the musket. A way of life and a peculiar scale of values, part Indian, part old regime, were swept into discard. This was doubtless inevitable, but it left us the poorer in ways that a shopkeeper could never fathom. What that old way of life had meant to men who had lived it was expressed, in exuberant fashion, to Alexander Ross on the shores of Lake Winnipeg in 1825, by a one time *voyageur* then over seventy years old:

> I have now been forty-two years in this country. For twenty-four I was a light canoe man. . . . No portage was too long for me; all portages were alike. My end of the canoe never touched the ground till I saw the end of . . . [the portage]. Fifty songs a day were nothing to me, I could carry, paddle, walk and sing with any man I ever saw. . . . No water, no weather, ever stopped the paddle or the song. I have had twelve wives in the country; and was once possessed of fifty horses, and six running dogs, trimmed in the first style. I was then like a Bourgeois, rich and happy: no Bourgeois had better dressed wives than I; no Indian chief finer horses; no white man better harnessed or swifter dogs. . . . I wanted for nothing; and I spent all my earnings in the enjoyment of pleasure. Five hundred pounds, twice told, have passed through my hands; although now I have not a spare shirt to my back, nor a penny to buy one. Yet, were I young again, I should glory in commencing the same career again. I would spend another half-century in the same fields of enjoyment. There is no life so happy as a voyageur's life; none so independent; no place where a man enjoys so much variety and freedom as in the Indian country.[5]

NOTES

Chapter 1: The Nature of the Canadian Frontier

[1] H. P. Biggar (ed.), *The Works of Samuel de Champlain*, 6 vols. (Champlain Society, Toronto, 1922), vol. I, p. 209.

[2] On the concept of the metropolis in Canadian history, see the article by J. M. S. Careless, "Frontierism, Metropolitanism, and Canadian History," *The Canadian Historical Review*, vol. XXXV (March, 1954), pp. 1–21.

[3] R. Glover, "The Difficulties of the Hudson's Bay Company's Penetration of the West," *The Canadian Historical Review*, vol. XXIX (September, 1948), pp. 240–254; Adolph B. Benson (ed.), *Peter Kalm's Travels in North America*, 2 vols. (New York, 1966), vol. I, pp. 363–365, 373. Kalm discusses the relative merits of the Canadian canoes and those used by the New York settlers. The York boat, built of pine with a 28-foot keel, was flat bottomed, sharp prowed, sides bow and stern sharply angled, propelled by oars and sail. Such a boat cost £20 to £25, was manned by from eight to twelve *voyageurs* carried a cargo of 3 tons, was easily carried or dragged over a portage, and would last two seasons.

[4] Marcel Trudel, *Histoire de la Nouvelle France*, vol. I: *Les Vaines tentatives, 1524–1603* (Montreal, 1964), p. 168.

[5] Gabriel Sagard, *The Long Journey to the Country of the Hurons* (G. M. Wrong, ed.; Champlain Society Publications XXXV, Toronto, 1939), pp. 134–137; Fr. J.-F. de St. Cosme, Michilimackinac, 13 Sept. 1698, *Rapport de l'Archiviste de la Province de Québec, 1965* (hereafter cited as *RAPQ*), p. 37; Etienne de Carheil à Champigny, Michilimackinac, 30 d'aoust 1702, Public Archives of Canada, Series M. vol. 204, part 1, pp. 177–178.

[6] The first such appointments were made by Governor General Le Febvre de La Barre in 1684, Morel de la Durantaye being appointed to command at Michilimackinac and the Chevalier de Baugy at St. Louis des Illinois.

[7] "Les Srs de Vaudreuil et Raudot se servira autant qu'ils pourront des Missionaires en des occasions qui se presenteront pour porter leurs ordres dans la profondeur des terres." Vaudreuil et Raudot an Ministre, Que, 15 Nov. 1707, Archives Nationales, Colonies, Series C11A, vol. XXVI, p. 12; see also, Memoire Instructif des Mesures que J'ay pris pour la Guerre Resolue Contre les Iroquois . . . Denonville, 26 aoust 1686, Archives Nationales, Colonies, Series F3, vol. 2, pp. 218–221; W. J. Eccles, *Canada Under Louis XIV* (Toronto, 1964), p. 249.

[8] Vaudreuil et Bégon au Ministre, Que., 20 sept. 1714, *RAPQ, 1947–1948*, p. 273.

[9] Baron de Lahontan, *New Voyages to North America*, 2 vols. (R. G. Thwaites, ed.; Chicago, 1903) vol. I, p. 54.

[10] See Richard J. Hooker (ed.), *The Carolina Backcountry on the Eve of the Revolution* (Williamsburg, Va., 1955.)

[11] For examples of *coureurs de bois* being brought to book for misbehavior, see Le Gardeur de St. Pierre à Beauharnois, Fort des Miamis, 1741, Archives du Seminaire de Québec, Fonds Verreau, carton 5, no. 5; Beauharnois à St. Pierre, Mtl. 22 juillet 1742, *ibid.*, No. 13, La Galissonière à M. de St. Pierre, commandant à Missilimakinac, de Québec le 4 7bre 1748, *ibid.*, No. 53.

[12] On aspects of this problem on the Pennsylvania frontier, see Francis Jennings, "The Frontier Trade of the Susquehanna Valley," *Proceedings of the American Philosophical Society*, vol. CX, no. 6 (December, 1966), pp. 407–424.

¹³ Francis Parkman, *A Half Century of Conflict,* 2 vols. (Centenary Edition; Boston, 1922), vol. I, p. 223.

¹⁴ Pierre-François-Xavier de Charlevoix, S.J., *Histoire de la Nouvelle France,* vol. III: *Journal d'un voyage fait par ordre du Roi dans l'Amérique septentrionale adressé à Madame la Duchesse de Lesdiguières,* 3 vols. (Paris, 1744), vol. III, pp. 79–80.

¹⁵ Guy Frégault, *La Guerre de la Conquête* (Montreal and Paris, 1955), pp. 218–227; L. H. Gipson, *The British Empire Before the American Revolution,* 8 vols. (New York, 1949), vol. VII, pp. 145–153.

Chapter 2: New France 1524–1629: A Commercial Outpost

¹ H. P. Biggar (ed.), *The Voyages of Jacques Cartier* (Publications of the Public Archives of Canada, no. 11, King's Printer, Ottawa, 1924), pp. 60–62.

² H. P. Biggar (ed.), *A Collection of Documents Relating to Jacques Cartier and the Sieur de Roberval* (Publications of the Public Archives of Canada, no. 14, King's Printer, Ottawa, 1930), pp. 102–403 *passim.*

³ Marcel Trudel, *Histoire de la Nouvelle France,* vol. I: *Les Vaines tentatives, 1524–1603* (Montreal, 1963), p. 130.

⁴ Harold A. Innis, *The Fur Trade in Canada* (Toronto, 1962), pp. 4–15.

⁵ H. P. Biggar, *The Early Trading Companies of New France. A Contribution to the History of Commerce and Discovery in North America* (Toronto, 1901), pp. 104–106.

⁶ George T. Hunt, *The Wars of the Iroquois* (Madison, Wis., 1960), pp. 56–65.

⁷ *Chronological List of Canadian Censuses,* Dominion Bureau of Statistics, Demography Branch, Ottawa.

⁸ Gabriel Sagard, *Histoire du Canada et voyages que des frères Mineurs Recollects y ont faicts pour la conversion des Infidèles depuis l'an 1615,* 4 vols. (Paris, 1866), vol. II, pp. 430–431.

⁹ Gabriel Sagard, *The Long Journey to the Country of the Hurons,* G. M. Wrong, ed.; Champlain Society Publications, XXXV, Toronto, 1939), pp. 57–58.

¹⁰ Frère Denis Jennes, Recollect à M. Le Cardinal de Joyeuse, Québec, 15 juillet 1615, Bibliothèque Nationale, Paris, Series Cinq Cents de Colbert, vol. 483, p. 581.

¹¹ For a detailed study of this encounter, see A. G. Zeller, *The Champlain-Iroquois Battle of 1615* (The Madison County Historical Society, Oneida, N.Y., 1962).

¹² Lawrence H. Leder (ed.), *The Livingston Indian Records 1666–1723* (Gettysburg, Pa., 1956), p. 128.

¹³ They were Frs. Charles Lalemant, Ennemond Massé, Jean de Brébeuf, lay brothers Gilbert Burel and François Charton.

¹⁴ Gabriel Sagard, *The Long Journey to the Country of the Hurons,* pp. 52–53.

Chapter 3: Commerce and Evangelism, 1632–1662

¹ Claude Delisle: Mélanges du 2 Jan. 1634, Bibliothèque Nationale, Paris, Fonds Français, vol. 9711, p. 183.

² George T. Hunt, *The Wars of the Iroquois* (Madison, Wis., 1960), p. 33.

³ Relation d'un voyage de Paris au Canada. Montréal le 14 octobre 1741, *Rapport de l'Archiviste de la Province de Québec, 1947–1948* (hereafter cited as *RAPQ*), p. 24.

⁴ *Chronological List of Canadian Censuses,* Dominion Bureau of Statistics, Demography Branch, Ottawa.

⁵ On the role played by the *Compagnie de St. Sacrement* in the founding of Montreal, see the article by E. R. Adair, "France and the Beginnings of New France," *The Canadian Historical Review,* vol. XXV (September, 1944), pp. 246–278.

⁶ Reuben G. Thwaites (ed.), *The Jesuit Relations and Allied Documents,* 73 vols. (Cleveland, 1896–1901), vol. 22, pp. 207–209.

[7] Dollier de Casson, *A History of Montreal 1640–1672* (translated and edited by Ralph Flenley; London, Toronto, and New York, 1928), p. 101.

[8] Ordonnance de M. Raudot, intendant . . . Montréal, 26 May 1707, Archives Nationales, Colonies, Series CIIA, vol. 26, p. 256.

[9] R. P. George d'Endemare au R. P. François de la Vie, Fort Richelieu, 2 sept. 1644, Bibliothèque Nationale, Collection Moreau, vol. 841, pp. 251–252.

[10] Extrait du Conseil d'Etat du 5 mars 1648, Archives Nationales, Colonies, Series CIIA, vol. 2, pp. 22–23; Memoire du Canada, M. de la Chesnaye 1695, Archives Nationales, Colonies, Series F3, vol. 2, pp. 5–8; Gustave Lanctot, *A History of Canada*, vol. I: *From Its Origins to the Royal Regime, 1663*, (Cambridge, Mass. 1963), pp. 183–198; Leon Gérin, *Aux Sources de Notre Histoire* (Montreal, 1946), pp. 143–161.

[11] Canada, Memoire du Sr. Gaudais du Pont à Mgr. Colbert . . . , Archives Nationales, Colonies, Series CIIA, vol. 2, pp. 88–90.

[12] Extrait du registre du Con.ᵉˡ *ibid.*, vol. I, p. 296.

[13] Marcel Trudel, *Histoire de la Nouvelle-France*, vol. II: *Le Comptoir 1604–1627* (Montreal, 1966), pp. 348–351.

[14] In 1649 Fr. Charles Garnier asked his brother to pray God to grant him a martyr's death, and among Father Lallemant's papers was found, after his death at the hands of the Iroquois, "a paper from which we learned that, before coming to New France, he had devoted and consecrated himself to Our Lord for the purpose of receiving from his hand a violent death, either in exposing himself among the plague stricken in Old France, or in seeking to save the Savages in the New." Thwaites, *Jesuit Relations*, vol. XXXIV, p. 229. See also, Chas. Garnier à son frère, Sainte-Marie, 12 aoust 1649, *RAPQ, 1929–1930*, p. 41.

[15] In the Royal Arrêt approving the establishment of the Community of Habitants in 1645, it is stated that one of the main purposes of the colony was "the advancement of the glory of God, and the honour of this Crown by the conversion of the savage peoples, to bring them to a civilized life under His Majesty's authority . . .". *Edits, Ordonnances Royaux, Declarations et Arrêts du Conseil d'Etat du Roi concernant le Canada* (Quebec, 1854), p. 29.

[16] Thwaites, *Jesuit Relations*, vol. VII, p. 55.

[17] *Ibid.*, vol. XXXIII, pp. 143–145.

[18] *Ibid., vol. IV*, p. 197; vol. X, pp. 89–90.

[19] *RAPQ*, 1929–1930, pp. 14–15.

[20] *Ibid.*, pp. 23–24; Thwaites, *Jesuit Relations*, vol. IX, pp. 299–300.

[21] Although the Jesuits were tolerant of the Indians in matters of dress, the Sulpicians were not. They were extremely critical of the Jesuits for, among other things, not making the squaws wear long skirts and the braves trousers, and seemingly condoning their loose morals. See, Copie d'un Memoire dressé par un Missionaire de St. Sulpice établi à Montréal, Public Archives of Canada, transcript, Documents St. Sulpice, Registre 25, vol. 1, Part I.

[22] Thwaites, *Jesuit Relations*, vol. IX, pp. 299–300.

[23] Hunt, *The Wars of the Iroquois*, p. 40.

[24] Thwaites, *Jesuit Relations*, vol. XXXIV, p. 83; vol. VIII, p. 89; vol. XXXII, p. 99.

[25] *Ibid.*, vol. XXXIII, p. 69; vol. XXXIV, pp. 87, 99, 122–137, 197.

[26] *Ibid.*, vol. XXXIV, pp. 202–227; vol. XLIX, p. 223; vol. LI, p. 123; Hunt, *Wars of the Iroquois*, pp. 94–95.

[27] Thwaites, *Jesuit Relations*, vol. XXVIII, p. 67; *RAPQ*, 1929–1930, p. 41.

[28] P. Camille de Rochemonteix, *Les Jesuites et la Nouvelle-France au XVIIᵉ siècle*, 3 vols. (Paris, 1896), vol. II, pp. 153–155.

[29] There are innumerable accounts of Indian torture, in the *Jesuit Relations* and also in Sagard's, *The Long Journey to the Country of the Hurons*, pp. 161–163. Aubert de la Chesnaye, a leading figure in New France *ca.* 1650–1700, in his Memoire de Canada,

1695 (Archives Nationales, Colonies, Series CIIA, vol. 13, pp. 440–454) states that the Iroquois had been the first to torture their prisoners to death to frighten their more numerous foes into submission, but the other nations had merely reciprocated in kind. See also Nathaniel Knowles, "The Torture of Captives by the Indians of Eastern North America," *Proceedings of the American Philosophical Society*, vol. LXXXII, (Philadelphia, 1940), pp. 151–225.

30 On Sulpician hostility to the Jesuits, see the memoire referred to in note 21 above.

31 The best study to date of this vexed problem is the article by André Vachon, "L'eau de vie dans la société indienne," *Canadian Historical Association Report*, 1960.

Chapter 4: Institutions and Environment

1 S. L. Mims, *Colbert's West India Policy* (New Haven, Conn., 1912), pp. 75–81.

2 *Ordonnances des Intendants et Arrêts portant règlements du Conseil Supérieur de Québec*, 2 vols. (Quebec, 1800), vol. II, p. 128.

3 On this aspect of immigration, see Gustave Lanctot, *Filles de joie ou Filles du Roi* (Montreal, 1952).

4 See W. J. Eccles, "Social Welfare Measures and Policies in New France," XXXVI *Congreso Internacional de Americanistas, Espana, 1964. Actas Y Memorias* (Seville, 1967), vol. IV, pp. 9–20.

5 Reuben G. Thwaites, *Jesuit Relations and Allied Documents*, 73 vols. (Cleveland, 1896–1901), vol. LI, pp. 167–177.

6 Vaudreuil au Ministre, Que., 15 mai 1713, *Rapport de l'Archiviste de la Province de Québec, 1947–1948* (hereafter cited as *RAPQ*), p. 203.

7 In 1690, for example, when Governor Frontenac received word that a Boston fleet was in the Gulf of St. Lawrence headed for Quebec, he was able to mobilize the entire manpower of the colony and muster it at Quebec before the New Englanders managed to put their forces ashore. Similarly, in offensive operations an army could be put in the field in a matter of weeks, a large detachment in days. See W. J. Eccles, *Frontenac: The Courtier Governor* (Toronto, 1959), pp. 230–243.

8 See Edmond Esmonin, *Etudes sur la France des XVIIᵉ et XVIIIᵉ siècles* (Paris, 1964), pp. 13–165.

9 For a detailed account of some of these early conflicts, see W. J. Eccles, *Frontenac: The Courtier Governor*, pp. 31–74, 127–156, 309–327.

10 *Edits, Ordonnances Royaux, Déclarations et Arrêts du Conseil d'Etat du Roi concernant le Canada* (Quebec, 1854) p. 233; Colbert à Frontenac, St.-Germain-en-Laye, 8 mai 1675, *RAPQ, 1926–1927*, p. 100.

11 The registers of the Ordonnances des Intendants, twenty volumes of manuscript copies, are at the Archives de la Province de Québec. They are briefly calendared in Pierre-Georges Roy, (ed.), *Inventaire des Ordonnances des Intendants de la Nouvelle France*, 4 vols. (Quebec, 1919).

12 Lettre du Roy à M. de Courcelles . . . , Paris, 3 avril 1669, Archives Nationales, Colonies, Series B. vol. 1, pp. 115–117; Colbert à Courcelles, Paris, 11 mars 1671, *ibid.*, vol. 3, pp. 38–39.

13 André Lachance, *Le Bourreau au Canada sous le régime français* (Cahiers d'Histoire No. 18, La Sociéte Historique de Québec, 1966), pp. 43–44.

14 Claude de Ferrière, *Corps et Compilation de tous les Commentateurs anciens et modernes sur la Coutume de Paris*, 4 vols. (Paris, 1714), vol. II, p. 262.

15 In October 1705 the attorney general reported to the Sovereign Council that a soldier condemned to be hanged for the rape of an eleven-year-old girl would freeze to death if retained in the cells much longer. This posed a problem since the colony lacked the services of a hangman at the time. To spare him further suffering, a condemned murderer was brought from Acadia and given the choice of accepting the vacant post

and executing the soldier or returning to Acadia to be hanged himself. He accepted the post and the soldier went to the gibbet in Montreal on November 23 before the winter had become too severe. *Jugements et Délibérations du Conseil Supérieur de Québec* (Quebec, 1889), vol. V, pp. 157–158, 191–193. See also *ibid.*, vol. III, pp. 71–72.

[16] *Ibid.*, vol. I, pp. 129–130, 174–175.

[17] Le Roi à Vaudreuil et Bégon, Versailles, 19 mars 1714, *RAPQ, 19 17–1948*, p. 241.

[18] Ordonnance du Roy, St. Germain, 24 mai 1679, Archives Nationales, Colonies, Series B, vol. 8, pp. 17–18; Pièces Judiciaires, 23 fev. 1719, Archives Judiciaires de Montréal.

[19] Règlement pour les salaires des officiers de Justice du pays de Canada, 1 may 1678, Archives Nationales, Colonies, Series F3, vol. 5, pp. 28–31; *Inventaire des Ordonnances des Intendants de la Nouvelle France*, vol. II, pp. 122–123.

[20] Addition au Memoire du Roy à MM de Vaudreuil et Bégon, Marly, 24 juin 1712, *RAPQ, 1947–1948*, p. 145. That this intention was heeded by at least some of the senior officials was made manifest in 1704 when the governor general and the intendant reported to the minister that, upon learning that the commandant at Montreal had exceeded his authority by seizing without due process of law a canoe load of furs belonging to local merchants whom he suspected of illegal trading with the Ottawa, "the Sieur de Ramezay has suffered the dishonor, despite the prestige of his office, to be condemned to restore the seized furs, and pay the costs, to those from whom he had seized them by main force." The fact, however, that Governor General Vaudreuil and de Ramezay were not on good terms may have had some bearing on this case. See Vaudreuil et Beauharnois au Ministre, Que., 14 nov. 1704, *RAPQ, 1938–1939*, p. 62.

[21] Edit du Roi, 1717, Public Archives of Canada, Series AC/G2, vol. 192–1, pp. 8–10. For examples of cases where poverty was not allowed to bar a man from obtaining justice, see *Jugements et Délibérations du Conseil Souverain de la Nouvelle France*, vol. III, pp. 576–577, 596, 635–637, 626–627, 656, 664; *Inventaire des Insinuations du Conseil Souverain* (Quebec, 1929), p. 274.

[22] See Marcel Giraud, "Tendances humanitaires à la fin du règne de Louis XIV," *Revue Historique*, vol. CCIX, 1953, pp. 217–237.

[23] The view that New France was a despotism, "without open discussion of public issues, a world of suppression of thought in which governmental policy affecting the most vital issues of the people was carried out without their consent expressed either directly or indirectly. . . ." (L. G. Gipson, *The British Empire Before the American Revolution*: vol. V, pp. 342–343) is not in accord with a substantial body of evidence. This was also, of course, the view of Francis Parkman, enunciated in *The Old Regime in Canada* (Boston, 1887), pp. 394–395, 400–401. Professor Y. F. Zoltvany has decisively refuted this opinion by citations from primary sources. See K. A. MacKirdy, J. S. Moir, and Y. F. Zoltvany, *Changing Perspectives in Canadian History* (Toronto, 1967), pp. 16–31.

[24] Colbert à Frontenac, 13 juin 1673, *RAPQ, 1926–1927*, p. 25.

[25] This concept of social responsibility is made manifest in the lengthy instructions given each intendant upon appointment. For example, the official instructions to Jean Talon, the first intendant of New France, contained this among several similar injunctions: "The King, considering all his Canadian subjects from the highest to the lowest as though, they were virtually his own children, and wishing to fulfill the obligation he is under to extend to them the benefits and felicity of his rule, as much as to those who reside in France, the Sieur Talon will study above all things how to assist them in every way and to encourage them in their trade and commerce, which alone can create abundance in the country and cause the families to prosper." *RAPQ, 1930–1931*, p. 9.

[26] MM de Vaudreuil et Raudot au Ministre, Que., 3 nov. 1706, *RAPQ, 1938–1939*, p. 154; Le Roe à MM de Vaudreuil et Raudot, Versailles, 30 juin 1707, *RAPQ 1939–1940*, p. 361. See also Allana G. Reid, "Representative Assemblies in New France, "*The*

Canadian Historical Review, Vol. XXVII (March, 1946), pp. 19–26. Unfortunately the minutes of these assemblies appear not to have survived. In the correspondence of the governors and intendants mention is made of a few of them, but only when the problems discussed were not resolved satisfactorily.

27 La Roi à MM de Vaudreuil et Raudot, Marly, 10 mai 1710, *RAPQ, 1946–1947,* p. 375.

28 For example, Ordonnance que homologue un acte d' assemblée des habitants de Boucherville pour l'élection de deux syndics chargés de gérer la commune de la dite seigneurie, *Inventaire des Ordonnances des Intendants,* vol. II, p. 127.

29 When it was proposed to levy a tax for local purposes, an assembly of those who would be called on to pay the tax was convened to determine the amount needed, how much each person or institution should pay, according to his means, and the method of collection. This was tantamount to taxation with representation. For an example of such a procedure, the levying of a tax to repair the stone wall encircling Montreal, see *Inventaire des Ordonnances des Intendants,* vol. II, p. 53.

30 Vaudreuil et Bégon au Ministre, Que., 20 sept. 1714. *RAPQ, 1947–1948,* pp. 281–282.

31 Most, but by no means all, of these "immigrants" had been captured by French and Indian war parties. The Canadian authorities made every effort to ransom the English prisoners held by the Indians. The younger children were cared for by the Ursulines or the Sisters of the Congregation of Notre Dame. At the end of King William's War, most of the prisoners refused to return to the English colonies; those under twelve had to be forced to return by the French authorities who declared them to be too young to decide such an important issue themselves. On this particular case, see W. J. Eccles, *Frontenac: The Courtier Governor,* pp. 268–269. In the ensuing War of the Spanish Succession well over one hundred prisoners elected to remain in Canada at the end of hostilities. Those who had become Roman Catholics and requested naturalization papers were granted them, becoming French subjects. According to one compilation by P. G. Roy in *Bulletin des Recherches Historiques,* vol. XXX (August, 1924), pp. 225–232, some 134 letters of naturalization were issued during this war. How many others remained in the colony and did not request *Lettres de nationalité* is not known. Likely those who acquired little property would see no need to bother. In 1714 Governor General Vaudreuil informed the king that the English colonial authorities had sent envoys to Canada who had been given very opportunity to persuade their nationals to return, but with very little response. He further stated that he had done nothing whatsoever to encourage them to remain and had made every effort to prevent others from doing so. It is interesting to note in passing that one child captive, Esther Wheelwright of York, Maine, was cared for by Vaudreuil as his foster daughter and subsequently entered the Ursuline order, eventually becoming mother superior. It is perhaps not without significance that in the 1966 Montreal telephone directory the name Langlois, the archaic form of l'Anglais, takes up two pages. On this question of British residents of New France, see *RAPQ, 1938–1939,* p. 61; *RAPQ, 1946–1947,* p. 38; *RAPQ, 1947–1948,* pp. 185, 243, 252–253, 262; *Inventaire des Insinuations du Conseil Souverain,* pp. 119–121; *Inventaire des Ordonnances des Intendants de la Nouvelle France,* vol. I, p. 120.

Chapter 5: Society and the Frontier

1 *Chronological List of Canadian Censuses,* Bureau of Statistics, Demography Branch, Ottawa.

2 Adolph B. Benson (ed.), *Peter Kalm's Travels in North America,* 2 vols. (New York, 1966), vol. II, pp. 416–417.

3 Le Roi à Vaudreuil et Raudot, Versailles, 6 juillet 1709, *Rapport de l'Archiviste de la Province de Québec,* 1942–1943 (hereafter cited as *RAPQ* p. 408.

[4] E. B. O'Callaghan and J. R. Brodhead, *Documents Relating to the Colonial History of New York*, 15 vols. (Albany, 1856–1883), vol. IV, p. 693.

[5] Benson (ed.), *Peter Kalm's Travels in North America*, vol. II, p. 600.

[6] Papiers La Pause. *RAPQ, 1931–1932*, pp. 66–67.

[7] Denonville au Ministre, Que., 13 nov. 1685, Archives Nationales, Colonies, Series C11A, vol. 7, pp. 89–95.

[8] Memoire instructif sur le Canada, 10 may 1691, *ibid.*, vol. 11, pp. 262–268.

[9] Benson (ed.), *Peter Kalm's Travels in North America*, vol. II, pp. 522, 563.

[10] Etienne de Carheil, S.J. à Champigny, Michilimackinac, 30 d'aoust 1702, Public Archives of Canada, Series M, vol. 204, part 1, pp. 177–179; Fr. J.-F. St. Cosme, Michilmackinac, 13 sept. 1689, *RAPQ, 1965*, p. 37.

[11] In a dispatch to the minister, Vaudreuil stated, "tous les françois qui ont épousé des sauvagesses sont devenus libertins feneans, et d'une independence insuportable, et que les enfans qu'ils ont esté d'une feneantise aussy grande que les sauvages mesmes, doit empescher qu'on ne permette ces sortes de mariages." Vaudreuil et Raudot au Ministre, Que., 14 nov. 1709, *RAPQ, 1942–1943*, p. 420.

[12] Charlevoix, *Histoire de la Nouvelle France*, vol. II: *Journal d'un voyage fait par ordre du Roi dans l'Amérique septentrionale addressé à Madame la Duchesse de Lesdiguières* (Paris, 1744), pp. 247–249.

[13] Papiers La Pause. *RAPQ, 1931–1932*, p. 67. See also Fernand Ouellet, "La mentalité et l'outillage économique de l'habitant canadien 1760. . . ." *Bulletin des Recherches Historiques* (1956), pp. 131–136.

[14] Memoire sur les affaires du Canada, Avril 1689, *RAPQ, 1922–1923*, p. 7.

[15] *The American Gazetteer*, 3 vols. (London, 1762), vol. II, entry under Montreal.

[16] Relation d'un voyage de Paris à Montréal en Canadas en 1737. *RAPQ, 1947–1948*, pp. 16–17.

[17] See Benson (ed.), *Peter Kalm's Travels in North America*, vol. II, pp. 446–447, 558; H. R. Casgrain (ed.), *Voyage au Canada dans le nord de l'Amérique septentrionale fait depuis l'an 1751 à 1761 par J.C.B.* (Quebec, 1887), p. 169.

[18] Benson (ed.), *Peter Kalm's Travels in North America*, vol. II, pp. 558, 626.

[19] Richard Colebrook Harris, *The Seigneurial System in Early Canada* (Madison, Wis., 1966), p. 81.

[20] Robert Mandrou, *Introduction à la France moderne. Essai de psychologie historique 1500–1640* (Paris, 1961), pp. 17–39.

[21] Mme Bégon à son gendre, Rochefort, 8 déc. 1750. *RAPQ 1934–1935*, p. 129.

[22] Champigny au Ministre, Que., 20 oct. 1699. Archives Nationales, Colonies, Series CllA, vol. 17, pp. 106–110.

[23] Benson (ed.), *Peter Kalm's Travels in North America*, vol. II, p. 536.

[24] For a revealing account of one such protestation, which could have become dangerous, and the cool way it was subdued without the *habitants* concerned being treated at all harshly, see Vaudreuil au Conseil de la Marine, Que., 17 oct. 1717, Archives Nationales, Colonies, Series CllA, vol. 38, pp. 123–124. It is interesting to note that in this dispatch Vaudreuil is justifying his having had the ten ringleaders summarily arrested and kept in cells for nearly two months without trial. He considered that the circumstances had warranted the use of his exceptional powers, which permitted arrest and imprisonment without trial only in cases of sedition and treason. The Council of Marine subsequently approved his action in this instance. The common sense attitude of the government toward the governed is illustrated in another incident, which at first appeared to be a seditious assembly but was treated as being much less serious. See Raudot au Ministre, Que, 11 nov. 1707, *ibid.*, vol. 26, pp. 202–203.

[25] Mandement de Jean éveque de Québec, 26 avril 1719, ("Trivia," Cameron Nish), *William and Mary Quarterly*, 3rd Series, vol. XXIII (July, 1966), pp. 477–478.

[26] See Les Mariages à la Gaumine, *RAPQ, 1920–1921*, pp. 366–407.

²⁷ Mme de Contrecoeur à son Mari, Montreal, 23 mai 1755. Fernand Grenier (ed.), *Papiers Contrecoeur et autres documents concernant le conflit Anglo-Français sur l'Ohio de 1745 à 1756* (Quebec, 1952), p. 349. The context in which the proverb is cited is quite revealing.

²⁸ Pierre-François-Xavier de Charlevoix, S.J. *Histoire de la Nouvelle France*, vol. III: *Journal d'un voyage fait par ordre du Roi dans l'Amérique septentrionale addressé à Madame la Duchesse de Lesdiguières* (Paris, 1744), p. 79.

²⁹ Arrest du Conseil d'Estat qui permet aux Gentilshommes de Canada de faire Commerce, du 10 mars 1685, Archives Nationales, Colonies, Series F3, vol. 7, p. 214; Le Roy au Sr. de Meulles, Versailles, 10 mars 1685, *ibid., Series B*, vol. 11, p. 99.

³⁰ Roland Mousnier, "L'evolution des institutions monarchiques en France et ses relations avec l'état social," *XVIIᵉ Siècle*, 1963, nos. 58–59.

³¹ Extrait des Registres du Conseil d'Estat, 10 avril 1684, Bibliothèque Nationale, Collection Clairambault, vol. 448, p. 369; Champigny au Ministre, Que., 10 mai 1691, Archives Nationales, Colonies, Series CllA, vol. 11, p. 255; Memoire Instructif sur le Canada, *ibid.*, pp. 265–267.

³² Le Ministre à M. de Vaudreuil, Versailles, 30 juin 1707, *RAPQ, 1939–1940*, p. 375; Résumé d'une lettre de Mme de Vaudreuil au Ministre, Paris, 1709. *RAPQ, 1942–1943*, p. 416; Mémoire du Roy à MM de Vaudreuil et Raudot, à Marly, 10 May 1710, *RAPQ, 1946–1947*, p. 376; Archives du Seminaire de Quebec, Fonds Verreau, carton 5, no. 62.

³³ Benson (ed.), *Peter Kalm's Travels in North America*, vol. I, 343–346, 375–376, 392–393; vol. II, pp. 446–447, 558, 626, 628.

Chapter 6: The Fur Trade Frontier, 1663–1700

¹ Colbert à Talon, Versailles, 5 jan. 1966, *Rapport de l'Archiviste de la Province de Quebec, 1930–1931* (hereafter cited as *RAPQ*), p. 41.

² *Ibid.*, p. 42.

³ Reuben. G. Thwaites (ed.), *The Jesuit Relations and Allied Documents,* 73 vols. (Cleveland, 1896–1901), vol. XXXXIX, p. 162; Hubert à Colbert, La Rochelle, 27 nov. 1666, Bibliothèque Nationale, Mélanges Colbert, vol. 142, p. 220; Memoire de Talon sur l'état présent du Canada, *RAPQ, 1930–1931*, p. 63.

⁴ *Jugements et Délibérations du Couseil Souverain de la Nouvelle France,* 6 vols. (Quebec, 1885), vol. 1, pp. 524, 636; Novembre 1666, Canada, Memoire de plusieurs choses touchant le Canada, Sr. Fussambert, Public Archives of Canada, Series F2A, carton 13.

⁵ Memoire sur la ferme du domaine d'Occident, 28 dec. 1698, Archives Nationales, Colonies, Series CIIA, vol. 16, p. 207; Memoire sur la Ferme . . . 1699., *ibid.*, vol. 17, p. 236; Arrêt du Roy, au camp de Condé, 16 may 1677, *ibid.*, vol. 4, pp. 169–170.

⁶ Colbert à Talon, Versailles, 5 jan. 1666, *RAPQ, 1930–1931*, p. 43.

⁷ Talon à Colbert, Que., 10 nov. 1670, Archives Nationales, Colonies, Series CIIA, vol. 3, p. 81.

⁸ Colbert à Frontenac, 17 mai 1674, *RAPQ, 1926–1927*, p. 58.

⁹ On the founding of Fort Frontenac and the subsequent controversy, see W. J. Eccles, *Frontenac: The Courtier Governor* (Toronto, 1959), pp. 38–50, 79–85, 104–107.

¹⁰ Colbert à Duchesneau, Paris, 28 avril 1677, Archives Nationales, Colonies, Series B, vol. 7, p. 79.

¹¹ Frontenac au Ministre, Que., 25 oct. 1696, *ibid.*, Series CIIA, vol. 14, pp. 157–161; Mèmoire écrit par l'officier envoyé par Frontenac commander à Missilimakina en 1694, *ibid.*, vol. 13, pp. 149–151.

¹² On La Salle's career, see E. B. Osler, *La Salle* (Toronto, 1967). Francis Parkman's epic work, *La Salle and the Discovery of Great West* (Boston, 1869), is doubtless a great literary work, but as history it is, to say the least, of dubious merit. On this work, see

the article by W. R. Taylor, "A Journey into the Human Mind: Motivation in Francis Parkman's *La Salle,*" *William and Mary Quarterly,* 3rd Series, vol. XIX (April, 1962).

¹³ Relation des Voyages et des découvertes du Sr. de la Salle, Bibliothèque Nationale, Collection Clairambault, vol. 1016, pp. 49–84.

¹⁴ Duchesneau au Ministre, Que., 13 nov. 1680, Archives Nationales Colonies, Series C11A, vol. 5, p. 168; Memoire du Sr. Patroulet demandé par Mgr. a Paris le 25 janvier 1672, *ibid.,* vol. 3, p. 274.

¹⁵ "Onontio" was a Mohawk word meaning big mountain. Charles Jacques de Huault de Montmagny, governor of the colony 1636–1648, made a strong impression on the Iroquois who asked what his name signified. Upon being told, they deemed it fitting, and from then on all governors general of Canada were given this name by the Indian nations, Iroquois and Algonkin alike.

¹⁶ See Emma Helen Blair, *The Indian Tribes of the Upper Mississippi Valley and Region of the Great Lakes,* 2 vols. (Cleveland, 1911), vol. I, pp. 208–209, n. 148; Pierre-François-Xavier de Charlevoix, S.J., *Histoire de la Nouvelle-France,* 3 vols. 4th ed.; Paris, 1744), vol. III, p. 142.

¹⁷ M. Dudouyt à Mgr. de Laval, Paris, 9 Mars 1681, Archives du Seminaire de Québec, Lettres, carton M, no. 52.

¹⁸ Edit du Roy, Versailles, 2 May 1681, Archives Nationales, Colonies Series B, vol. 8, pp. 86–87; Ordonnance du Roy, Versailles, 2 May 1681, *ibid.,* pp. 88–89; Louis XIV à Duchesneau, 30 avril 1681, *ibid.,* Series C11A, vol. 5, p. 342.

¹⁹ Thwaites, *Jesuit Relations,* vol. 59, p. 250; ibid., vol. 60, p. 172.

²⁰ On the outbreak of French-Iroquois hostilities, see W. J. Eccles, *Frontenac: The Courtier Governor,* pp. 107–126.

²¹ La Barre au Ministre, Que., 1682, Archives Nationales, Colonies, Series C11A, vol. 6, p. 60.

²² See Arthur H. Buffinton, "The Policy of Albany and English Westward Expansion," *Mississippi Valley Historical Review,* vol. VIII (March, 1922), pp. 327–366.

²³ On Anglo-French rivalry in Hudson Bay, see E. E. Rich, *The History of the Hudson's Bay Company 1670–1870,* vol. I: *1670–1863* (London, 1958), pp. 116–132, 192–249, 327–354.

²⁴ For Colbert's frank comments on his son's meager abilities, see Pierre Clément (ed.), *Lettres, instructions et Mémoires de Colbert,* 7 vols. (Paris, 1861–1873), vol. III, part 2, pp. 9–10, 12–13.

²⁵ Le Chevalier de Baugy, *Journal d'une expédition contre les Iroquois en 1687* (Paris, 1883), pp. 155.

²⁶ Bégon à de Villermont, La Rochelle, 10 déc. 1688, Public Archives of Canada, transcript, Bibliothèque Nationale, Fonds Français, vol. 22800, p. 181.

²⁷ E. B. O'Callaghen (ed.), *Documentary History of the State of New York,* 4 vols. (Albany, 1850), vol. III, pp. 784–786; *Calendar of State Papers Colonial, America and West Indies 1697–1698* (London, 1862–1912), p. 499; *ibid., 1699,* p. 71.

²⁸ For contemporary accounts of this abortive expedition, see E. Myrand, *Sir William Phips devant Québec* (Quebec, 1895).

²⁹ Colonies, febvrier 1695, Commerce due Castor de Canada: de Lagny à Daguisseau, Archives Nationales, Colonies, Series C11A, vol. 13, pp. 399–408.

³⁰ E. B. O'Callaghan and J. R. Brodhead (eds.), *Documents Relating to the Colonial History of New York,* 15 vols. (Albany, 1856–1883), vol. IV, pp. 337–338.

³¹ Mémoire du Sr Riverin sur la traittre et la Ferme des Castors de Canada, 1696, Archives Nationales, Colonies, Series C11A, vol. 14, pp. 280–285.

³² Le Sr de Boishebert à M. le Chevalier de Callières. Missilimakina, 30 aoust 1702, Public Archives of Canada, transcript, Series C11A, vol. 20, pp. 150–156.

³³ Extrait des depesches de Canada de l'année 1700, Archives Nationales, Colonies, Series C11A, vol. 18, p. 27; Extrait des lettres du Canada 1701. *ibid.,* vol. 19, p. 47.

Chapter 7: The Imperial Frontier, 1700–1750

[1] Projets sur la Nouvelle Angleterre, Canada, 1701, Archives Nationales, Colonies, Series C11A, vol. 19, pp. 233–234. (To the French, the term New England included New York.)

[2] F. H. Hammang, *The Marquis de Vaudreuil* (Bruges, 1938), pp. 120–122.

[3] Vaudreuil au Ministre, Que., 8 nov. 1711, *Rapport de l'Archiviste de la Province de Québec, 1946–1947* (hereafter cited as *RAPQ*), p. 453.

[4] Vaudreuil au Ministre, Que., 14 oct. 1703, Archives Nationales, Colonies, Series C11A, vol. 21, p. 52; Vaudreuil au Ministre, Que., 19 8bre 1705; *RAPQ, 1938–1939*, p. 90; Vaudreuil au Ministre, Que., 28 juin 1708, *RAPQ, 1939–1940*, p. 423.

[5] Vaudreuil au Ministre, Que., 14 9bre 1709, *RAPQ, 1942–1943*, pp. 431–432.

[6] *Jugement et délibérations du Conseil Supérieur de Québec* (Quebec, 1889), vol. V, pp. 1027–1028; Vaudreuil et Bégon au Ministre, Que., 12 nov. 1712, *RAPQ, 1947–1948*, pp. 183–184; E. R. Adair, "Anglo-French Rivalry in the Fur Trade during the 18th Century," *Culture*, vol. VIII (1947), pp. 434–435.

[7] Yves F. Zoltvany, "The Problem of Western Policy under Philippe de Rigaud de Vaudreuil (1703–1725)," *Canadian Historical Association Report, 1964*, pp. 9–24.

[8] *Ibid.*

[9] Le Sr. d'Aigremont au Ministre, Que., 14 nov. 1708, Archives Nationales, Colonies, Series C11A, vol. 29, pp. 26–77.

[10] Memoire pour prendre possession de Niagara . . . Joint à la lettre du Sr. Charon, 28 oct. 1706, Archives Nationales, Colonies, Series C11A, vol. 25, p. 298; Vaudreuil et Raudot au Ministre, Que., 14 nov. 1708; *ibid.*, vol. 28, p. 35.

[11] Jean Lunn, "The Illegal Fur Trade out of New France, 1713–1760," *The Canadian Historical Association Report, 1939*, pp. 61–76; Adolph B. Benson (ed.), *Peter Kalm's Travels in North America*, 2 vols. (New York, 1966), vol. I, p. 343; Vaudreuil et Bégon au Ministre, Que., 20 sept 1714, *RAPQ, 1947–1948*, p. 275.

[12] D'Aigremont au Ministre, Que., 14 nov. 1708, Archives Nationales, Colonies, Series C11A, vol. 29, p. 69.

[13] Vaudreuil et Raudot au Ministre, Que., 15 nov. 1707, *ibid.*, vol. 26, p. 12; Memoire du Roy à MM de Vaudreuil et Raudot, à Marly le 10 May 1710, *RAPQ, 1946–1947*, p. 376; Memoire du Roy à Vaudreuil et Bégon, Paris, 15 juin 1716; *RAPQ, 1947–1948*, p. 306.

[14] *Chronological List of Canadian Censuses*, Dominion Bureau of Statistics, Demography Branch, Ottawa.

[15] Vaudreuil et Beauharnois au Ministre, Que., 15 oct. 1703, Archives Nationales, Colonies, Series C11A, vol. 21, pp. 13–14; Vaudreuil et Raudot au Ministre, Que., 30 avril 1706, *ibid.*, vol. 24, pp. 9–10; Journal du Sr de Montigny . . . 13e mars 1705, *RAPQ, 1922–1923*, pp. 293–298; Raudot et Vaudreuil au Ministre, Que., 14 nov. 1708, *RAPQ, 1939–1940*, pp. 457–458; Vaudreuil au Ministre, Que., 3 nov. 1710, *RAPQ, 1946–1947*, p. 400; Vaudreuil au Ministre, Que., 27 juin 1712, *RAPQ, 1947–1948*, pp. 150–151; Vaudreuil au Ministre, Que., 14 nov. 1709, *RAPQ, 1942–1943*, p. 434; Vaudreuil au Ministre, Que., 3 nov. 1710, *RAPQ, 1946–1947*, p. 397.

[16] Articles de Capitulation accordés pour la Redition du fort du Port Royal à la Cadie Entre M. Daniel Auger de Subercase . . . et M. François Nicholson, Bibliothéque Nationale, Fonds Français, vol. 10207, pp. 205–206; Lettre de M. Nicholson à M. Subecase le 3 Oct. 1710, Lettre de M. Subercase à M. Nicholson datée le 12 oct. 1710, *ibid.*, pp. 207–208.

[17] Le Ministre à M. de Vaudreuil, à Marly le 10 May 1710, *RAPQ, 1946–1947*, p. 378; Vaudreuil et Bégon au Ministre, Que., 12 nov. 1712, *RAPQ, 1947–1948*, pp. 174–176; Vaudreuil au Ministre, Que., 14 nov. 1713, *ibid.*, pp. 236–237; Ministre à Vaudreuil, Versailles, 19 mars 1714, *ibid.*, p. 250; Memoire du Roy à MM de Vaudreuil et Bégon,

Versailles le 19 mars 1714, *ibid.*, p. 240; Memoire du Roi à MM. de Vaudreuil et Bégon, Paris, 15 juin 1716, *ibid.*, pp. 298–299.

18 Yves F. Zoletvany, "The Problem of Western Policy under Philippe de Rigaud de Vaudreuil (1703–1725)," *The Canadian Historical Association Report, 1964*, pp. 9–24.

19 Beauharnois au Commandant d'Oswego, Que., 14 juillet 1729, Affaires Etrangères, Series Amérique, vol. 7, pp. 232–234; Beauharnois à Burnet, Que., 20 juillet 1727, *ibid.*, pp. 235–237; *Inventaire des Ordonnances des Intendants*, II, p. 16.

20 Memoire de M. de Vaudreuil au comte de Toulouse, *RAPQ, 1946–1947*, p. 405.

21 The Comte de la Galissonière stated that those engaged in the Albany smuggling trade insisted that the Indians would accept none other than English cloth, but that this was a means to protect the smugglers' vested interest in contraband goods; he maintained that Languedoc cloth had driven English cloth off the Levant market and could do the same in Canada. See Galissonière au Ministre, Que., 20 oct. 1748, Archives Nationales, Colonies, Series C11A, vol. 91, pp. 67–71.

22 Five- to eight-man canoes cost, in the mid-eighteenth century, 300 *livres* and lasted from four to five years if properly handled. Each canoe was equipped with paddles, sail, a large cooking pot, large sponge, and "gomme de ouatape" for recaulking the seams en route, all of which cost 30 *livres*. The bow and stern men were paid 250 *livres* each, the men in the middle 200, for a three-month trip. The men's supplies, consisting of hard tack, leached corn, salt pork or jerked venison, brandy, tobacco, powder, and lead cost 45 *livres* per man. An eight-man canoe was 35 feet long (33 old French feet), 5 feet beam, 2½ feet deep. Trois Rivières was the main center for canoe making. A master builder earned as much as 6000 *livres* a year. In comparison to the *voyageurs*, the officers, chaplains, and storekeepers at the western posts lived quite well. Some officers at least had Negro slaves as body servants. For rations, they were issued per year, a barrel of wine, 48 quarts of brandy, 20 pounds of butter, 1 pound of pepper and some other spices, 20 pounds of candles, a bushel of peas, 48 quarts of molasses, and enough pork, beef, and flour to allow a daily ration of ½ pound of pork, 1 pound of beef, and 2 pounds of bread. The old French *livre* (pound) approximated three quarters of an English pound. Surgeons received the same rations, with the omission of wine, a further indication that the medical profession did not enjoy a particularly high status under the old regime. See Memoire sur les postes du Canada . . . par le Chevalier de Raymond, *RAPQ, 1927–1928*, p. 341; Louis Franquet, *Voyages et mémoires sur le Canada* (Quebec, 1889), p. 17; Rations de MM les offiiers, aumoniers et garde-magasins, 23 août 1748, P.-G. Roy (ed.), *Inventaire des ordonnances des intendants de la Nouvelle France conservées aux archives provinciales de Québec*, 4 vols. (Quebec, 1919, vol. III, p. 109; Journal de Marin, fils, *RAPQ*, Tome 41, 1963, p. 292.

23 Archives Judiciares de Montréal, Congés et Ordonnances 1721–1730; P.-G. Roy (ed.), *Inventaire des ordonnances des intendants de la Nouvelle France*, vol. II, p. 274.

24 Galissonière au Ministre, Que., 23 oct. 1748, *ibid.*, pp. 231–233.

25 Mme Bégon à son gendre, Mtl, 28, 29 mars, 2 avril 1749, *RAPQ, 1934–1935*, pp. 52, 54.

26 Louis Franquet, *Voyages et mémoires sur le Canada* (Quebec, 1889), pp. 29–30.

27 Journal de Marin, fils, 1753–1754, *RAPQ*, Tome 41, 1963, pp. 237–308. For other accounts of attempts by post commandants to keep the peace in the west, particularly between the Cree tribes and the Sioux, see Archives du Séminaire de Québec, Fonds Verreau, Carton 5, nos. 24, 33, 54.

28 Yves F. Zoltvany, "The Frontier Policy of Philippe de Rignaud de Vaudreuil (1713–1725)," *The Canadian Historical Review*, vol. XLVIII (September, 1967), pp. 227–250.

29 La Galissoniàre à M. de St. Pierre Commandant à Missilimakinac, Que. 4 7bre 1748. Archives du Seminaire de Québec, Fonds Verreau, carton 5, no. 53; see also Beauharnois à M. de St. Pierre, Mtl. 28 aoust 173 . . . (last figure torn off) *ibid.*, no. 12; M. Neul (?) à St. Pierre à Grand Portage, Que., 15 may 1752, *ibid.*, no. 38½; Mémoire

sur l'Etat de la Nouvelle France 1757, Bougainville, *RAPQ, 1923–1924*, p. 51; Marcel Trudel, *L'esclavage au Canada français* (Quebec, 1960), p. 71.

[30] Roland Mousnier et Ernest Labrousse, *Histoire Générale des Civilizations.* Tome V le XVIIIe Siècle (Paris, 1955), p. 213; Paul Vaucher, *Robert Walpole et la politique de Fleury (1731–1742)* (Paris, 1924), pp. 298–302.

[31] *Ibid.*, pp. 296, 302.

[32] Galissonière au Ministre, Que., 23 oct. 1748, Archives Nationales, Colonies, Series C11A, vol. 91, pp. 231–233; *Collection de manuscrits contenant lettres, mémoires et autres documents historiques relatifs à la Nouvelle-France,* 4 vols. (Quebec, 1883–1885), vol. III, pp. 348–361.

[33] Maurice Filion, *Maurepas ministre de Louis XV, 1715–1749* (Montreal, 1967), pp. 54–55, 137, 140.

[34] Walter L. Dorn, *Competition for Empire 1740–1763* (New York, 1963), p. 171.

[35] Galissonière au Ministre, Que., 1 Sept. 1748, Archives Nationales, Colonies, Series C11A, vol. 91, pp. 116–123.

Chapter 8: The Military Frontier, 1748–1760

[1] Raymond à Jonquière, Fort des Miamis, 4 et 5 spt 1749, Archives Nationales, Colonies, Series C11A, vol. 93, pp. 58–64, 66–68.

[2] Quoted in Lawrence Henry Gipson, *The British Empire Before the American Revolution,* vol. IV, p. 217.

[3] *Documents Relating to the Colonial History of New York* (E. B. O'Callaghan and J. R. Brodhead, eds.; Albany, 1856–1883.) (hereafter cited as *NYCD*), 15 vols., vol. X, p. 269.

[4] Mme Bégon à son gendre, Mtl., 13 juin 1749. *Rapport de l'Archiviste de la Province de Québec* 1934–1935 (hereafter cited as *RAPQ*), p. 74.

[5] *NYCD*, vol. X, pp. 242–245.

[6] Fernand Grenier (ed.), *Papiers Contrecoeur et autres documents concernant le conflit anglo-français sur l'Ohio de 1745 à 1756* (Quebec, 1952), p. 17; Duquesne à Marin, Mtl, 20 juillet 1753; *id à id*, Mtl, 22 juillet 1753, Archives du Seminaire de Québec, Fonds Verreau, carton 5, no. 62.

[7] Guy Frégault, *François Bigot administrateur français,* 2 vols. (Montreal, 1948), vol. II, pp. 64–72; Mme Bégon à sons fils, Rochefort 17 and 23 déc. 1750, *RAPQ, 1934–1935*, pp. 132–134.

[8] Grenier (ed.), *Papiers Contrecoeur,* pp. 99–100; H.-R. Casgrain (ed.), *Voyage au Canada dans le nord de l'Amérique septentrionale fait depuis l'an 1751 à 1761 par J.C.B.* (Quebec, 1887) pp. 62–63.

[9] Grenier (ed.), *Papiers Contrecoeur,* p. 84.

[10] *Ibid.*, pp. 60–61, 93, 99–100, 105–107, 113–116.

[11] *Ibid.*, pp. 116–117.

[12] *Ibid.*, pp. 130–131.

[13] It is impossible to give a clear-cut verdict on Washington's conduct. Despite his own and later historians' attempts to justify his action, it still remains dubious to some. Certainly the French were convinced that Jumonville and his men had been shot down, without warning, at a time when England and France were at peace. Their reaction was a mixture of extreme anger and contempt at the circumstances surrounding the incident.

[14] Both Parkman and Gipson state that upon learning of Jumonville's death Duquesne sent Villiers with Indian reinforcements to the Ohio. Duquesne's letter to Contrecoeur dated June 20 makes it plain that he had not yet received word of the clash, but his letter of the 24th acknowledges Contrecoeur's of June 2 informing him of it. Villiers arrived at Fort Duquesne on June 26; clearly, he could not have traveled from Montreal to Fort Duquesne in two days. In fact, on June 15 Villiers was at the Chataugua

portage, on the point of leaving for Fort Duquesne with 130 allied Indians and 20 French. The garrison at Fort Duquesne consisted at this time of 900 men, at least 130 of them Indians, not 1400 as stated by Parkman. See Grenier (ed.), *Papiers Contrecoeur*, pp. 183–185; Parkman, *Montcalm and Wolfe* (1964 edition), p. 118. Gipson also states (vol. VI, p. 36) that on June 27 a council of war held by Contrecoeur and his officers "conforming to orders given by Duquesne on May 29 with reference to measures that should be taken to avenge the death of Jumanville," which had occurred on May 28. But as noted above, Duquesne did not learn of Jumonville's death until sometime between June 20 and 24. Gipson further states that the council agreed that "should de Villiers find in advancing that the English had retired from the King's lands, he should nevertheless continue his march into the region of their settlements and proceed to destroy the habitations and to treat them as enemies until he had secured ample satisfaction and a change of conduct on their part. In other words, reprisals were to be made even to the extent of ravishing the English frontier settlements." The reference given is Mém. et Doc., Amérique, 10, vol. I, pp. 110–113; this being a series of original documents in the Archives du Ministère des Affaires Etrangères, Paris. It is therefore rather startling to discover, when consulting Contrecoeur's orders to Villiers dated June 28, 1754, that he gave no such instructions. Villiers was ordered to seek out the English force and, if possible, destroy it, "to chastise them for the murder that they had committed on us in violation of the most sacred laws of civilized nations." If the English force had retired, Villiers was to pursue them as far as necessary to satisfy the honor of the King's arms. Should they be entrenched and Villiers saw no way of giving battle, he was to destroy their animals and try to fall on their supply convoys. "Despite their unheard of action the Sr de Villiers is enjoined to avoid all cruelty so far as it is in his power." There is no mention whatsoever of attacking the English settlements, only of attacking convoys bringing supplies to the English force at Fort Necessity. A transcript of these orders is to be found in *RAPQ, 1922–1923*, p. 347; the original is in the Judicial Archives at Montreal.

[15]Grenier (ed.), *Papiers Contrecoeur*, p. 251. The "Capitulation du Fort Necessité" is printed in *Papiers Contrecoeur*, pp. 202–205, this being a copy at the Archives du Séminaire de Québec. The only other contemporary copy is in the Archives Judiciaries de Montréal. There are a few very minor variations in the two, the odd word transposed, an occasional word omitted without the sense being altered. Much ink has been spilled by historians eager to defend Washington against the charge that he had behaved dishonorably in the Jumonville affair and that he subsequently admitted his guilt by signing de Villier's terms for the capitulation of Fort Necessity. Washington's defense rests largely on his ignorance of French and the incompetence of his interpreter Jacob Van Braam. It seems a little odd that it was only at this late date that Van Braam's linguistic inadequacy was discovered, for he had accompanied Washington as interpreter, on his earlier expedition to Fort de la Rivière aux Boeufs to deliver Dinwiddie's letter demanding that the French vacate the Ohio country. Washington spent four days with the French officers and was well entertained. That Washington employed Van Braam on his second expedition to the Ohio would seem to indicate that he had confidence in his abilities as an interpreter. That Van Braam had an adequate command of French is established by his request, when being tried at Quebec in 1756 for high treason (he was acquitted) along with Robert Stobo, that his trial be conducted in French rather than English. In any event, in such an important issue as the signing of the terms of the capitulation of Fort Necessity it was incumbent on Washington, regardless of circumstances, that he made sure he understood what he was signing. His subsequent actions, however, make it clear that he had no intention of honoring the terms of the capitulation; thus it would have mattered little to him what the document contained. All things considered, there remains quite a wide "credibility gap." For Duquesne's opinion of Washington, see Grenier (ed.), *Papiers Contrecoeur*, p. 251.

[16] Grenier (ed.), *Papiers Contrecoeur,* pp. 223–224.

[17] "Je veux bien que vous gardiés tour les amenagemens imaginables pour ne vous mettre dans votre tort vis à vis des anglois. . . ." Duquesne à Contrecoeur, Que., 21 oct. 1754, *ibid.,* pp. 265, 305.

[18] *Ibid.,* pp. 95, 126, 128, 209, 224, 248–249, 252, 256, 265.

[19] *Ibid.,* pp. 321, 371, 375, 382, 386.

[20] *Ibid.,* pp. 215, 219, 227, 389; Archives du Seminaire de Québec, Fonds Verreau, carton 5, nos. 60, 62.

[21] Memoire sur les postes du Canada . . . par le Chevalier de Raymond. *RAPQ., 1927–1928,* pp. 326; Papiers La Pause, *RAPQ, 1933–1934,* pp. 207–208; Journal de Bougainville 1756, *RAPQ, 1923–1924,* p. 318; Journal du marquis de Montcalm . . . Henri-Raymond Casgrain (ed.), *Collection des manuscrits de maréchal de Lévis,* 12 vols. (Montreal and Quebec, 1889-1911), vol. VII, p. 349. The moral climate in Canada at this time is made plain by Mme Bégon in her letters to her son-in-law dated December 1750, *RAPQ, 1934–1935,* pp. 132, 134.

[22] M. de Machault to M. Duquesne, 6 nov. 1754. *NYCD,* vol. X, p. 270.

[23] On the military incompetence of the English colonies, see Gipson, *The British Empire Before the American Revolution,* vol. VI, chap. 3 *passim.*

[24] *Ibid.,* pp. 99–126; Julian S. Corbett, *England in the Seven Years War,* 2 vols. (London, 1907), vol. I, pp. 32–56; Roland Mousnier et Ernest Labrousse, *Histoire Générale des Civilisations, Tome V, Le XVIII Siècle* (Paris, 1955), p. 215; Guy Frégault, *La Guerre de la Conquête* (Montreal and Paris, 1955), pp. 160–161.

[25] Braddock's timetable called for him to leave his base at Alexandria, Virginia, on April 20, cross the Alleghenies on May 3, capture Fort Duquesne in June, and if the French destroyed it before retiring, build a new fort and garrison it with colonial troops. But by article 6 of the terms of the capitulation of Fort Necessity, signed by Washington, the British had agreed not to construct any posts or forts west of the height of land for one year from the date of signature, that is, July 3. In fact, Braddock's army crossed the height of land a few days after July 3; they honored the terms of the capitulation, but inadvertently.

[26] Gipson's statement in *The British Empire before the American Revolution,* vol. VI, p. 80, that Frenchmen led Indian war parties "against the frontier settlements of isolated families of Maryland and Virginia" to divert Braddock is refuted by Contrecoeur's letter of June 21 to the governor general in which he reported that the *cadets* sent out with one Indian party had just returned and reported that they had "done nothing as I had given them orders not to cross the height of land." Grenier (ed.) *Papiers Contrecoeur,* p. 366.

[27] Journal de Bougainville, 17 oct. 1757, *RAPQ, 1923–1924,* p. 313.

[28] In March 1759, Lieutenant Archibald Blane at Fort Ligonier reported to Colonel Henry Bouquet that the companies of Royal Americans, Highlanders, and Pennsylvanians in garrison were being exercised in marksmanship, those hitting the target receiving a "dram." The appended score sheet indicates that the Highlanders were much the better shots. Lieutenant Blane commented: "All the Pen.ᵃ that fire have not Riffles, nor do those that have make the best shots." S. K. Stevens and D. H. Kent (eds.), *The Papers of Col. Henry Bouquet,* 3 vols. (Harrisburg, 1951), vol. II, p. 67.

[29] On November 27, 1756, delegates from the Five Nations conferred with the French authorities at Montreal and congratulated them on the capture of Oswego. Significantly, their speaker "adroitly thanked the Marquis de Vaudreuil for in as much as he had destroyed Oswego, he had re-established the Five Nations in possession of land that belonged to them." Memoires du Chevalier de la Pause, *RAPQ, 1932–1933,* p. 327.

[30] M. Hennin à M. le Comte de Broglie, Versailles, 24 juin 1757, Archives Affaires Etrangères, Mémoires et Documents, France, vol. 536, p. 228.

[31] Quoted in B. Tunstall, *William Pitt Earl of Chatham* (London, 1938), p. 199.

[32] *NYCD*, vol. X, pp. 767–770, 824, 960–962; Casgrain (ed.), *Collection des manuscrits du maréchal de Lévis*, vol. V, p. 343, vol. VII, pp. 351, 370–371; *RAPQ, 1944–1945*, p. 155. (These are but a few examples of Montcalm's defeatist attitude. His journal is replete with it, and also with savage criticism and scathing remarks of and about all things Canadian.)

[33] *Collection de manuscrits contenant lettres et autres documents historiques relatifs à l'histoire de la Nouvelle France . . .* 4 vols. (Quebec, 1883–1885), vol. IV, p. 157.

[34] Doreil au Ministre, Que., 22 oct. 1757, 30 avril 1758. *RAPQ, 1944–1945*, pp. 113, 124.

[35] *Ibid.*, pp. 97, 121; Casgrain, *Collection des manuscrits du maréchal de Lévis*, vol. VI, pp. 111–113, 117, 121, 123, 124–125.

[36] Guy Frégault, *La Guerre de la Conquête*, pp. 304–307.

[37] Doreil au Ministre, Que., 28 juillet 1758, *RAPQ, 1944–1945*, p. 141.

[38] Doreil au Ministre, Que., 31 aoust 1758; *ibid.*, pp. 156–158.

[39] Repertoire des engagements pour l'ouest . . . 1670-1778. *RAPQ, 1932–1933*, pp. 245–259.

[40] Jeremiah Pearson His Book, 1759. Public Archives of Canada, M.G. 18, N 43.

[41] Relation de M. Poularies, *RAPQ, 1931–1932*, p. 97; Journal du siège de Québec du 10 mai au 18 septembre 1759, *RAPQ, 1920–1921*, pp. 185–186.

[42] Relation de M. Poularies, *RAPQ, 1931–1932*, p. 119; Bibliothèque Nationale, Manuscrits Français, Nouvelles Acquisitions, vol. 1041, pp. 44–63.

[43] Bourlamaque à Lévis, Longueuil, 1 sept. 1760, Casgrain, *Collection des manuscrits du maréchal de Lévis*, vol. V, pp. 121–122; *id à id*, St. Ours, 22 août 1760, *ibid.*, pp. 101–102; *id à id.*, Sorel, 16 août 1760, *ibid*, p. 91; *id à id*, Sorel, 15 août 1760, *ibid.*, pp. 88–90; *id à id*, Longueuil, 2 sept. 1760, *ibid.*, p. 124; *id à id*, Sorel, 30 août 1760, *ibid.*, p. 119; M. Bellot à M. de Bourlamaque, 22 août 1760, *ibid.*, p. 103.

[44] Lévis à M. le Maréchal de Belle Isle, De la Rochelle, le 25 nov. 1760, *ibid.*, vol. II, pp. 387–388.

Chapter 9: **The Closing of the Canadian Fur Trade Frontier**

[1] Répertoire des engagements pour l'ouest conservés dans les Archives Judiciaires de Montréal, *Rapport de l'Archiviste de la Province de Québec, 1932–1933*, pp. 245–268; 1942–1943, pp. 371–397.

[2] Fernand Ouellet, *Histoire économique et sociale du Québec 1760–1850* (Montreal, 1966), pp. 101–109.

[3] Memoire du Sr Riverin sur la traitte et la Ferme des Castors de Canada, 1696, Archives Nationales, Colonies, Series C11A, vol. 14, pp. 280–285. It is intriguing to speculate that had Riverin's proposal been heeded then, what is today the Dominion of Canada might still be under the French flag.

[4] Fernand Ouellet, "Le Nationalisme canadien-français: De ses origines à l'insurrection de 1837," *The Canadian Historical Review*, vol. XLV, no. 4, (December, 1964) p. 287.

[5] Alexander Ross, *The Fur Hunters of the Far West*, 2 vols. (London, 1855), vol. II, pp. 236–237. Quoted in P. B. Waite, *Canadian Historical Document Series*, vol. II, Pre-Confederation, 3 vols. (Toronto, 1965), p. 145.

BIBLIOGRAPHICAL NOTES

The primary source material for the history of New France is extensive but rather scattered. Little of the correspondence and accounts of the private companies that administered the colony prior to 1663 is known to have survived. In 1671 the government in France took steps to conserve official documents, and some pertaining to Canada, written during the preceding eight years, were preserved; many, however, had already been lost. In 1760, when the French officials returned to France, all but documents of purely local interest, mainly those concerning property, were taken with them. The bulk of the correspondence between colonial officials and the metropolitan authorities is conserved in various archives in Paris. The principal depositaries are the Archives Nationales, the Bibliothéque Nationale, the Archives du Ministère de la Guerre, and the Archives du Ministère des Affaires Etrangères. Certain of the archives in the provinces contain material pertaining to Canada, for example those at La Rochelle, and more is being discovered as scholars widen their interests and their search.

In Canada the Public Archives at Ottawa hold some primary source material. The more important series of documents relating to Canada in the French archives have been microfilmed, and an extensive selection has been transcribed. The Quebec Provincial Archives possess considerable manuscript material, notably the registers of the intendants' *ordonnances,* the records of the Sovereign Council and the Quebec Prévôté, a number of notarial *greffes,* some important documents pertaining to the War of the Conquest, and much other material of particular interest to the social historian. In addition this depositary possesses transcripts and microfilm copies of much of the official correspondence in the French archives.

Certain of the religious orders have their private archives; that of the Grand Séminaire de Québec is exceptionally rich, particularly in material relating to the west. In Montreal the Archives Judiciares contain a great mass of original source material, notably documents pertaining to the western fur trade. Shortly before this book was completed a large cache of fur traders' records was discovered in the Château de Ramezay at Montreal; microfilm copies are held by the Public Archives, Ottawa, and the Minnesota Historical Society. The state archives of New York and Massachusetts also contain many significant documents relating to New France and Acadia.

Guides to Manuscript Material

The Public Archives of Canada, Manuscript Division, have, since the 1950s, published periodically *Preliminary Inventories* of the manuscripts, and of the microfilm and transcript copies they possess of documents in the French and other archives. Several calendars of much of this material were published from 1891 to 1940. Exhaustive general listings of source material are contained in the two bibliographical guides by Henry Putney Beers, *The French in North America: A Bibliographical Guide to French Archives, Reproductions and Research Mis-*

sions (Baton Rouge, 1957), and *The French and British in the Old Northwest. A Bibliographical Guide to Archives and Manuscript Sources* (Detroit, 1964).

Printed Sources

Considerable primary source material pertaining to New France has been published in Canada, France, and the United States. For the early period H. P. Biggar, *A Collection of Documents Relating to Jacques Cartier and the Sieur de Roberval* (Ottawa, 1930), consists mainly of transcripts of documents in the Spanish archives at Simancas. There have been several editions of the *Jesuit Relations*, that by Reuben Gold Thwaites, *The Jesuit Relations and Allied Documents*, 73 vols. (Cleveland, 1896–1901), contains transcripts of the documents alongside an English translation; the translation in the earlier volumes could be better but the series is an invaluable source, particularly for the period prior to 1663. Joseph P. Donnelly, S.J., *Thwaites' Jesuit Relations: Errata and Addenda* (Chicago, 1967), is more *addenda* than *errata;* it contains a brief but informative essay on the history of the *Relations*. While this bibliography was in preparation the first volume appeared in a series that will contain annotated transcripts of all the known documents relating to the work of the Jesuits in North America. This first volume, Lucien Campeau, S.I. (ed.), *Monumenta Novae Franciae I La Première Mission d'Acadie* (1602–1616) (Quebec, 1967) is a monument to scholarship.

Word from New France. The Selected Letters of Marie de l'Incarnation, translated and edited by Joyce Marshall (Toronto, 1967), throws light on the religious climate of the age as well as on events in the colony during the years 1639–1670.

The Rapport de l'Archiviste de la Province de Québec now published under the title *Rapport des Archives du Québec,* published annually since 1920, consists of transcripts of miscellaneous but very useful series of documents. Unfortunately in the past the transcriptions have contained some obvious, and some not so obvious, errors; included is the official correspondence of some of the senior officials, an inventory of the fur trade *congés* held by the Quebec Archives, a calendar of the *"engagements pour l'ouest"* conserved by the Montreal Judicial Archives, a great deal of primary source material on the War of the Conquest, and much relating to clerical affairs. An index to the first forty-two volumes (1920–1964), *Table des Matières des Rapports des Archives du Québec,* was published by the Imprimeur de Sa Majesté la Reine (Quebec, 1965). The Quebec Archives have also published calendars of various documents in its possession: *Inventaire des Ordonnances des Intendants de la Nouvelle-France conservées aux Archives provinciales de Québec,* 4 vols. (P.-G. Roy, ed.; Beauceville, 1919); *Inventaire des Insinuations de la Prévôté de Québec,* 3 vols. (P.-G. Roy, ed.; Beauceville, 1936–1939). The records of the Sovereign Council of New France (after 1703 Conseil Supérieur) for the years 1663–1716 were published by order of the Quebec legislature under the title *Jugements et Délibérations du Conseil Souverain de la Nouvelle-France,* 6 vols. (Quebec, 1885–1891). Unfortunately, certain of the transactions of the Council were, doubtless inadvertently, not included. For the years after 1716 a useful calendar has been published, *Inventaire des jugements et délibérations du Conseil Supérieur de la Nouvelle-France de 1717 à 1760,* 7 vols. (P.-G. Roy, ed.; Beauceville, 1932–1935). By order of the Legislative Assembly of the Province of Canada (the pre-Confederation political unit comprising present-day Quebec and Ontario) a three-volume series was published with the individual titles, *Edits et ordonnances royaux, déclarations et arrêts du Conseil d'Etat du Roi concernant le Canada* (Quebec, 1854); *Arrêts et règlements du Conseil Supérieur de Québec, et ordonnances et jugements des intendants du Canada* (Quebec, 1855); *Complément des ordonnances et jugements des gouverneurs et intendants du Canada, précédé des commissions des dits gouverneurs et intendants et des différents officiers civils et de justice* (Quebec, 1856). The Collection *des manuscrits contenant lettres, mémoires et autres documents historiques relatifs à la Nouvelle France*, 4 vols. (Quebec, 1883–1885), is a rather haphazard selection. E.-Z. Massicotte, onetime archivist at Montreal, edited a useful calendar, *Montréal sous le régime français. Repertoire des Arrêts, Edits, Mandements, Ordonnances et Reglements Conservés dans les Archives du Palais de justice de Montréal 1640–1760* (Montreal, 1919).

Some of the Annual Reports of the Public Archives of Canada contain transcripts of documents dating from the French regime. A selection from the Paris documents was translated and edited by E. B. O'Callaghan and J. R. Brodhead, *Documents Relating to the Colonial History of New York*, 15 vols. (Albany, 1856–1883), but both the selection and translation leave something to be desired. The same stricture applies to *Documentary History of the State of New York*, 4 vols. (E. B. O'Callaghan, ed.; Albany, 1850). Transcriptions of correspondence concerning Antoine Laumet, alias La Mothe Cadillac, are contained in Michigan Pioneer Historical Society, *Historical Collections*, vols. XXXIII–XXXIV (Lansing, 1904–1905). P. Margry edited *Mémoires et documents pour servir à l'histoire des origines françaises des pays d'outre mer: Découvertes et établissements des Français dans l'ouest et dans le sud de l'Amérique septentrionale*, 6 vols. (Paris, 1876); this series has to be used with caution as the editor took liberties with the text of some of the documents to bolster his judgments on individuals, notably in extolling La Salle. Camille de Rochemonteix, S.J., *Relation par lettres de l'Amérique septentrionale (années 1709 et 1710)* (Paris, 1904), depicts some aspects of life in the colony under harsh wartime conditions. The letters of Mme Bégon serve a similar purpose for society at mid-century; these letters have been printed in the *Rapport de l'Archiviste de la Province de Québec, 1934–1935*. Much information can also be gleaned from Mgr. H. Tetu and Mgr. C. O. Gagnon (eds.), *Mandements, lettres pastorales, et circulaires des évêques de Québec*, 7 vols. (Quebec, 1887). On French relations with the Iroquois, two invaluable collections of documents are Peter Wraxall, *An Abridgement of the New York Indian Records* (C.H. McIlwain, ed.; Cambridge, Mass., 1915), and Lawrence H. Leder (ed.), *The Livingston Indian Records 1666–1723* (Gettysburg, Pa., 1956).

On the War of the Conquest a vast amount of primary source material has been published; most of it, however, is concerned with the central colony theater of operations and particularly with the 1759–1760 campaigns. Among the more useful collections is Abbé H.-R. Casgrain (ed.), *Collection des manuscrits du Maréchal de Lévis*, 12 vols. (Montreal and Quebec, 1889-1895). The manuscript copies of this series are in the Public Archives of Canada; in the published version the odd error of transcription has been detected but the series is of great value. Over the years the annual *Rapport de l'Archiviste de la Province de Québec* has printed a great deal of primary source material on the war; journals, memoirs, dispatches. The index to the *Rapports,* published in 1965 and listed above, should be consulted under the entry *Guerre.* A. G. Doughty with G. W. Parmalee, *The Siege of Quebec and the Battle of the Plains of Abraham,* 6 vols. (Quebec, 1901) is a collection of documents and a history; the documents are very useful, the "history" is not. Captain John Knox, *An Historical Journal of the Campaigns in North America for the years 1757, 1758, 1759 and 1760,* 3 vols. (Arthur G. Doughty, ed.; Champlain Society, Toronto 1914–1916) is a good account by an observant Irishman. For the war in the west, Fernand Grenier (ed.), *Papiers Contrecoeur et autres documents concernant le conflit anglo-français sur l'Ohio de 1745 à 1756* (Quebec, 1952), is indispensable. Also of value are the translations of pertinent documents in the *Illinois Historical Collection* (Theodore Calvin Pease and Raymond C. Werner, eds.), vol. XXIII; T. C. Pease and Raymond C. Werner, *The French Foundations, 1680–1693* (Springfield, Ill., 1934); vol. XXVII; T. C. Pease (ed.) *Anglo-French Boundary Disputes in the West, 1749–1763* (Springfield, Ill., 1936); vol. XXIX; T. C. Pease and Ernestine Jenison (eds.), *Illinois on the Eve of the Seven Years' War, 1747–1755,* (Springfield, Ill., 1940).

Travel Accounts, Journals, Contemporary Histories

Literary circles in France prior to the Conquest evinced considerable interest in Canada, and not a few histories and travel accounts were published in the seventeenth and eighteenth centuries. The original editions are now scarce and frequently those subsequently republished are better edited.

For the early period Ch. A. Julien, R. Herval, Th. Beauchesne (eds.), *Les Français en Amérique pendant la première moitié du XVIe siècle* (Paris, 1946), contains the texts of the journals of the early explorers, Gonneville, Verrazano, Cartier, and Roberval. H. P. Biggar, *Voyages of Jacques Cartier* (Ottawa, 1924), gives an English translation of Cartier's journals. A valuable critical study of these sources is Bernard G. Hoffman, *Cabot to Cartier: Sources for a Historical Ethnography of North Eastern North America, 1497–1550* (Toronto, 1961). H. P. Biggar (ed.), *The Works of Samuel de Champlain,* 6 vols. The Champlain Society, Toronto, 1922–1935); Marc Lescarbot, *The History of New France,* 3 vols. (W. L. Grant and H. P. Biggar, eds.; The Champlain Society, Toronto, 1907–1914); and Gabriel Sagard, *The Long Journey to the Country of the Hurons* (George M. Wrong, ed.; The Champlain Society, Toronto, 1939), give an English translation along with the French texts. Gabriel Sagard's *Histoire du Canada et voyages que les Frères Mineurs Recollects y ont faicts pour la conversion des Infidelles* (Paris, 1636), was reissued in 4 vols., (Edwin Tross, ed.; Paris, 1866). Pierre Boucher, *Histoire Veritable et Naturelle des Moeurs et Productions du Pays de la Nouvelle-France* (Paris, 1663), reissued in Montreal in 1882, is of particular value.

The history of the colony by François Du Creux, S.J., *Historiae canadensis seu Novae-Franciae libri decem, ad annum usque Christe MDCLVI* (Paris, 1664), was based on contemporary Jesuit accounts, oral and written. J. B. Conacher edited for the Champlain Society publications a translation with an introduction by Percy J. Robinson, *The History of Canada or New France,* 2 vols. (Toronto, 1951–1952). The manuscript of Dollier de Casson's "Histoire de Montréal" is in the Bibliothèque Mazarine, Paris. Inaccurate transcripts were printed by the Société Historique de Montréal (1868) and by the Literary and Historical Society of Quebec (1871). The Public Archives of Canada had a more accurate transcript made (1919–1921), and this was later published, with an English translation, under the title *A History of Montreal 1640–1672 from the French of Dollier de Casson* (Ralph Flenley, ed.; Toronto, 1928).

The journals of the hospitals at Quebec and Montreal provide considerable detailed information: Juchereau de La Ferté de Saint-Ignace, Jeanne-Françoise, et Marie-Andrée Duplessis de Sainte-Hélène, *Les annales de l'Hôtel-Dieu de Québec, 1636–1716*, (Albert Jamet, ed.; Quebec and Montreal, 1939); Marie Morin, *Annales de l'Hotel-Dieu de Montréal* (collated and annotated by A. Fauteux, E. Z. Massicotte, and C. Bertrand; introduction by E. Morin; Montreal, 1921). Pierre Esprit Radisson's controversial account of his explorations and adventures in North America was published by the Prince Society of Boston in a limited edition of 250 copies under the title *Radisson's Voyages* (Boston, 1885). A new edition, correcting what are claimed to be misplacings of parts of the narratives and thereby clearing away the author's apparent inconsistencies, is Arthur T. Adams (ed.), *The Explorations of Pierre Esprit Radisson* (Minneapolis, 1961). Louis Armand de Lom d'Arce, Baron de Lahontan, officer in the Troupes de la Marine, wrote a lively and imaginative account of events in the colony at the end of the seventeenth century. It was, however, written some thirty years after the events described and is frequently inaccurate; despite this some of his observations have value. The English version was edited by R. G. Thwaites, *New Voyages to North America*, 2 vols. (Chicago, 1905).

Chrestien Leclercq, *Premier établissement de la foy dans la Novelle France* (Paris, 1691), makes manifest his order's hostility toward the Jesuits. An English translation was edited by John Gilmary Shea, *First Establishment of the Faith in New France*, 2 vols. (New York, 1881). Of greater value is the history of the colony written by Pierre-François-Xavier de Charlevoix, S.J., who taught at Quebec from 1705 to 1709 and in 1721 traveled from Quebec to Louisiana by way of the Great Lakes. In his *Histoire et description générale de la Nouvelle France, avec le journal historique d'un voyage fait pare ordre du Roi dans l'Amérique septentrionale*, 3 vols. (Paris, 1744), he utilized primary source material in the archives of the Ministry of Marine; he also garnered information from persons who had been involved in the events depicted or who were at one remove. He did not, however, always exercise enough critical judgment of his source material, too often accepting it at face value. An English translation was made and edited by John Gilmary Shea, *History and General Description of New France*, 6 vols. (New York, 1866–1873). Louise Phelps Kellog translated and edited Charlevoix's account of his voyage to Louisiana, *Journal of a Voyage to North America* (Chicago, 1923).

On French activities in the west and relations with the indigenous tribes, the following are among the more useful: Le chevalier de Baugy, *Journal d'une expédition contre les Iroquois en 1687* (Paris, 1883); Nicholas Perrot, *Mémoire sur les moeurs, coustumes et relligion des sauvages de l'Amérique septentrionale*, (Tailhan edition, Paris and Leipzig, 1864); M. de Bacqueville de la Potherie, *Histoire de l'Amérique Septentrionale* (Paris, 1753). The best edition of Jean-Louis Hennepin's rather mendacious account of his travels is the critical one edited by R. G. Thwaites, *Louis Hennepin, A New Discovery of a Vast Country in America; Reprinted from the Second London Issue of 1698* . . . , 2 vols. (Chicago, 1903). The memoirs of La Mothe Cadillac and Pierre Liette, *The Western Country in the 17th Century* (Milo Milton Quaife, ed.; Chicago, 1947) provide information on the mid-western tribes. The Caxton Club edition of Henri Joutel, *A Journal of La Salle's Last Voyage,* was recently republished (New York, 1962). Louise Phelps Kellog, *Early Narratives of the Northwest: 1634–1699* (Madison, Wis., 1917), and Emma Helen Blair (ed.), *The Indian Tribes of the Upper Mississippi Valley and Region of the Great Lakes,* 2 vols. (Cleveland, 1911–1912), give the accounts of several early French travelers in the west in English translation. L. J. Burpee (ed.), *Journals and Letters of Pierre Gaultier de Varennes de la Vérendrye and His Sons* (The Champlain Society; Toronto, 1927), is one of the more significant collections but the English translation bears checking.

Descriptive of society in the colony in the closing years of the French regime are Louis Franquet, *Voyages et mémoires sur le Canada* (Quebec, 1889), and *Voyage au Canada dans le Nord de l'Amérique Septentrionale fait depuis l'an 1751 à 1761 par J.C.B.* (Quebec, 1887). Especially valuable, since it is the only account by a foreign visitor, and a particularly discerning one, is Adolph B. Benson (ed.), *The America of 1750: The Travels in North America by Peter Kalm,* (New York, 1937). Reissued in 2 volumes, paperback format, New York, 1966.

Secondary Sources: General Accounts

The first significant history of New France was that of F.-X. Garneau, *Histoire du Canada depuis sa découverte jusqu'à nos jours,* 3 vols. (Quebec, 1845–1848). Garneau wrote this history in reaction to the slurs cast on French-Canadians, their supposed lack of a culture or a history, by Lord Durham in his famous Report. It has, therefore, a strong nationalist theme. Moreover, Garneau based his interpretation largely on that of Charlevoix (mentioned above) and many of the latter's errors were incorporated, even expanded, and accepted almost as holy writ by later historians. Despite these shortcomings Garneau's work was a tour de force and still has considerable merit, not least, readability. A strong clerical bias permeates F.-B. Ferland, *Cours d'histoire du Canada,* 2 vols. (Quebec, 1861-1865); he too relied heavily on Charlevoix. Etienne-Michel Faillon, *Histoire de la colonie française en Canada,* 3 vols. (Ville Marie, 1865–1866), gives a very detailed and well-documented account of events down to 1672, concentrating on the role of the clergy, particularly those of Montreal. An excellent example of the Whig interpretation of Canadian history is provided by William Kingsford, *The History of Canada,* 10 vols. (London, 1887–1898). On the French regime, Kingsford provides a narrative account remarkable mainly for its Anglo-Saxon bias and the number of factual errors. *The Cambridge History of the British Empire,* vol. VI, *Canada and Newfoundland* (London, 1930), notable chiefly for its pedestrian approach, devotes four of thirty-three chapters to New France, but they have little value for students today. The same stricture applies to *Canada and Its Provinces: A History of the Canadian People and Their Institutions,* 23 vols. (Adam Short and A. G. Doughty, eds; Toronto, 1914–1917).

Of the more recent histories, that by Abbé Lionel-Adolphe Groulx, *Histoire du Canada français depuis la découverte,* 2 vols. (Montreal, 1962), has a marked nationalist and clerical viewpoint. Gustave Lanctot has written a narrative account, *A History of Canada,* 3 vols. (Cambridge, Mass., 1963–1965), based largely on research done several years ago. Much more detailed and critical is Marcel Trudel. *Histoire de la Nouvelle France* (Montreal, 1963–1966). To date two volumes have appeared, carrying the history only to 1627; they are the best works yet published on this early period. Francis H. Hammang, *The Marquis de Vaudreuil: New France at the Beginning of the Eighteenth Century,* Part I; *New France and the English Colonies* (Bruges, 1938) is a scholarly treatment of colonial affairs at the turn of the century. In a class by itself is the epic series by Francis Parkman, *France and England in North America,* beginning with *Pioneers of France in the New World* (Boston, 1865) and closing with *Montcalm and Wolfe* (Boston, 1884). Written with a pronounced Anglo-American Protestant bias, they portray the inevitable victory of the forces of progress over the reactionary French Catholic regime in North America. Since Parkman's underlying premises were in accord with majority opinion in both the United States and Canada, his interpretation of the history of New France gained instant acceptance as definitive works by both Americans and English-speaking Canadians. Despite trenchant criticism by scholars, these works emulate the phoenix. George M. Wrong, *The Rise and Fall of New France,* 2 vols. (Toronto, 1928) follows closely Parkman's view of events but lacks his literary style. Morden Heaton Long, *A History of the Canadian People,* Vol. I: *New France* (Toronto, 1942), is well written and the material is better organized than in many such general histories, but it embodies no original scholarship, being based entirely on secondary and tertiary sources, too many of which had little merit, and contains a dismaying number of factual errors. The period 1663–1701 is treated in more analytical fashion in W. J. Eccles, *Canada Under Louis XIV, 1663–1701* (Toronto, 1964). The articles by E. R. Adair, "France and the Beginning of New France," *The Canadian Historical Review,* vol. XIII (September, 1944) and "The Evolution of Montreal Under the French Regime," *The Canadian Historical Review,* vol. XXIII (March, 1942) are valuable analytical studies.

Society and Institutions

The society and institutions of New France were, of course, based on and affected by changes in those of the mother country. The student of the history of the colony is obliged to have a thorough grasp of developments in France in the sixteenth, seventeenth, and eighteenth centuries. The A. de Boislisle edition of *Mémoires de St. Simon,* 41 vols. (Paris, 1879), contains in its multitudinous notes and appendices a mine of information on all aspects of French society and institutions in the age of Louis XIV. Marcel Marion, *Dictionnaire des institutions de la France aux 17ᵉ et 18ᵉ siècles* (Paris, 1923), is a valuable reference work. So too is the brief study by F. C. Green, *The Ancien Regime. A Manual of French Institutions and Social Classes* (Edinburg, 1958). Franklin L. Ford, *Robe and Sword: The Regrouping of the French Aristocracy after Louis XIV* (Cambridge, Mass., 1953), contains much that has meaning for New France. Particular attention must be paid to the work presently being done in the social history of the period by such scholars as Roland Mousnier, Robert Mandrou, Pierre Goubert, E. Labrousse, and Jean Meuvret, to mention only a few of the more eminent scholars. The journal, *Les Annales d'histoire économique et sociale,* cannot be ignored. In Canada the *Journal of Canadian Social History—Journal de l'histoire, sociale canadienne* (Carleton University and Université d'Ottawa), has just come into publication and should serve to stimulate research in this hitherto neglected field.

On the administrative framework of New France, Gustave Lanctot's doctoral thesis, *L'Administration de la Nouvelle France* (Paris, 1929), was a pioneering work. W. J. Eccles, *The Government of New France*, The Canadian Historical Association Booklet No. 18 (Ottawa, 1965), provides a brief general description but already requires minor revisions. R. du Bois Cahall, *The Sovereign Council of New France* (New York, 1915) is the best study of that important body. The article by Allana G. Reid, "Representative Assemblies in New France," *The Canadian Historical Review*, vol. XXVII (March, 1946), is illuminating. A thorough study of crime and punishment has yet to be made but the preliminary work by André Lachance, *Le Bourreau au Canada sous le régime français* (Cahiers d'Histoire No. 18, La Société Historique de Québec, 1966), is important despite the author's tendency to judge eighteenth century practice by modern standards.

Emile Salone, *La Colonisation de la Nouvelle-France: étude sur les origines de la nation canadienne-française* (Paris, 1906), and Ivanhoe Caron, *La colonisation du Canada sous la domination française* (Quebec, 1916), are still useful. Jacques Henripin, *La Population canadienne au début du XVIII° siècle* (Paris, 1954), is a pioneering and interesting application of quantitative methods. Guy Frégault, in his "Canadian Society in the French Regime" (The Canadian Historical Association Booklet No. 3; Ottawa, 1964), stresses the role of the colonial bourgeoisie and qualifies certain of the views expressed in his earlier work *La civilisation de la Nouvelle-France* (Montreal, 1944). One of the more useful works is the collection of analytical essays by the sociologist Léon Gérin, *Aux Sources de notre histoire* (Montreal, 1946). The article by Sigmund Diamond, "An Experiment in 'Feudalism': French Canada in the Seventeenth Century," *William and Mary Quarterly*, 3rd series, vol. XVIII (January, 1961), is an interesting but rather superficial study by a sociologist wherein the particular is too often assumed to be general, resulting in some sweeping generalizations of dubious validity. The article by the same author, "Le Canada français au XVII° siècle: une société préfabriquée," in *Annales; Economies, Sociétés, Civilizations*, mars-avril 1961, 16° année, no. 2, is merely a translation of the article in the *William and Mary Quarterly*: a few paragraphs are added to the introduction, the body of the article is exactly the same in both versions. The chapters dealing with New France in the work of yet another sociologist, S. D. Clark, *The Social Development of Canada: An Introductory Study with Select Documents* (Toronto, 1942), have little merit. Earlier studies of the seigneurial system have now been superseded by Richard Colebrook Harris, *The Seigneurial System in Early Canada* (Madison, Wis., 1966). Marcel Trudel, *L'Esclavage* (Quebec, 1960), provides a massive amount of information on the institution and its incidence. No worthwhile studies have yet been made of social groups, such as the *habitants,* the seigneurs, the clergy, the administrators, the military, or the *coureurs de bois.* Grace Lee Nute, *The Voyageur* (New York, 1931), is very superficial.

Some aspects of the role of the clergy have been examined but much remains to be done, Auguste Gosselin, *L'Eglise du Canada depuis Mgr. de Laval jusqu'à la conquête*, 3 vols. (Quebec, 1911–1914), is detailed but uncritical. C. de Rochemonteix, *Les Jésuites et la Nouvelle-France au XVII° siècle*, 3 vols. (Paris, 1895–

1896), and *Les Jésuites et la Nouvelle-France au VXII° siècle*, 2 vols. (Paris, 1906), are well-documented, scholarly studies by a Jesuit historian. Francis Parkman, *The Jesuits in North America* (Boston, 1867), despite his marked prejudice and his incomprehension of the seventeenth-century religious climate, gives a readable account based largely on the *Jesuit Relations*. Mack Eastman, *Church and State in Early Canada* (Edinburgh, 1915), fails to take account of the subordination of the clergy to the crown in the eighteenth century. Jean Delanglez, S.J., *Some La Salle Journeys* (Chicago, 1938), and *Frontenac and the Jesuits* (Chicago, 1939), are a corrective to the anticlerical attitude of Parkman. H. H. Walsh, *The Church in the French Era* (Toronto, 1966), is a rather uneven study by a sympathetic Protestant theologian.

The West and Acadia

A. S. Morton, *A History of the Canadian West to 1870–71* (London, 1939) gives a scholarly and detailed account of French activities in the west. J. B. Brebner, *The Explorers of North America, 1492–1806* (London, 1933), is more than useful. Louise Phelps Kellog, *The French Régime in Wisconsin and the Northwest* (Madison, Wis., 1925) stands in need of revision but provides a good outline of the main events. L. J. Burpee, *The Search for the Western Sea* (Toronto, 1908), is of little value. C. W. Alvord, *The Illinois Country 1673–1818* (Springfield, Ill., 1920), is outdated. The best studies to date of French western policy in the first quarter of the eighteenth century are the three articles by Yves F. Zoltvany, "The Problem of Western Policy under Philippe de Rigaud de Vaudreuil (1703–1725)," *Canadian Historical Association Report*, 1964; "New France and the West, 1701–1713," *The Canadian Historical Review*, vol. XLVI, (December, 1965); and "The Frontier Policy of Philippe Rigaud de Vaudreuil (1713–1725)," *The Canadian Historical Review*, vol. XLVIII (September, 1967). On the Canadian frontier *per se*, there are few studies. The article by Frederick Jackson Turner, "The Rise and Fall of New France," *Minnesota History*, vol. XVIII (December, 1937), was an interesting attempt, based largely on the meager secondary sources of the day, to apply his thesis to New France. A. L. Burt, "The Frontier in the History of New France," *Canadian Historical Association Report, 1940*, is a short and provocative article which sets out to prove that social values and institutions in New France were completely dominated by the frontier environment. Evidence supporting the argument is unduly stressed, that which would deny or qualify it is ignored or dismissed in cavalier fashion. No sources are cited and the presentation is more that of the *parti pris* advocate than the detached inquisitor. J. M. S. Careless, "Frontierism, Metropolitanism and Canadian History," *The Canadian Historical Review*, vol. XXXV (March, 1954), analyzes the response of Canadian historians to the Turner thesis.

There are few works of scholarly merit on Acadia. For the early period the surviving documentary evidence is scanty, and too many of the studies of this region suffer from the emotional involvement of the authors with the ultimate fate of the Acadians, some condemning the British, others defending their action. One of the few authoritative works that does preserve a detached viewpoint is J. B. Brebner, *New England's Outpost; Acadia Before the Conquest of Canada* (New York, 1927). D. C. Harvey, *The French Régime in Prince Edward Island*

(New Haven, 1926), stands alone. On Louisbourg and Cape Breton, J. S. McLennan, *Louisbourg from Its Foundation to Its Fall* (London, 1918), is well documented. Francis Parkman's treatment of the struggle for Acadia in *A Half Century of Conflict* (Boston, 1892), is unblushingly partisan. Thomas Pichon, *Lettres et mémoires pour servir à l'histoire Naturelle, Civile et Politique du Cap Breton* (La Haye, 1760), is a contentious account by an archtraitor.

Economic Affairs

Although the fur trade dominated the history of New France, nothing approaching a definitive study of it has yet been made. H. P. Biggar, *Early Trading Companies of New France. A Contribution to the History of Commerce and Discovery in North America* (Toronto, 1901), remains the best study of the early period. Harold A. Innis, *The Fur Trade in Canada* (New Haven, Conn., 1930), contains both profound insights and dubious generalizations. Innis sometimes fails to distinguish between *livres* value and *livres* weight of fur traded; he also frequently fails to distinguish between beaver and other furs, thus many of the figures he cites are erroneous or misleading. Regretfully Paul C. Phillips, *The Fur Trade*, 2 vols. (Norman, Okla., 1961), is so replete with errors that in the section dealing with the Canadian trade it is virtually worthless. The article by E. R. Adair, "Anglo-French Rivalry in the Fur Trade during the Eighteenth Century," *Culture*, vol. VIII (1947), pp. 434–455, is valuable, as is also that by Jean Lunn on the contraband trade with the English colonies, "The Illegal Fur Trade out of New France, 1713–1760," *Canadian Historical Association Report*, 1939. Guy Frégault, "La Compagnie de la Colonie," *Revue de l'Université d'Ottawa*, vol. XIV (December, 1960), is a masterly analysis of an extremely complex affair. E. E. Rich, *The History of the Hudson's Bay Company, 1670–1870*, vol I: *1670–1763* (London, 1958), is thorough.

On other aspects of the colony's economy little that is worthwhile has been done. Exceptions to this are the chapters dealing with the Canadian lumber trade in P. W. Bamford, *Forests and French Sea Power* (Toronto, 1956), and the articles by A. R. M. Lower, "The Forest in New France; A Sketch of Lumbering in Canada before the English Conquest," *Canadian Historical Association Report*, 1928, pp. 78–90; Allana G. Reid, "General Trade Between Quebec and France during the French Régime," *Canadian Historical Review*, vol. XXXIV (March, 1953); Allana G. Reid, "Intercolonial Trade During the French Regime," *Canadian Historical Review*, vol. XXXII, (September, 1951). No thorough study of agriculture in the colony has yet been published; F. W. Burton, "The Wheat Supply of New France," *Proceedings and Transactions of the Royal Society of Canada*, series 3, vol. XXX, broaches the subject and is sound. J. N. Fauteux, *Essai sur l'industrie au Canada sous le régime français*, 2 vols. (Quebec, 1861–1865), is superficial and uncritical but it does give some indication of the scope of economic activity. P. E. Renaud, *Les Origines économiques du Canada* (Mamers, 1928), lacks cohesion but contains masses of detail. Jean Hamelin, *Economie et Société en Nouvelle France* (Quebec, 1960), is an interesting preliminary study using quantitative methods but the evidence presented does not entirely justify the conclusions.

Indian Relations

Few works deal directly with this important topic. Diamond Jenness, *The Indians of Canada* (Ottawa, 1932) is a standard reference work. The Iroquois have been the subject of a few studies but the role of the Algonkin tribes has received little attention. Lewis H. Morgan, *League of the Iroquois* (Rochester, 1851), and William M. Beauchamp, *History of the New York Iroquois* (New York, 1905) have little value for the historian. Cadwallader Colden, *The History of the Five Indian Nations of Canada*, 2 vols. (New York, 1902; first published, Part I, 1727, Part II, 1747), was arguing a case and this has to be taken into account. George T. Hunt, *The Wars of the Iroquois* (Madison, Wis., 1940), is an interesting and scholarly work that stresses the economic factor but unfortunately fails to carry the study far enough chronologically. Allen W. Trelease, *Indian Affairs in Colonial New York* (Ithaca, N.Y., 1960), is disappointing; the French manuscript material bearing on the subject was not consulted. J. H. Kennedy, *Jesuit and Savage in New France* (New Haven, Conn., 1950), broaches this vital topic but not in depth; it is still, however, a work well worth consulting. The article by André Vachon, "L'Eau de vie dans la société indienne," *Canadian Historical Association Report*, 1960, offers more than the title suggests, giving significant insights into the clash of religious beliefs and cultures. A. G. Bailey, *The Conflict of European and Eastern Algonkin Cultures, 1504–1700. A Study in Canadian Civilization* (Saint John: New Brunswick Museum, 1937), and J.-P.-A. Maurault, *Histoire des Abenakis depuis 1605 jusqu'a jours* (Sorel, 1866), are useful studies. On French relations with the western Indians, Marcel Giraud, *Le Métis canadien. Son rôle dans l'histoire des provinces de l'ouest* (Paris, 1945), is a monumental work of scholarship. On the important topic of Indian subsidies, see W. R. Jacobs, *Indian Diplomacy and Indian Gifts: Anglo-French Rivalry along the Ohio and Northwest Frontier, 1748–1763* (Stanford, Calif., 1950).

Biographies

An invaluable reference work is the *Dictionary of Canadian Biography* (Toronto, 1966). To date only Volume I, which includes biographies of persons who died before 1700, has appeared. Mgr. Cyprian Tanguay, *Dictionnaire généalogique des familles canadiennes depuis la fondation de la colonie jusqu'a nos jours*, 7 vols. (Quebec, 1871–1890), is a basic work. New France harbored perhaps more than its share of colorful individuals and many of them found biographers. Others have been strangely neglected. Among the more worthwhile studies are Morris Bishop, *Champlain, the Life of Fortitude* (New York, 1948); Thomas Chapais, *Jean Talon, Intendant de la Nouvelle France (1665–1672)* Quebec, 1904); W. J. Eccles, *Frontenac: The Courtier Governor* (Toronto, 1959); Guy Frégault, *Iberville le conquérant* (Montreal, 1944); Nellis M. Crouse, *Lemoyne d'Iberville: Soldier of New France* (Ithaca, N.Y., 1954); E. B. Osler, *La Salle* (Toronto, 1967); E. R. M. Murphy, *Henri de Tonty: Fur Trader of the Mississippi* (Baltimore, 1941). On Antoine Laumet, alias LaMothe Cadillac, one of the more interesting scoundrels of the period, the articles by Jean Delanglez should be consulted: "Cadillac's early years in America," *Mid-America*, January, 1944; "An-

July, October, 1950; "Cadillac's Last Years," *ibid.*, January, 1951. Nellis M. Crouse, *La Vérendrye Fur Trader and Explorer* (Toronto 1956), could not be deemed a definitive work. The brief study by Roland Lamontagne, *La Galissoniére et le Canada* (Montreal, 1962) discusses some interesting aspects of the important governor's career. A significant and very useful study is that by Maurice Fillion, *Maurepas ministre de Louis XV (1715–1749)* (Montreal, 1967). Guy Frégault, *François Bigot, administrateur français*, 2 vols. (Montreal, 1948), is authoritative. Montcalm's biographers have been markedly partisan, either for or against. H.-R. Casgrain, *Montcalm et Lévis* (Tours, 1898), is hostile. Thomas Chapais, *Le Marquis de Montcalm (1721–1759Q* (Quebec, 1911, is prejudiced in his favor, and Georges Robitaille, *Montcalm et ses historiens; étude critique,* (Montreal, 1936), eulogizes him.

Colonial Wars

Useful reference works are the scholarly study by André Corvisier, *L'Armée française de la fin du XVIIe siècle au ministère de Choiseul*, 2 vols. (Paris, 1964), and G. Lacour-Gayet, *La Marine militaire de la France sous le règne de Louis XV* (Paris, 1910). As yet no serious study of the Troupes de la Marine or the colonial militia has been made. George F. G. Stanley, *Canada's Soldiers, 1604–1954* (Toronto, 1954), of necessity treats their role rather cursorily. Military organization in New France is briefly outlined in chapter 12 of W. J. Eccles, *Frontenac: The Courtier Governor* (Toronto, 1959). Gerald S. Graham, *Empire of the North Atlantic. The Maritime Struggle for North America* (Toronto, 1950), provides a general context. By the same author, *The Walker Expedition to Quebec: 1711* (The Champlain Society Publications, 1953), contains Walker's defense of his conduct, additional documents, and a scholarly introduction. Francis Parkman, *A Half Century of Conflict* (Boston, 1892), and *Montcalm and Wolfe* (Boston, 1884), are grippingly written but markedly lack detachment, viewing the final British victory as not only inevitable but highly desirable. Howard H. Peckham, *The Colonial Wars, 1689–1762* (Chicago, 1964), is based on superficial knowledge of the history of New France and is riddled with errors. Lawrence Henry Gipson, *The British Empire before the American Revolution*, vols. 4–8 (New York, 1939–1954), is a very detailed study, lacking in scholarly detachment on some issues; it is severely critical of the British colonial war effort but espouses the British imperialist cause in partisan fashion. On the eastern theater, J. C. Webster, *The Forts of Chignecto. A Study of the Eighteenth Century Conflict between France and Great Britain in Acadia* (n. p., 1930) is a brief study by an amateur historian. J. S. McLennan, *Louisbourg from Its Foundation to Its Fall: 1713–1758* (London, 1918), is well documented and deals with some of the broader aspects of the Acadian conflict.

On the War of the Conquest not a little has been written in both French and English, and of widely varying quality. Historical inevitability and ethnic bias all too frequently color the treatment of events. In addition historians have tended to be partisan in their judgments on the strife between the French and Canadian military leaders, some defending Montcalm, others Vaudreuil. Guy Frégault, *La Guerre de la conquête* (Montreal, 1955), espouses Vaudreuil's side in the disputes and can find little good to say of Montcalm; it is still the best study to date of toine Laumet, alias Cadillac, commandant at Michilimackinac," *ibid.*, April, July, October 1945; "The Genesis and Building of Detroit" *ibid.*, April, 1948; "Cadillac at Detroit," *ibid.*, July, October, 1948; "Cadillac Proprietor of Detroit," *ibid.*, the course of the war. Henri-Raymond Casgrain, *Guerre du Canada, 1756–60, Montcalm et Lévis,* 2 vols. (Quebec, 1891), is also highly critical of Montcalm and his officers. Parkman, in the works mentioned above, is a staunch advocate for Montcalm, as is also G. M. Wrong, *The Fall of Canada: A Study in the History of the Seven Years' War* (Oxford, 1914). The latter work is superficial and has little to recommend it. Julian S. Corbett, *England in the Seven Years' War: A Study in Combined Strategy,* 2 vols. (London, 1918), is more useful for activities in European waters than for the Canadian campaigns. Stanley M. Pargellis, "Braddock's Defeat," *American Historical Review,* vol. XLI (1936), pp. 251–259, is dated; the limitations of the eighteenth-century musket were not taken fully into account, and the effectiveness of guerrilla tactics against regular troops trained for such warfare had not been demonstrated as clearly in 1936 as it was to be in subsequent years. Several studies of the 1759 siege of Quebec were published in 1959; the best is C. P. Stacey, *Quebec 1759. The Siege and the Battle* (Toronto, 1959). Two articles by Colonel Stacey should also be consulted: "Generals and Generalship before Quebec, 1759–1760," *Canadian Historical Association Report,* 1959; "Quebec, 1759: Some New Documents," *The Canadian Historical Review,* vol. XLVII (December, 1966). The article by E. R. Adair, "The Military Reputation of Major-General James Wolfe," *Canadian Historical Association Report,* 1936, is a useful antidote to the panegyrics published over the years.

INDEX